A CRUISE IN THE CORPS

1951 to 1954

The View from the Ranks

Semper Fi!

Jerry G.
AKA BONES

Gerald D. Ginnelly

928-277-1152

CASTLE ROCK
PUBLISHING

A Cruise in the Corps

The View from the Ranks

By Gerald D. Ginnelly

Copyright © 1999 by Gerald D. Ginnelly

Published by:
Castle Rock Publishing
1712 Pine Woods Rd.
Prescott, AZ 86305 U.S.A.

Copies may be obtained by writing to:
Dano & Dad
PO Box 2052
Prescott, AZ 86302.

Outline map of the Korean Peninsula was drawn by the USMC. The vignettes were taken from a USMC group photo of Platoon 136 at MCRD, PI, SC. The photo of the bridges on the Imjin R. was provided by the U.S. Army. All other photos,except those credited to James Milliken and Sam Camarato, were taken by the author.

Cover design: Ronald H. Smith
Cover Photo: Korean Marines in fake pull-back from MLR in Punchbowl, Mar. 1952

Library of Congress Catalog Card Number: 99-64322
First printing August 1999 by Castle Rock Publishing, Prescott, AZ
Printed in the U.S.A.

Library of Congress Cataloging-in-Publication Data
Ginnelly, Gerald D.
    A Cruise in the Corps: The View from the Ranks / Gerald D. Ginnelly, — First
Edition
    p. 250
    Includes bibliographical references
    ISBN 0-9640308-4-5
    1.Korean War, 1950-1953 — Personal narrative, American. 2. United States
    Marine Corps — biography   I. Title
951.9/042/092

Dedicated to my father and all Marine Engineers

The Old Creed

Duty
Honor
Country

Joseph F. Ginnelly, 1166090, Mentor, Ohio
NG Painesville, O. May 7/17. Br. Cleveland, O.
20 6/12 yrs. Co. M 145 Inf to Nov 1/18; Hq Co 145
Inf to disch. Corp July 25/17; Sgt Oct 2/17;
Bn Sgt Maj Oct 29/18. Meuse-Argonne; Ypres-Lys;
Defensive Sector. AEF June 15/18 to Mch 27/19.
Hon disch May 1/19. Awd French C de G with bronze star.

3

**GRAND QUARTIER GÉNÉRAL
DES
ARMÉES FRANÇAISES DE L'EST
ÉTAT-MAJOR
BUREAU DU PERSONNEL**

ORDRE No. 13.258 "D." (EXTRAIT)

Aprés approbation du Général Commandant en Chef les Forces expéditionnaires Américaines en France, le Maréchal de France, Commandant en Chef les Armées Françaises de l'Est, cite à l'Ordre du REGIMENT:

Sergeant-Major de Bataillon Joseph F. Ginnelly, du 145° Régiment d'Infanterie Américain:

"Sous-Officier plein de bravours, a accompli son devoir avec une vaillance et un courage remarquables pendant l'offensive des Flandres du 31 Octobre au 4 Novembre, et du 9 su 11 Novembre 1918."

["NCO bravely fulfilled his duty with valor, and remarkable courage during the Flanders offensive from Oct. 31 to Nov. 4 and from Nov. 9 to Nov. 11, 1918"]

Au Grand Quartier Général, le 6 Fevrier 1919

Le Maréchal
Commandant en Chef les Armées Françaises de L'Est
PÉTAIN

NB. Citation to award the Croix de Guerre by Marshal Foch in February, 1919 at a regimental ceremony in France.

— GDG

TABLE OF CONTENTS

PREFACE

When my children were in their teens they would ask me why I never talked about my time in the service. I said, "Remember that old saw about only remembering the good things? Well then, I don't remember anything." I kept no notes or diary of that time and I never thought about those days until I went to a reunion of Charlie Co. 2ndEng Bn. at Camp Lejeune in April, 1998. After talking with the guys, some of whom were with me in Korea, it all came flooding back. Or some of it did. My own Dad went through some trying times in France and Belgium in WWI and he said little about it. In those days we kids did not speak to an adult until spoken to. Since my Dad did not have much to say, we never broached the subject until we went off to war ourselves. Now that my father is gone, I want to know everything that he went through from basic training to the trenches. Although he was a literate man, he wrote nothing down about his life back then. I decided that no matter how routine my service years were, I would write it all down for my children and grandchildren. They should know what we went through, no matter how mundane our work was to us. The trouble is that now that I've put it all down, I don't want them to read it until they are eighteen.

In modern warfare all men cannot be in a line outfit or on a recon team. It is said that for every rifleman on the lines recently, there are up to ten men supporting him. Someone has to deliver the rations, ammunition, ordnance, fuel, etc. Someone has to maintain all the mechanized equipment like tanks, amtracs, planes, helicopters, trucks and modern weapons and do all the other tasks to make the riflemens' job easier. With the combat engineers, someone has to build the roads and bridges, clear and lay mine fields, bring up timbers and barbed wire to help fortify our line positions. For those servicemen like myself who did not have to serve in a line company, rest assured that your work in the rear with the gear was appreciated by the infantry. When they called us rear echelon poges, we didn't have to say, "You'd better smile when you say that Mac." They knew we'd be there to bring the supplies up take the dead and wounded back. They knew that the engineers risked their lives all the time with mines, booby traps and in general demolition work. On that point, I don't think you'll see many books about Marine combat engineers at work and learn how they lived in the field. This book does just that.

Remember this admonition David gave to his troops after a victory over the Amalekites. He told those who did the actual fighting that they would have to share their booty with the detail assigned to the rear guarding their supplies. The combat types were grumbling to David about having to share with those who did not fight. David settled it with these words, "They also serve who only stand and wait." That phrase is the modern essence of Verses 21-26 from the first book of Samuel, Chapter 30.

It is not easy to recall the details nearly fifty years after the events, so I apologize for any errors in names, times, places or events that have appeared in the text. Several of the men who were there have tried to keep me straight and have reminded me of things that happened in Korea that have slipped my aging gray cells. They are Jim Milliken, Bill Hepinger, John Chapin and Sam Camarato formerly of Able Engineers. I thank them for their help. I also acknowledge the peer review of Al Essbach, Gaylord Walker and my two brothers, Tom and John Ginnelly. Walter G. Rockwood provided technical advice. Ron Smith of Castle Rock Publishing put the text and photos into book form, typeset and pre-pared the material for the printer. I give special thanks to my wife Beverly for putting up with this long project with patience and support.

— *G. D. Ginnelly, June 1999*

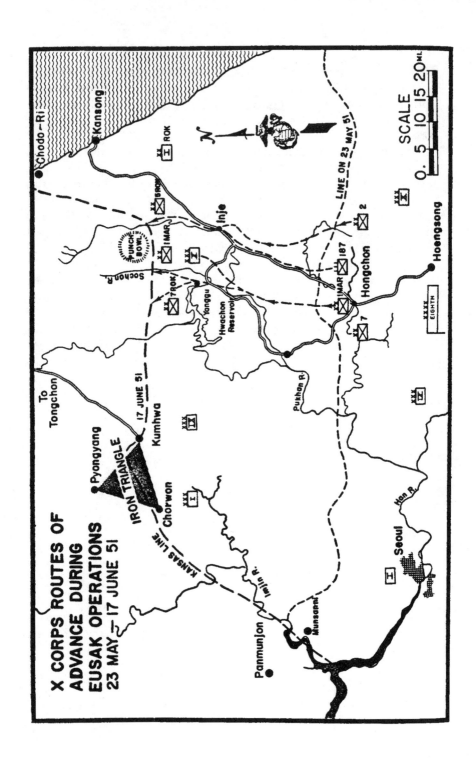

X CORPS ROUTES OF
ADVANCE DURING
EUSAK OPERATIONS
23 MAY — 17 JUNE 51

PART ONE
TRAINING AND TRAVEL

PART ONE: TRAINING AND TRAVEL

MILITARY SERVICE OPTIONS

Christmas day in the Punchbowl was like any other winter day in Korea. We were just across the 38th parallel in North Korea where the cold comes down from Siberia and Manchuria. For Able Co. it was a rare day off. The weather was normal for winter, bitter cold and overcast. Most of the men opted to stay in their tents close to the stove and rest up. The big event of the day was a dinner of roast turkey with all the down home fixings. Guys who got them, opened presents from home, the rest were happy just to have letters and Christmas cards from loved ones. The only Marines astir outdoors were those on watch and a few hunters out in the field.

We were in as much of a holiday mood as one can be out here in the middle of a strange country. We thought nothing much could happen on a day when we celebrate Peace on Earth and Goodwill Toward Men. That was until the news about Budde spread from tent to tent. Among the braver souls who thrived on cold weather, three friends Sgt. Elkins, and PFCs. Blanco and Budde, decided to go hunting. They lived in the same tent and Budde was always accusing Blanco of swiping his wool socks. The argument was settled once and for all on Christmas day.

While they were hunting, Budde tripped a bouncing Betty. The mine leaped up in front of him and went off blasting him in the groin. Budde knew he was a goner as he lay there on the frozen ground, his life seeping away. I'm told that while his partners tried to give him first aid, he told Blanco, "You can have all my socks now. I won't be needing them." It reminded me of the scene in "All Quiet on the Western Front," where the German soldier who had just lost both legs to a shell, tells his buddy from his hospital bed that he can have his boots. He had been admiring them for months.

This senseless accident put a damper on what holiday spirit we had been able to scare up. It was the sort of thing we did not write home about, but it did make me wish I was still back home in Detroit. Every time this happened I asked myself, "What am I doing here anyway?"

When the Korean War broke out in June 1950 I had been working for the City of Detroit for a year and a half as a tree surgeon. The North Korean communists had crossed the 38th parallel into South Korea clobbering the South Korean Army and the small contingent of U.S. Army troops on garrison duty there. The U.S. Government's response was to call up the reserves and send active duty units to Korea to stem the invasion. Meantime the United Nations was putting together an international military contingent to assist the U.S. and South Korean Forces.

As I turned 20 in August, many young men of draft age were nervous about the service. Heavy casualties in American units in Korea were reported in the daily press adding to the sense of unease. It was a constant topic of conversation among my friends. What should we do — sit tight and wait for the draft notice from Selective Service, or enlist now and get it over with?

I have often been asked why I joined the Marine Corps. My answer varied from 1) my father bet me $1,000 that I could not hold a steady job for more than a year, 2) the court ordered me off the streets and the service was an option, and 3) I was simply dodging the draft in my peculiar way. Only the last is true. The other two applied to my brothers. The older went the court route, the other was offered the bribe to ship over.

Some guys, like my future brother-in-law, were safe in college with deferments. Because I had never finished high school, the option of a college deferment was out. I had the alternatives of enlisting, being a conscientious objector (C.O.), or joining the reserves. A buddy, Ted Kilberg, and I went down to the Federal Building in Detroit and made the rounds of the military recruiters. Most young men did not want to die or be maimed in combat, so thought the Air Force or the Navy would be the safest place to be. The Marines and the Army would be the worst place.

One friend of ours, Kurt (Snooky) Korvanen, was already safely in the Air Force. Dick Hayes, another friend, was home on leave over Christmas of 1950. Looped over the left shoulder on his green Marine uniform, Dick sported the Pogey Rope of the 6th Marines, 2nd Marine Division, FMF, stationed at Camp Lejeune, NC. This decoration, more correctly known as the *Fourragere*, was awarded to the 6th Marine Regiment by the French Army for its distinguished service as part of the American Expeditionary Force (AEF) in WWI at the battle of Belleau Wood, near Chateau Thierry. Dick was on his way to a line company in the First Marine Division of the Fleet Marine Force, (1stMarDiv, FMF) Korea.

Ted and I found that the Air Force and the Navy had a waiting list for six months before accepting new applications for enlistment. When we went around to the Army and the Marines, there were no takers in the office and no waiting list. Months earlier I had enlisted in the U.S. Naval Reserve on Jefferson Ave. as a hedge, which gave me a classification of 5-C. This meant that I would not be drafted into the Army, but could ask for active duty in the Navy if I would start striking for a useful (to the Navy) rating, i.e. a specialty. At the time I was interested in meteorology and they had a rating in what they called aerography. However, I was still in the lowest rank when events caught up with me.

During the winter of 1950-51 the Ist MarDiv., and some Army units pushed the North Koreans back into the North and were headed for the Yalu River when 300,000 Red Chinese soldiers entered the war without warning. The Marines and Army troops were completely surrounded by the Chinese in weather that was more than -30⁰ F. at the Chosin Reservoir (known to Marines as Frozen Chosin). The survivors still call themselves "The Chosin Few." The Marine, Army, and British units fought their way out to Hungnam on the coast and were evacuated by ship to Pusan at the south eastern tip of the Korean peninsula in December 1950.

When the news of the Chinese invasion and the predicament of the Marines hit the U.S., it added to our concern about the future. Our government was involved in a war in which men were dying or coming home wounded, which caused a certain amount of anxiety among the young. We didn't know what to do and fretted about what kind of future we might have, if any.

During those winter months, while the Marines were freezing their butts, or getting them shot off at Frozen Chosin, I was floundering in indecision. I was only 20 and I hung around with a wild bunch of Finns who did a lot of carousing . Some weeks I didn't go home, didn't go to work and worst of all, I failed to show up at the weekly USNR meetings. Or when I did show up, I didn't present the proper attitude toward my military obligations. Wearing peg pants and sporting a James Dean duck's ass haircut were frowned upon by the Chief Bosun Mate for some reason.

The USNR unit sent a letter to my draft board requesting that my classification be changed from 5-C to 1-A—prime draft material. This was followed up with letters from Selective Service, which I ignored until I received a notice to report for a physical exam for induction into the Army. Now it was getting serious. When other guys went to take their induction physicals, they usually disappeared soon afterward into some Army Camp for basic training. I was uneasy. This was it and some evasive action was required. I absolutely refused to be sucked into the Army without checking out the now dwindling options.

Ted Kilberg went with me across the Detroit River to Windsor, Ontario where he played hockey. The recruiter for the Canadian Army was not encouraging. He explained that if we enlisted in that Army there were several things we could look forward to: 1) an enlistment of seven years with five years of that time overseas, 2) we would lose our U.S. citizenship, and 3) we would not receive any benefits under the U.S. G.I. bill. The Canadian option was clearly out so we went back to Detroit to ponder the only remaining option. I think the Canadian recruiter was lying about No. 1 just to discourage us. Why would a normal man volunteer for seven years of service when he only had to serve two as a draftee in his own Army. Why did I go through all these twists and turns to avoid being drafted? In my family it would be a stigma not to volunteer when the country faced a crisis while others were already enlisting and reservists were leaving for Korea.

On the February 1, 1951, Ted and I went down to the Detroit Federal building to give ourselves up. Because neither of us wanted to serve even two years (drafted) in the Army, we entered the recruiting office of last resort, the U.S. Marines. We encountered a few other guys like ourselves who were adrift in the same sinking boat. The recruiting Sergeant was very convincing, but told us a lot of lies. We signed on the dotted line and a couple of days later went to the U.S. Naval Reserve Center to take a mass physical exam with a bunch of others on their way into the Navy or the Marines.

I was skinny but very strong from doing all that tree work. It was a typical military physical. Turn your head, cough twice and you're in. Well there was a little more to it than that. One doctor was feeling my hands and feet and said, "Why did you say on this form that you never had any broken bones and no severe burns, when I can feel where four bones in your hand had been broken recently? I told him that I'd forgotten about that. He just glared at me, probably thinking, "What a twit, maybe he won't know it when he gets wounded in Korea either."

Looking at the three by four inch scar on the inside of my upper right arm, he said, "What about this burn here. It looks quite severe and skin has been grafted over it. I suppose you forgot about that too?" I explained how I got pulled up into a wringer on an old Easy copper tub washing machine when I was only two years old. I was stuck hanging there with the rotating rollers pulling the muscles out until I was rescued. He wanted to know why I was doing the wash when I was only two. Some smartass doctor.

When this washer incident happened, the doctor at the time told my parents that I would never be able to have full use of that arm. Well he didn't know my mom. She was one tough mother. As soon as the graft healed, my mother stood over me every day while I worked out with an old fashioned flat iron. It was one of those cast iron jobs that were heated on the wood cook stove. Now they are used for doorstops. For almost a year she had me lifting that iron every day to build up the muscles that had been damaged.

When I told them I was joining the Marines, my folks told me that I couldn't pass the physical exam because of the arm injury. But, I had no trouble with the physical, because the Marines were looking for what they called "warm bodies." Back in the Civil War and WWI, we were known as cannon fodder. Warm bodies to feed to the hungry cannons of war.

On February 4, I went to the City of Detroit offices to see about my pay and to tell them I quit so I could enlist. The Personnel Chief told me that they were going to overlook all of my absences from work over the past few months, because they understood what I was going through and that my job would be waiting for me when I came home. I was surprised by all that concern, which I never expected from bureaucrats. But most of the older city employees served in WWII, which had ended only five years earlier.

The enlistment was effective on February 6, 1951. The night before, we all mustered at a downtown Detroit movie theater to watch the film, The Sands of Iwo Jima, starring John Wayne, courtesy of the USMC. I think it was supposed to whip us up into a frenzy of patriotism, but it didn't help to see all those Marines getting shot and blown up even though the Japanese got the worst of it.

I said goodbye to my family the next morning and went to the train station with Ted Kilberg. I was thinking about my Dad, because I was 20 years and six months old when I enlisted. Joe Ginnelly was exactly the same age when he enlisted in the Army in WWI. The U.S . declared war on Germany on April 6, 1917 and he enlisted in the Ohio National Guard, which was just being mobilized, on May 17. He had just finished his second year at Cornell University.

There were at least 40 of us in our group as we boarded the train under the watchful eyes of the Marine officer and NCOs from the recruiting office. They had done their job and knew what was in store for us at the other end of this trip. If we had known what our fate would be in boot camp, most of us would have let the Selective Service System (SSS) draft us into the Army for two years. As we pulled out of the station and were leaving the Detroit suburbs, I looked out over the soot blackened snow and grimy ice. I was glad to be leaving and to be off into the great unknown.

As the train rolled south, we were sizing each other up. I'm sure that some of these guys were looking at me, the skinniest one in the group, thinking that I would not last a week of the intense harassment and training we would undergo. Now, 48 years later, I remember only one guy in our car, other than Ted Kilberg that is. This guy was pretty hefty, and had a big mouth — a real wise ass. He was proud of his long blond hair and told us he would be the toughest Marine at Parris Island (PI). We found out later he fit the image of the Hollywood Marine. All looks, no substance.

Most of the rest of us were pretty quiet, knowing we were in for a complete change of lifestyle at the end of the line. When we crossed the Mason-Dixon line we were sitting in the last car in the train. All of us were white, and being Yankees we were not aware of the way things were done in the South. The conductor came into our car and told us we couldn't sit here. We had to move forward to another car. When we asked why, he curtly told us that this car was reserved for coloreds only. We looked around and said we don't see any coloreds here. He told us not to get smart with him. If we didn't move forward he would take it up with our military escort. So we went forward to another car.

One of the cities we stopped in was Augusta, Georgia. We were allowed out on the platform to walk around and saw a few things that surprised most of us Yankees. Not only were there four rest rooms (toilets) at the station, one each for the sexes and for whites and coloreds, but the Southerners thought enough of coloreds to have a separate drinking fountain for them. The rest rooms and the drinking fountains were plainly marked with signs for colored or for white. For the first time in our lives, us Yankees were exposed to real life in the South and started wondering what kind of a country we were living in.

BOOT CAMP, PARRIS ISLAND, SC

When we pulled into Beaufort, South Carolina we could see green USMC buses waiting at the station. The train had no sooner stopped, when the cars were invaded by swarms of drill instructors (DIs) who screamed obscenities at us while shoving and crowding us to the doors and herding us onto the platform. All the time they were accusing us of being a bunch of "pansies, wimps, and candy asses who wouldn't make a pimple on a fighting man's ass." They told us we were a sorry lot and they had the impossible task of making something useful (to them) out of the flotsam (me) and jetsam (Ted) of the civilian world.

In a few minutes, the DIs gave up trying to get us into some sort of formation and herded us out to the buses all the time yelling, " Move it, move it, you damn cruddy civilians. Get your asses on that bus. Faster! Step on anyone in front of you." Three DIs got onto each bus. They continued to harass us in our seats, trying to put the fear into us for what was to come. The buses passed through town and onto the Marine Corps Recruit Depot (MCRD) where boys are turned into men and men into machines of a sort.

The buses stopped at a tent city where we were driven off like cattle by the relentless and caustic barrage of abusive language of the DIs. Our very own DIs were waiting for us and took over the herd. They immediately began to show us who was boss. The lead DI ordered his two assistants to get us into some semblance of a formation so that he could lay down the law. We stood at what we assumed to be attention and tried to look like Marines even though our multicolored civvies made us look like a raggedy-assed mob.

The three DIs were dressed in their winter uniform, a khaki shirt with military creases, green woolen trousers, and spit-shined cordovan dress shoes. This was topped off with the symbol of the DI; a wide brimmed, tan campaign hat with a large Marine emblem (globe and anchor) in front. The DIs were neat and we came to know this appearance as that of John J. Squared Away—the image every Marine would strive for soon after boot camp.

The lead DI demanded our rapt attention, which he got in a few seconds. He looked us over and told us his name, Staff Sergeant Sicklick. Right away, the smart asses like myself were working out ways we could twist this lovely name into the satire it deserved: Sgt. SickDick, Sgt. LickDick, Sgt. SlickDick, SlackDick, SickleLick, SickleDick, SuckDick, or Sicko for short. I decided on Sgt. SickDick, but needless to say, we were so afraid of him all through boot camp, that I never, ever heard his name misused. Why is that? Because we learned to hate him and curse his name only to ourselves. SSgt. Sicklick was stocky with a hint of a gut pressing his duty belt. He had a kind of hound dog look about him, blood hound that is. I could imagine him growing jowls in a few short years. He had a rather commanding presence, which became overpowering as the weeks wore on. When we saw SSgt Sicklick later wearing his green battle jacket, we came to respect him more for the two hash marks on his sleeve and the ribbons on his chest. We guessed from the hashmarks that he had at least ten years of service and from the battle stars on one of his six ribbons, he must have been in the war in the Pacific.

SSgt.Sicklick was about the meanest looking person I had ever seen, and that is a compliment after growing up on the streets of Detroit. He carried his police nightstick and kept swatting it into his other hand for emphasis. He proceeded to tell us that we were just a bunch of cunts to him and his impossible task was to turn us into real men. He assured us that he could not only take any one of us, but could take us in twos or threes. He said that he had the power of life and death over us and we believed him. His eyes were penetrating. We felt them boring into every one of us. He was already searching for any weakness, probing for the fault that he would correct with his nightstick.

He warned us that we would learn to obey him without thinking. He would have complete control over our lives night and day for the next 11 weeks. The survivors would go off to Korea and other posts. He didn't say what would happen to the chaff. He warned us that he was on active duty only for our benefit. His peacetime job was that of a police officer in New York City. He had seen everything there, so we would not be able to put anything over on him. He said he had eyes in the back of his head and we later came to believe it. SSgt. Sicklick barked out his commands in a gravelly voice, which was normal for a DI after months of this training duty.

Sgt. Sicklick further told us that we would bend to his will starting today and that when he told us to shit, we would squat and ask," What color sir?" We were to jump to attention whenever a DI addressed any of us and stand there rigidly awaiting his next command. We were never to speak to a DI, or an officer without first requesting permission to do so. I have forgotten the exact ritual, but if we ever had the nerve to do so, we had to address a DI as follows while standing at attention, "Private Smith requests permission to speak, sir." I didn't know anyone who ever wanted to do such a crazy thing. It was suicidal to confront him for any reason. He made "house calls", which brought his ugly kisser and nasty personality right into your face. You had to be nuts to go looking for grief by reminding him that you even existed.

One of the most important things you learned that first day at PI was not to attract the DI's attention. When he was jumping all over some other poor bastard for an infraction (or just for being alive), you tried to make yourself small and unnoticeable. When he was raising hell with some poor skinhead out in front of the platoon we all stood at attention. What he said or made the fool do was so funny, we would almost burst out laughing inside. You had to suppress any glee, because if the DI caught you laughing, smirking, or even looking at the victim, you would soon join him.

It may be human nature, but the DI tended to pick on anyone who stood out—the very tall, very short, the clumsy, the super stupid, the uncoordinated, the would be smart ass, etc. Trying to become completely unnoticed became an obsession to most of us throughout boot camp. I was successful most of the time, but took my lumps when I deserved them and even when I didn't. Maybe this had something to do with us learning to become a part of the scenery when patrolling in enemy territory later. A pretty clever training method.

The first day at PI was spent in becoming sanitized to suit the Corps as our new family. We formed up and went for the famous haircut on the base, where we were rendered completely bald by former sheep shearers posing as barbers. SSgt. Sicklick stood by and personally supervised the hair loss of the blond loudmouth recruit on the train. The DI stood menacingly in front of him with arms akimbo, nightstick in one hand, watching the operation which transformed this smart assed civilian into a skinhead boot. At one point the DI held his hand up to signal the barber to stop. He sarcastically asked the trembling recruit who was trying to screw himself into the chair, " Lad, do you want to keep your nice long sideburns?"

The not-so-loud mouth was so shook up he could barely speak, but managed to nod is head in the affirmative. The DI got into his face, the brim of his campaign hat pressing into the kid's forehead and said, "Answer me when I ask you a question you creep!" The kid squeaked out a "Yes sir, I do want them." The DI laughed and signaled the barber to zip the burns off, saying, " Then hold up your hands and catch them." The kid caught them while the DI roared. That was one of the few times any of us boots ever saw Sgt. Sicko laugh.

When we left the barber shop it was mass confusion as we sought out our friends. Ted Kilberg and I passed each other a couple of times without recognizing each other. We sure looked funny or at least I thought Ted looked funny, I wouldn't see my new hairless do until I went to the head later.

To most of those in the military, GI means General or Government Issue. It is the stuff that is issued to everyone and we received our basic share in boot camp. From the barber shop we were marched off to the supply sergeant's domain. As we passed along a counter inside, the supply types sized us up and hurled various items of clothing at us—such as: skivvies, socks, field and dress; boondockers; dungaree shirt, dungaree trousers, trousers, shirts, field scarf, cap fore and aft, towel, washcloth, belt, with military brass buckle, dungaree cap.

A seabag was issued along with a packet of tie-ties. These small cords were used to secure rolled up clothing for proper stowing in the seabag. We were issued an olive-drab field jacket, which was supposed to keep us dry and warm but it wasn't much good. A waterproof poncho with a hole in the middle was issued for foul weather. The poncho had green camouflage on one side and brown-tan camouflage on the other. A white bag was issued for laundry..

As for the stylish colors offered, they were Marine standard. The dungarees including cap were light green, skivvies were dark green or white, boondockers (field shoes) light brown, dress socks dark brown, work socks khaki. The seabag was light brown and the tie-ties white. The belt was khaki, towel and washcloth, green.

All gear was stowed in the seabag. Then we right shouldered seabags and marched back to place them near our metal cots. We were allowed a few minutes to get into Marine skivvies, dungarees, socks and boondockers. Right after dressing, we were told to roll up our civvies in whatever jacket or coat we arrived in. Then we were marched to a room near the Post Office, provided with wrapping paper and string to do up our old clothes, and wrote our home address on the parcel. The USMC mailed them home for us. We were informed that our old skivvies, which we had put in a big pile, were sent off to be burned. They weren't taking any chances with us bringing in any microscopic livestock.

We immediately formed up again and were marched back to the supply building. This time we were issued the military accoutrements for the infantryman. This stuff is known as the web gear (heavy canvas) or 782 gear in Marine lingo which comprised all the items we would need for living and fighting in the field.

Later that day we also visited another supply shed to be issued a mattress, sheets, pillow and cover, two blankets, one steel bucket, and one brush, scrub, Model 1815 A1—a brush that hadn't changed since the days of the Horse Marines. We deposited this gear on our cots. Then it was off to the armory to be issued one M-1 Garand rifle and one bayonet with sheath and leather rifle sling. Each rifle was covered with cosmoline, a petroleum product something like Vaseline but thicker and darker. The rifle was wrapped in an oilcloth type fabric. All this was to prevent rusting while the rifle was in storage, probably from WWII.

We marched to a special area where there were long tables for us to clean the cosmoline off and learn how to disassemble the M-1. This was not a fun job as the rifle had to be cleaned meticulously of every trace of the goop. An instructor had shown us the proper way to field strip (take apart) the rifle beforehand, naming the parts as he deftly broke one down to its main components.

We were provided with some rags and cans of cleaning solvent to help remove the tenacious preservative from the rifle. As we worked, the DI hovered over us with dire threats of punishment if we got any cosmoline on our dungarees. When we finished, the DIs and the rifle instructor circulated among the platoon checking the progress and sending each boot back into formation as his rifle passed inspection.

As soon as we were all in formation, we were given rudimentary instruction in close-order drill and in the basic manual of arms. Then we came to attention, dressed right, right shouldered arms, right faced and marched in cadence back to the tents. The DI calling out at first: left, right, left, one, two, three, four, left, right left. Then he lapsed into the DI vernacular that we had heard from other DIs drilling their boots— one, hup reep, for yur leup, right, leup, then repeated until we fell into the cadence rhythm. The junior DIs skirted around the marching platoon like sheep dogs to find the boots who could not get it right, tapping them on the shoulder and screaming in their ears, "Your other right you idiot." or "Get in step you clodhopper, you ain't behind your plow horse now." There was a farmer from Michigan in our platoon who was picked on for weeks because he naturally walked as though he was stomping through the furrows. He was taken out to the parade ground every night after chow for a week for special instruction in troop and stomp.

During the second week, we were marched back to the supply shed to be issued our winter green uniforms made of fine wool. This time the distribution was somewhat more civilized. Because we might be wearing these uniforms on graduation day and when we went back home on leave, the USMC wanted them to fit properly. As I entered the warehouse I was told to step up on a platform about two feet high. A supply guy measured the inseam leg length and waist and wrote the figures on a piece of paper. I went to the next supply type who measured my neck size, shoulder width, sleeve length, and chest girth and added them to the chit.

At the counter I gave the chit to the supply NCO who called out the measurements to his helpers in the racks where the folded clothing was arranged by sizes. I was handed the battle jacket, overcoat and other items rounding out the cold weather uniform.

Before receiving the trousers the supply sergeant asked me, "For the trousers, which way do you dress, left or right?" Like all the other boots ahead of me, I looked puzzled and said, "What?" SSgt. Sicklick who was standing behind me, nudged me in the back with the end of his nightstick and said, "The sergeant wants to know which side of your crotch your pecker hangs in because the trousers are made to accommodate your equipment on the right or the left. Do you know, or do you have to look?" I got it and said, "Hanging to the left sir." The supply man shouted towards the shelves, trousers, waist 28" and length 34", dressed left." And that's what I got. This business about which way the penis hangs had been turned into a friendly form of greeting by coarse old salts. Instead of saying Hi in the morning, one might be greeted with, "How's your hammer hanging Hector? To the left or to the right?" Which usually drew the retort, "Same as yours I expect, peckerhead." A common form of repartee among enlisted types.

The next stop was to be measured for dress shoes and issued two pairs of cordovan blucher style jobs made on a Navy last. These shoes are so comfortable that I still wear the same style years later. A style known to my kids as the ultimate in frumpy. From there we marched back to the tents to stow our gear, listen to a lecture (in formation) on how to wear the new issue winter uniform, and to learn how to spit shine our new shoes.

There were some items of clothing not issued to my platoon for some reason. One was the traditional green woolen blouse, a neat looking, long, belted outer jacket worn with the green trousers, green cap and dress shoes. We were not issued the dress blue uniform, which the public sees on Marines on posters and at parades. Dress blues were provided only to those going on to sea duty aboard naval vessels, those going to recruiting duty, band or drum and bugle units, Marine barracks guard type duty, and embassy duty.

Also missing, a white covered barracks cap with a shiny visor, normally worn with dress blues, but it also had a green and a khaki cover to be worn with those uniforms. None of these items were issued because we were all destined for one of the amphibious units of the Fleet Marine Force (FMF), Most of us were going to the 1st Marine Div. fighting in Korea and a few to the 2nd Marine Div. at Camp Lejeune. We would be in dungarees all the time except on liberty ashore or for parades and inspections on post.

At every formation the DI gave us instruction in Marine terminology. Most of the words came from the Navy's names for things. The floor or ground was the deck and the wall was a bulkhead. Upstairs was above decks and downstairs, below decks, a stairway was a ladder and a hall a passageway. The toilet was the head, a door a hatch, a window a porthole, the ceiling was the overhead. The kitchen was the galley and the dining hall the mess hall. Out in the country was the boondocks, where Marines spend much of their time. What takes one to the boondocks? Boondockers of course, those shoes to be worn for work, for field hikes, and long marches. A necktie became a field scarf, fore and aft cap was a pisscutter or a cunt cap. We also had to learn some words for getting out of the way if we ever happened to be standing in a bunch, as aboard ship in a passageway. When you heard the words, "gangway, make a hole, make way, or coming through," you had to get out of the way for an officer or chief, approaching. Aboard ship it could be corpsmen with someone on a litter, or a fire, or damage control team rushing to some crisis.

The company commander was the skipper, The first sergeant was the top (for top sergeant) and the technical sergeant was the gunny. The gunner was a warrant officer, somewhere in the limbo-land between a master sergeant and a second lieutenant. The senior officers called the lesser ones mister. To us a second lieutenant was a shavetail, or a 90-day-wonder if he graduated from Quantico. Of course, we never used those terms within an officer's hearing.

On returning from one of our first trips to the supply shed, we came to a somewhat controlled halt on the tarmac, which ran between the rows of tents. The DI wasn't satisfied with the performance so he had us face right then had the assistant DIs show us how to come to a stop as he called cadence. He said, " When I call Platoon...... Halt., You take two more steps and bring your feet together as the DIs are doing." We left faced and marched around the area while we practiced coming to a halt with SSgt. Sicklick yelling, " Damnit, let's get it together girls." Eventually we did.

Back at the tents we fell out (were dismissed) and ordered into our tents to stow our rifles in their rack and make up our sacks. The DIs split up and showed the boots in each tent how to make up a tight sack with hospital corners on sheets and the blanket. The made-up sack had to be so taut that a quarter would bounce off the blanket.

About half way through this exercise the DI yelled, " Platoon 136, Fall in!" He and the other DIs rousted everyone from the tents and into formation where we lined up as best we could. We stood at attention, while SSgt. Sicklick showed us how to form up, with each boot in his assigned place and how to come to attention with heels together and feet out at about a 45 degree angles, eyes straight ahead, back straight, stomach in, chest out and fingertips at your thigh side.

The DI showed us how to dress right—left arm extended and fingertips just touching the man to your left and shuffling to the side to form a straight line in ranks. Then the command to open ranks, i.e. one step forward for all except the last rank. This gave the DI better access for examining each skinhead during inspections. The head DI started at the first rank harassing boots along the way about appearance. He stopped in front of me in the second rank, examining my ruddy face and the various and sundry zits thereon and had this advice, "That problem will clear up lad when we make sure you shave everyday and are forced to do without all that junk food and pogey bait you've been eating 'til now."

We started to learn some of the Marine lingo he was laying on us one word at a time. We still weren't sure what a poge was, but it must be someone looked down upon by the entire Corps. Perhaps an undesirable such as a homosexual, an anathema to the Corps. And of course, pogey bait was the sort of thing that a poge would eat, such as candy, pastries and the like.

When he finished telling me that, he said, "Do you get that, Marine?" I replied, "Yes." He stuck his face in mine and said, "What?," shouting now and glaring at me, 'Yes what? You say, yes sir you boney fuck." I said, "Yes sir." He said, "What? I can't hear you. Speak up, skinhead." I said, "Yes Sir." a little louder. He reached up and jerked my cap visor down over my eyes, saying, "Louder, I can't hear you." At least now I can't see him, what a relief. But he spent another few minutes making me shout it out, then went down the line harassing every boot. I noticed a distinct odor on the DI's breath. An aroma I associated with Hamtramck, a Polish enclave in Detroit. I'm sure it was garlic, probably from kielbasa he got from home.

While he was giving us the business, his two aides were going through the tents ripping up our (or so we thought) well made bunks. They took off the blankets, stripped off the sheets, pillow case and dumped the mattress and all on the floor. I mean on the deck. When we were dismissed, we were told to get back inside and make up the sacks properly. We had exactly four minutes to do it. It seemed like only two minutes had passed when the DI yelled, " Platoon 136, Fall In." We fell in and formed up. He shouted, "You're too slow. Get back inside and get those sacks made up right." We did, and two minutes later came the order to fall out again. This went on for an hour of in and out. The access to each tent was through the flaps which were closed overlapping each other, although usually closed only for inclement weather. The DIs had their fun yelling and pushing us through the flaps all the time telling us that we were too slow. In some cases the DI's boondocker was applied to rumps as we scurried like rabbits into our warrens.

At just about dark, we fell out for another harassment drill, but to our surprise we were then marched off to the mess hall for evening chow. We marched in single file to the chow line and our trays were loaded by the mess servers. We were allowed about 20 minutes to wolf it down. The real chow hounds like myself, went back for seconds. There was little conversation, since SSgt. Sicklick was sitting nearby at the DI's table watching us with his beady eyes.

LEARNING THE WAYS OF THE CORPS

As we marched around Parris Island those first few weeks, I thought the base quite eerie. I had never been around a place where the entire facility was heated by a steam generating power plant through overhead and underground pipes. All buildings there were heated by steam, but our tents, of course, had no heat at all. Much of the steam was vented at the places where it was used, which meant that there were clouds of steam billowing up from valves at the mess hall, the head, barracks, etc. This made the experience of being on PI creepy and menacing, especially in the dark. I'm sure that Alfred Hitchcock or Vincent Price must have been hired as a consultant on the design of this base for maximum effect on intimidating new arrivals.

If we were told in formation that we were never, ever to go anywhere except in marching formation, or if we had to go to sick bay alone we needed the DI's permission, I didn't hear it. I was soon to be lumped into the ten percent who didn't get the word. After chow we were back in our tents sitting on our upturned buckets practicing field stripping our rifles and adjusting the leather sling to maximum tautness. After we finished these kinds of chores we could spend a half hour writing letters. We were never allowed to sit or lie on our sacks. They were for sleeping at night only from lights out 2200 hours (10PM) until 0500 hours when we heard reveille.

On this first evening when I thought my chores were all finished, Ted Kilberg and I took our towels and headed for the shower. Everyone else was in their tents, including the DIs. We sauntered down to the head and took a nice hot shower. We didn't wonder why the shower room was empty. We put our dungarees back on and were just about back to our tent when SSgt. Sicklick emerged from his tent and spotted us. He shouted, "Hold it right there you two. Where in the hell have you been, out swimming?" We came to attention facing him and said, "No sir, we went to take a shower." Then he went ballistic and started the "I can't hear you!" routine. Now he was so mad, his red face was glowing in the dark. He shouted, "You two, over there, backs to that tent, facing me." Followed by, "Platoon 136 fall in, pronto."

The rest of the guys fell in, some in skivvies, some without shoes, some without dungaree tops and formed up standing at attention in front of us. Then he placed himself between us and the other 70 boots. Arms akimbo, he said, "Didn't you shitbirds get the word, you don't take a shower, you don't take a shit, you don't do a fucking thing around here, unless you are told to do it. And when we do it, we do it in formation and by the numbers. We do everything together, because that is what your training is all about."

Then he asked them, "Do you see these two shitbirds in front of you?" They all said, "Yes sir." Then he made them go through the I can't hear you routine so they shouted louder and louder and after ten minutes they finally did it in unison.

He told them, "These two just sashayed down to the head to take a shower like they were still at home. And I'm going to punish them, by sticking it to the rest of you. If you think that it is unfair, too bad. Life is not fair. You are dismissed to get your rifles and fall in again."

He made them go in and out of the tents for a half hour, while we just stood there with wet towels around our necks, wondering what the hell was going on. The DI called out his assistants and had them show the other skinheads how to do physical training exercises with a 9.5 pound rifle. Then they opened ranks and really got into these very demanding workouts with their M-1s. As they were doing this, he would shout taunts at them, saying that we were standing their smirking and loafing while they were being put through the mill. He was provoking them to take out their frustrations on us. We were the real source of their present pain.

Now and then, the DI would turn to the two of us and tell us to repeat twenty times, "I'm a shitbird." This we did with fervor, all the time being admonished to shouts of, "Louder, I can't hear you." The rest of the troops might have thought this was funny, but were beginning to flag with fatigue and glaring at us, the goof ups, the goof offs. The DI's venom was beginning to take on them and he could tell they were ready to be turned loose on us.

After about an hour of this crap, the DI dismissed the platoon to stow their rifles and fall in again with towels and soap. As they fell into formation, he called attention to the two empty spaces in the ranks. He pointed to us and said, "The whole platoon will now march to the showers. The two shitbirds here in front of you are responsible for your going through these rifle PT drills when you all should have been asleep an hour ago. Now get your asses into the showers and when you come out, I want to see some bruises on these two idiots." He wanted them to beat us up, at least a little, to enforce some group discipline.

Ted and I were ordered back into ranks and we were all marched off to the showers with the DI calling out cadence, "One Hup reep, por yur left, hup reep, por yur lep, etc." All the way to the head I was worried shitless (sometimes this condition leads to pissing your pants, which in turn leads to dehydration and hence constipation). When we got into the head, we stripped and took showers in the large shower room. Ted and I hovered in the middle of the room, waiting for the first fist to be planted on one of us, but nothing happened.

No one said anything. There were no words of condemnation, none of encouragement. Why the silence? Simple. They knew that the DI was in the adjacent dressing room listening for any hint of sympathy from the rest of the platoon. Then they would be punished again.

But as we two stole glances at the rest of the recruits while we showered, we could see in their eyes that they understood what the DI was trying to do. From now on, the whole platoon would be punished for the errors and transgressions of one skinhead. The other boots knew that it could have been one of them in our boondockers, or shower shoes as it were. They realized that in the coming weeks, each one of them could be the victim in a situation like this.

And so ended the fist day of boot camp as we marched back to the tents and after a 15 minute harangue by the DI on discipline and group cooperation, unit integrity, etc. were dismissed to hit the sack. We had committed the worst blunder possible on our first day in boot camp. Ted and I had attracted attention to ourselves. Once you have done that, the DI would normally focus all his wrath on you until you left boot camp. In plain English, he picked on you because you fucked up early in your career. On the good side, the first day was over.

The next morning we were roused at reveille and marched to the head for the other of the three esses, shit and shave. We had taken care of the other S last night when I got two showers out of the USMC. As we fell in for the breakfast chow formation we began to get a little fatherly advice from SSgt. Sicklick. He said, "Although we normally make you hit the sack at taps, (2200 hours), there are exceptions. What you must know is that you are now in the USMC where there are 24 hours in day, (long pause) and then there is the night. For those of you who are afflicted with constipation, we have a cure for that here and at every other Marine Corps facility. It is called GI coffee. And since you may have noticed that it is made in an urn, we call it "urine coffee", possibly to be construed as made from weasel urine. If you drink several cups of that hot java every morning at chow, you will soon be loose as a goose." The rumor circulated later that the coffee was really made by collecting and boiling the dirty socks from a platoon just in from a two day march.

Looking back on it, he was right about the DI's idea of what a boot's day would be like. He was right about the coffee too, it works like a charm, although now that I am a seasoned civilian citizen, any hot liquid ingested early upon arising works just as well. Serving a number of years in the Far East will also cure constipation in westerners forever.

From that first day on we learned close order drill, known as troop and stomp. The British call it square bashing. First we had learned all the standing in one place drills then we spent the rest of the day learning the manual of arms. When we got that down pat, we had to learn the marching part of the troop and stomp routine to commands which began with the call to attention, but sounded like, "Platoon, Ten Hut." This was followed by right shoulder arms, then left face. When the platoon guide moved to his position at the right front of the platoon, the DI shouted, "Forward 'arch," (forward march) and we all started out in step—sort of. We marched down to the end of the platoon street and at the end we heard, "Column right, 'arch" and the platoon guide and boots in front smartly followed that command and we all did the same when we got to the corner.

As we headed for the parade ground we look like a herd trying to follow the cadence of our DI. Other DIs passed by with their platoons marching smartly. They've been at it for weeks now. But their DIs can't resist ribbing our DI. They call out, "What's that thing there, SSgt. Sicklick, looks like a disorderly mob to me. You'll never make Marines out of that bunch of galoots."

Our DI ignores the catcalls and shouts, "Continue to march," calling cadence for us, "One hup, reep, por yur lep, right lep, one," etc. By this time the other passing DI has ordered his platoon to," Count cadence, count." And they sing out in unison, "One two, three, four, one, two, three, four, etc." All day long we pound the tarmac on the parade ground learning the movement drill, the troop and stomp, the DIs swirling around the platoon searching for the uncoordinated, the slow learners, the inept, the hapless. When a victim is found they ride him with taunts, stop the platoon, haul him out in front and put him through the drill, hollering in his ears until he gets it right.

We learn to come to a halt without running into the guy in front of us. At noon we go back to the tents, secure the rifles in the racks and march off to chow. On some days we march off to lectures on various subjects such as instruction in completely stripping your rifle, cleaning, oiling an putting it back together. There were lectures on health and sanitation and there seemed to be a couple of guys in our platoon who were very shy about being exposed to water as in washing. As time went on and shower rules were relaxed slightly, these two cowboys were not taking their daily shower. How they got away with it 'til then, I don't know.

When they started to reek, the DI ordered us all into the showers and told ten other boots to take their GI soap, scrub brushes and a pail of sand in with them. The guys with the cleaning equipment were ordered to grab the two cruds and hold them while the rest of the detail scrubbed their hides with some sand, brown GI soap and the brushes. The rest of us took our showers as usual while the protests of the cruds filled the steamy room. There were no more shower shirkers after that. These two rednecks gleamed bright pink after their sand scrubbing.

I'm sure that for some young guys, just 17 or 18 years old, having never been away from home, were shocked by some of the goings on at boot camp. They just could not believe there were people who had an aversion to bathing. During the personal hygiene lectures, the instructor said something, even I would never forget. In the course of warning about drinking water and about VD, he said, "Remember this! All women are infected and all water is contaminated until proven otherwise. As for the women, this goes for your mother and your sisters as well." Now I'm sure they were trying to scare the simple, but they surely must have offended the mama's boys present.

These lectures were usually given in a Quonset hut just big enough to hold all of us on benches. It would get hot and stuffy and we always had to wear our helmets to lectures. As the lecturer of the day droned on, heads would nod. A DI roamed around us watching for boots going to sleep and when he saw a head nod he came up from behind and crashed his long pole on the nodder's helmet; ringing your bell so to speak. They must have gotten the idea from church practice in the old days.

At one lecture, the expert warned us about finding more than one boot in a sack after taps. Most of us thought this was a nutty comment. Then there were remarks about anyone caught playing drop the soap in the shower with anybody else. A lot of us were pretty naive, and had to have this explained to us, including me. Then the same speaker told us that the medical people had devised a way of looking up your butt, and determining whether or not, something had been introduced into your bum at some time or other. Most of us didn't know what he was talking about, but the gist of it was explained. If any of you are so inclined as to climb into some one else's sack while he is in it, or if you play drop the soap with another, then you will be found out. The punishment for such illicit sexual behavior was a court martial and then the guilty one is drummed out the front gate with an Dishonorable (undesirable) Discharge. I guess the threat can't get much plainer than that.

Some lectures were accompanied by training films made by the military on subjects like venereal disease (VD). One such film showed a sailor who got the clap from some nice girl who seemed like the girl next door. The film also showed what a chancre looked like on some unlucky GI's dick. It was a very ugly and gross ulcer to say the least. He had syphilis and was in deep trouble with the military. Then they gave a list of the lame excuses given by GIs who had gotten VD. This Marine says to the Doc, " I must have got if off a toilet seat." The Doc in turn asks, "What were you doing, screwing some broad on a toilet seat."

While on the subject of VD, we were subjected to a 'milk it down routine" at our physical exam prior to enlistment and periodically until you left the Corps. I'm sure this was SOP in the other services also. The idea was to find anyone who had the clap (gonorrhea), which came to be known as Gone to Korea. First you were instructed en masse in the details of detecting the clap in men. First, drop your drawers as the corpsman or doctor approaches you. When he faces you, grab the base of your penis with thumb and forefinger, squeeze while pulling forward to see if anything comes out of the urethra at the business end. If a white exudate appears and it isn't toothpaste, you are in big trouble. To the Docs, this was a sure sign that there is an infection, probably the clap, and he had you report to sick bay for treatment and to catch hell for having VD. We were told that it was a court martial offense.

There were some guys who were not circumcised and who didn't do a good enough job of cleaning inside the fold of the foreskin. Material of sebaceous origin would accumulate there called smegma by those who know that kind of stuff.. It is of cheesy texture, which prompted the DIs to get in on the short arm inspection. If you showed any smegma during the process the DI's comment was loud and clear to embarrass you into better hygiene. Sgt. Sicklick would say, "What's the matter with you lad? You're not from Wisconsin. You have no business growing cheese." If you've never heard of smegma before, its because it has no common name and was one of those unmentionable things back then. That is until you got to boot camp, where you couldn't hide anything personal.

Short-arm inspections were simply called pecker checks by the troops. We had to go through it a couple of times during boot camp just to get us used to the indignity. Or perhaps they were looking for a latent case from one of us screwing some chick on the train to PI.

Although we were afterward tempted to call the corpsmen pecker checkers, we never did because our lives depended on these Navy medics when we got into combat. We were taught to have every respect for these noncombatants who went willingly into battle to give us first aid, bind our wounds, etc. The Navy corpsman was the first medical person you saw along the line of evacuation from the lines. They also took care of our everyday ailments too small for the MDs to bother with wherever Marines served. A few years later I was in graduate school with another veteran from California who had served in the Army as a medic. His name was Richard Painter and he was such a nice guy, I never did call him DickPainter. I'm sure that's what the soldiers he treated called him when he wasn't around.

There seemed to be no end to the ways a DI could waste an entire day driving us through nonsensical drills. On one particular day SSgt. Sicklick could find no better way to entertain himself, other than to see how fast we could change clothes. We had our full complement of clothing and he wanted us to become intimately familiar with our new wardrobe.

When we returned from morning chow and head call the DI checked us over in our dungarees. Then he told us to fall out and don our khaki uniforms, dress shoes and socks. He gave us so many minutes to do it and called us to fall in again. If it wasn't fast enough he would order us back in the tents and back out again. He would give us a quick inspection and if a field scarf was missing on a man, or knotted incorrectly, it was back inside for all and back out again. The tent doors were secured to make it more difficult for us to wriggle through the canvas flaps. Then he would order us inside to put on the green uniform and fall in again. Same routine. If an emblem was missing, put on crooked, or any other infraction, it was back in again.

For a change of routine, he would have us fall out in dungarees, boondockers, leggings, field pack and blanket roll, rifle, cartridge belt, helmet—the works. If someone had his bayonet on his cartridge belt instead of his pack (as instructed), or if his camo helmet cover was green instead of brown, it was in and out again. The pack and roll always made it very awkward trying to get through the tent flaps, which slowed us down and pissed him off. He had a thing about seeing the loose end of straps on anyone's pack. These straps were part of the pack and used for securing a blanket roll around the top and sides of the pack and for tying a sleeping bag or other stuff below. The DI had a name for the loose ends—he said, "I'll have no Irish pennants flying from the packs of men in my platoon."

Then it might be back into greens, with overcoat and the grabass went on like this all day, much to the chagrin of every boot. Then back into dungarees and leggings, poncho and helmet with green camo out on the cover. This kind of thing made you mad enough to want to ship out for Korea tomorrow just to take out your frustrations on the enemy. Maybe that was the intent.

Tradition dies hard in the military. Even in 1951, the daily routine was organized around bugle calls. When my brother John went into the

Navy in 1942 he became a bugler right out of boot camp and served on fleet flagships, etc. until the Navy went to taped bugle years later. Somewhere around our row of tents there was a huge megaphone on a swivel. The duty bugler pointed the megaphone in one direction and sounded reveille, then he turned the megaphone in the opposite direction and blew the tune again to wake up the sleepers all around. At 0800 and sundown, he blew colors as the post flag was raised and lowered in front of the base commanding general's office. At chow time, he blew mess call, and at 2200 hours he blew taps—time for lights out.

The daily grind after morning chow and head call, always started with a formation where we all stood at attention in our assigned spot. Information (the skinny or the word) was passed down from the training command through the DI to each skinhead. Sometimes it was about the schedule for that day. Otherwise, it was to get the word out. A variety of the items were brought to our attention.

One day we were told that from now on, when asked for our names, we were to give our last name first, then first name and middle initial, then rank, then serial number. So when I went up to the paymaster, or whomever, in the future I had to stand at attention and say, "Ginnelly, Gerald D., Pvt. 1234567" From then on we were all to be known by our rank and last name. We had just been given our serial number and had to memorize it and our rifle serial number as well.

Another day, early on, we were asked if any one of us was related to a congressman, cabinet member or any high government official, or general, admiral, or prominent civilian. If so, we had to report the relationship at once to the DI. We could only guess that in the past, some pansy son of an important person had been abused and insulted in the normal course of boot training. He wrote to his Daddy (Warbucks), who reported the physical and mental torture of mamma's boy to a senator, who in turn called the Commandant of the Marine Corps and told him that the USMC budget would be cut if the abuse didn't stop.

At other formations we were told about administrative items. One was signing up for the National Service Life Insurance. An admin type who was there to explain the details said it was optional and left the forms with us. As soon as he was gone, the DI passed out the application forms and told us there will be 100% participation as your folks could use the $10,000 after they learn about your death in combat in Korea.

There were no married guys in my platoon, because at that time, the USMC was only allowing single men to enlist. It used to be the same in the Canadian Mounties, (RCMP). Only bachelors were allowed to join.

One day we were urged to participate in a one time offer on a brass plaque with the USMC emblem in red on the top half and under that your name engraved and a dedication to a loved one, in my case it reads," To Mom and Dad 2/6/51." There was room below that for engravings of all the future campaign ribbons, medals, etc. We had to buy this thing or else, even though it seemed to be a racket. I recall that it cost $10. The only sour note on my plaque was at the delivery to my home. It was mailed COD and my brother, a swabbie on leave, answered the door and had to pay for the plaque. When he opened it he was somewhat miffed—just what every anchor clanker needed, a Marine plaque. Stiffed again for the bill.

SSGT. SICKLICKS CONDITIONING METHODS

At other formations we were being conditioned for what might come in the future. We were being psychologically toughened for the big blow. The day we were issued our dog tags (the British call theirs identity disks), we were told to wear them on the chain around the neck at all times. The stainless steel tags were stamped with last name, first name, middle initial, serial number., blood type, religion (P, C, J, etc.) and USMC The DI told us explicitly that there were two tags, one to be fixed to your grave marker in the field (Korea) and the other to be jammed tightly between your two top middle incisors right where you died. We gave this a lot of thought while fondling our new jewelry, but there wasn't much one could do about it now.

One of the things that we were told during the first few days was that the DI had some limits to his power over us. For example, he said that he was operating under new restrictions in turning us into combat-ready Marines. One was that now he could not call us just any old thing. He was forbidden to call us a motherfucker or a son of a bitch. Aside from that he could call us anything he wanted and he did. While he strutted in front of us swinging his nightstick and slapping it into his palm, he said that a DI was no longer allowed to touch a recruit, i.e. with his hand (fist). We were momentarily relieved at this encouraging state-ment, until he followed with the news that he could still, however, kick the shit out of us and then shook the nightstick at us, saying using that club on us didn't constitute touching—at least as far as the DIs were concerned.

I guess that this token spasm of leniency in training methods was brought on by the ruckus raised by a boot who complained about his treatment to his father a VIP in Washington, D.C. It wasn't much, but we appreciated any breaks accorded to us. We did learn after boot camp that prior to the end of WWII, boot training was much more onerous and the discipline extremely harsh. In other words we were having an easy time of it.

SSgt. Sicklick made no bones about what would happen to any boot who didn't do as he was told and do it quickly. If any boot dared to challenge him directly or take him on, he reminded us that he could whip any one of us at any time, if it came to that. He also explained something about the backup resources he had at his disposal. He arranged for a long lecture on the Uniform Code of Military Justice (UCMJ), which we needed to know but bored us to tears. The DI with the long stick played tunes on the nodding helmets, but we did get the gist of it. We could not win so we'd better toe the line.

According to the enlisted types who fancied themselves as sea lawyers, the UCMJ was an abomination. They said that during the first few years of the UCMJ, many who were guilty of crimes got off, whereas many of the innocent were severely punished. I learned later that the old line officers and NCOs preferred the old system. Under the old code, the officer presiding over Captain's Mast or in a court martial proceeding could mete out a penalty which helped to correct the path of the wayward sailor or Marine. It was a diet enforced in solitary confinement, called bread and water and known among the old salts as "Piss and Punk." My brother told me of a smart aleck poojie he knew aboard his ship. At his trial aboard ship the captain sentenced the man to, "Ten days in the brig on bread and water. Defendant, do you have anything to say for yourself?" The fool retorted, "Sir, I can do that standing on my head." To which the captain replied, "Well then, ten more days to get you back on your feet." To reassure the gentle souls who do not understand life aboard a Navy vessel, the prisoner was always allowed to have one full meal every third day. The pharmacist mate checked on his health daily. We must have order and discipline aboard at all times. These strict measures go back hundreds of years in the Navies of the world.

The Marine Corps lately (since the Korean war) has revised their handling of untrainable and uncooperative recruits and those who cannot accept any kind of regimentation or discipline. Now they just throw you out if you cannot adjust to the training. In the old days, you were subjected to all kinds of harassment in the name of discipline. If that didn't work, you were not allowed to graduate with your platoon but were recycled, i.e. kept in training with a new platoon, until you got the message and caved. Who in their right mind, would want to go through boot camp two or three times. Perhaps only a masochist.

One sure thing, was that if you kept resisting the training and the authority, sooner or later you would cross the line and violate the code (UCMJ). This could be done by running away, by taking a poke at or threatening a DI or anyone else, refusing to carry out a direct order, falling asleep, or wandering away from your post on guard duty or watch, etc. As we marched around the base, we could not help but notice the daily appearance of a number of Marines alone or in twos, marching along with another Marine close on their heels. The Marine in the rear wore a duty belt and holstered, loaded pistol. The DI called these little groups to our attention and said, "What you see there are prisoners we call poojies, and the Marine guard, the chaser. The prison chaser is escorting the poojie to or from the brig, to his court martial or somewhere else. You don't want to know what happens to you if you end up in the brig. It is such an awful place, we're not allowed to tell you about it. Just stay out of the brig. We were also warned that if you ever walked between a poojie and his chaser, you might end up in the brig yourself for interference.

One special attraction we often witnessed while standing in line outside the door of the mess hall at noon chow was the reading of orders for Courts Martial. An NCO with MP brassard would march up to the steps of the building with a poojie being escorted by a chaser. They had just come from the poojie's trial and were here to announce the verdict in public so that the rest of us would get the message. The clouds of steam around the steps added to the drama of the ritual.

The poojie stood there facing the steps with his head down and the chaser stood at parade rest one step behind him. The MP mounted the steps and facing us held up the court document, cleared his throat and boomed out, "The Marine before you, Private John Doe has just been found guilty of manslaughter in the death of another Marine. He has also been convicted of being AWOL for six months and for threatening an officer when arrested and brought back to camp. He has just been reduced in rank from corporal to private and has been sentenced to 25 years at hard labor in the Portsmouth Naval prison. He will forfeit all pay and allowances from this day and will receive a Bad Conduct Discharge (BCD) from the Marine Corps.

The MP would then fold up his paper, say, "As you were men," and march off toward the brig with his chasers and their charge. The poojie would soon be off to that infamous prison and would rue his crime for the rest of his life. We were not allowed to enter the mess hall until the ritual was over.

In those days there were only a few ways to leave Parris Island. One was to keep at it and graduate, then go on to another post. Or if you cracked up under the pressure, there was the strait jacket route with a medical (mental) discharge. If you did something really serious and you survived the brig, you might end up in Leavenworth or Portsmouth Prison as a poojie.

We were warned against trying to swim off the island as there had been some who went that way and drowned. Parris Island was so isolated, that to us it seemed like Devil's Island. We were told there were alligators swimming around out there, and the guys who were from non-alligator states believed it. We had one always smiling boot from Florida named Bush. We called him the alligator humper. He called it wrestling and he allowed that he wasn't afraid of them. There were a few other ways to get a Bad Conduct Discharge (BCD) or Dishonorable Discharge (DD) as an undesirable. This included those caught in homosexual acts, deserters, spies and whatever constituted a felony in civilian life. We were warned that those who received BCD, or DD could not vote and would receive no GI Bill benefits.

At one formation we received the word that we would take a special kind of test. We were marched to a small building and entered in groups of about 20. The room was empty except for 20 small desks, each about one foot square and attached to the outer bulkhead at waist level. Each desk had a pencil and one sheet of letter size paper on it. We stood facing the desks and were instructed to draw a picture of a man on one side and a woman on the back of the sheet. We were allowed ten minutes to make the drawings. Most of us had no artistic ability, so dithered moments away. I sort of drew stick figures with long hair on the female, a hat and a skirt, purse on arm, etc. For the guy, he stood in side profile with sombrero, long trousers, boots, moustache, goatee, sideburns, pistol, cartridge belt and the works. I printed his name below, BAD BASCOMB, Wanted Dead or Alive! In my drawings as well as most every other boot's, we must have drawn one figure notably male and the other obviously female to the observer.

We discussed the test later in the evening in our tent while cleaning rifles and shining shoes. We concluded that it was some kind of psychological test. It was a way of screening us all for potential mental cases who would not fit into service life. The USMC wanted you to be a little crazy, otherwise why would you enlist in the Corps, knowing you would be going off to a war. Our convictions proved to be true when about a week later five boots in our platoon were gone and we never saw them again. It had to do with their drawings. The shrinks went over all of the drawings carefully sorting out the dozen or so which caught their attention. They called in these 12 and each one was worked over by a couple of Navy psychiatrists who evaluated their mental state. Five were deemed to be potentially dangerous or disruptive to a combat unit in the future, and were quietly discharged for the good of the service.

Many months later at new posts we noticed that here and there, the shrinks missed a few nut cases who ended up hurting other marines, committing suicide or killing someone else. I regret to say now, that normal servicemen can often act like school children in dealing with an individual who is somewhat different than the rest of us. I remember an odd looking creature who was short and looked very much like Elmer Fudd. I can't remember his real name, but we all called him Herman. He was not in my boot platoon, but I went through advanced infantry training with him at Camp Pendleton, California and he served in Korea also. He was ribbed and teased endlessly by others in his unit. One morning he was found dead by his own hand in his barracks.

In 1958, my wife's cousin was shot in the head while in the kitchen of her apartment in Honolulu and died on the floor while her two small children sat there wondering what happened to her. This homicide was unsolved for over a year until a Marine from a guard detachment at the Navy base was being interviewed by an officer for a routine update of his security clearance. In the middle of the interview, the Marine blurted out," I didn't mean to kill her." He said this several times and the interviewing officer wondered what the hell he was talking about.

Later under interrogation by the Criminal Investigation Division (CID), he said that one night just after dark he was walking through the parking lot of an apartment complex in town. He fired his pistol at a porch light on the second floor, then saw a young women doing the dishes in the kitchen next door and fired his pistol at her, hitting her in the head. Apparently he had just flipped his lid and wanted to kill someone. The case was a landmark and mentioned in Life magazine because it was the first trial of a military man to be held in a civilian court after Hawaii had become a state. One wonders if there was anything weird about his drawings in boot camp, which slipped by the shrinks. There is a fine line between training men to be killers and to get them to concentrate on a declared enemy and not to practice on other Marines or innocent civilians.

Sometime early on, it may even have been during the recruiting process, we were all subjected to a comprehensive written examination, known as the General Classification Test (GCT). The purpose of the GCT was to allow the Corps to sort out who might be eligible for Officer's Candidate School (OCS) or for certain types of technical training. In most cases, college graduates who enlisted were offered a chance to go to OCS as a matter of course. In order for the rest of us to qualify for OCS, a score of 120 on the GCT was required. My score was 119. The story of my life, always on the edge.

During the second week of boot camp our numbers shrunk by one more warm body. It turned out that one lucky guy who had a very high IQ, also had two years of college and scored very well on the GCT. The Corps brain trust felt that this guy was an asset, so pulled him out of boot camp and sent him off to a university to finish his B.S. degree. We speculated that as soon as he graduated he would be sent to Quantico to the USMC/OCS for platoon leaders school, which was every bit as tough as boot camp for enlisted men and maybe even tougher.

The most popular building on any Marine base, is the mess hall. This is especially so at boot camp. Even though we were only allowed about 20 minutes sitting down for each meal, it was a respite as well as a repast. No one harassed us. We could speak to each other freely, keeping one eye on our DIs at their table. Because of all the physical activity, marching or running everywhere, we were always hungry. We were not allowed to use the PX, except on a couple of special organized occasions and even then we were not allowed to buy any pogey bait. The desserts at the mess hall had to satisfy our sugar cravings.

I never heard any complaints about the food in the PI mess hall. It was something any New Zealander would love. When I lived there in the mid 1960s, the Kiwis told me they didn't care what was on their plate at mealtime as long it was hot and there was plenty of it. We had plenty to eat in boot camp and it was good food. I was famished most of the time and always went back for seconds of anything. If they were short of second servings, I filled up on bread and butter.

The joke was that if you drank a lot of liquid with the extra slices of bread, the bread would swell up in your stomach making you feel full. But as soon as you took a leak later, you were hungry again. Us chow hounds were always on the lookout for more grub at our table. If someone was off their feed, we would ask him, "Are you going to eat that?" If he said no, I would spear it before someone else got it. One way to piss off some chow hound boot was to ask him, " Do you want two pieces of cake? " Thinking he was going to get a second piece from us he'd say, "Sure." Then you'd point to the one on his tray and say, "Well, just cut that one in half."

One of the most boring tasks in the military is guard duty and standing watches. In order to get us used to this type of duty, which would plague us all no matter where we went from PI, we were given every opportunity to pull this task. In boot camp we mainly stood two kinds of watches, one a bit silly, one not so. The serious one was fire watch which was maintained usually from taps to reveille or from dusk to dawn.

A clothesline watch was instituted whenever we were going to have an inspection. We all had a certain amount of clothing, i.e. so many socks, shirts, skivvies, etc., which had to be laid out in a prescribed manner on your bunk during clothing inspections. We called it junk on the bunk. Every bit of clothing except what you wore during the inspection had to be on the bunk with your name showing. If you were missing an article of clothing, you could not very well borrow someone else's, because they had their name on it.

We had no access to washing machines, but washed our clothes by hand the way it had been done in the Corps for many years. Each area had flat concrete tables with water taps and we actually looked forward to every opportunity to wash our clothes. New dungarees were stiff and shiny and marked one as a new boot. One way to become salty looking was to take the sheen off the dungarees by washing them often with GI soap and a scrub brush.

Sometimes we had junk on the bunk inspection with 782 gear, which only had US printed on each item. If a boot was missing a piece of gear, here were the instructions from the DI, "I will not have any boot missing equipment. A Marine never steals, but a good Marine is never without. The night before an inspection, I will not notice if any of you who need an item of 782 gear sneak over to the area of the neighboring platoon. If you are caught, I never said that." So this is why there was a clothes line watch. We all wore the same clothing and sometimes if you needed some article for inspection, you might just find an unstamped item on the clothesline of the next platoon.

The fire watch was a very serious assignment. We lived in rows of tents that were highly flammable because of the waterproofing chemical applied to the outside surface. The door flaps were secured over each other in inclement weather, making it slightly difficult to get out in an emergency. The tents were about a yard apart but tied together at the sides and at every third or fourth tent was a 55 gallon drum of water and a bucket hung on a post. The boot on fire watch patrolled the platoon area watching for fire or anything else unusual like some boot from another platoon on a midnight requisition for clothing or equipment for an upcoming inspection. Usually a fire watch or clothesline watch was for two hours or until you were relieved.

Guard duty was done on four hour shifts and was a more formal affair. You had to memorize the General Orders, which told you how to conduct yourself on guard duty. There were ten of them and I can only remember part of the second one: I will walk my post in a military manner.........! Over the last hundred years, Marines have made up their own version of the General Orders, and I can only recall two. I will walk my post in a military manner and take no shit from the company commander. Another went, I will walk my post from flank to flank and take no shit from any rank. These were but dreams in the minds of the bored sentries pounding their posts from midnight to four AM in some Godforsaken part of the world.

At any time during your particular hours on post, you might be approached in the dark by a figure looming out of the gloom. You moved your rifle to port arms and called out, " Halt, who goes there?" The answer was usually, "The Officer of the Day." And you had to say, "Advance and be recognized." This he did and because he was your boss while on guard duty, you knew who he was. Sometimes it was the sergeant of the guard, sometimes one of the DIs. They almost always asked how it was going, and gave you some simulated situations to find out how you would deal with them. Invariably they asked you to recite the General Orders or asked if you had been given any special orders for the post. The most difficult part of standing watches or guard duty was the midnight to four AM shift and trying to stay awake.

All that stuff I had heard about spit and polish in the Marines turned out not to apply to us in the FMF. There were only two items that had to be polished, the dress shoes and brass belt buckle. This pleased me to no end. Our boondockers, or field shoes, were made of that rough inside out leather so only had to be cleaned of mud and were never polished. Our USMC emblems were dark brown and had a dull finish. We were instructed not to try polishing them.

During inspections, the DI resorted to his own methods to remind you that something was amiss with your clothing. If a button anywhere on your dress shirt was not properly secured (buttoned) he would whip out his pocket knife and deftly cut it off . As he handed the button to you, his usual comment was, "What the hell do you think the button is for, knot head?" This forced us to remember that little detail, particularly with the collar button. No one wanted him to be placing the tip of his knife near your throat for any reason. It also made you concentrate on fastening each button on your fly and hip pocket.

There were few pockets on Marine dress clothing. The DI made a fuss about carrying things in your pockets which made the uniform look sloppy. When we left boot camp, most of us sewed up the front pockets on the trousers. There was only one pocket on the hip for a thin wallet. Since our pay was meager, our wallets were always thin anyway. When we went on liberty later, we carried what we needed under our trousers in the long dress socks. I didn't have a wallet so carried my folding cash in my socks along with liberty card, ID card, a pack of cigarettes, and matches. The green woolen uniform battle jacket at least had an inside pocket and two outside.

Communications in boot camp between DI and skinheads was primitive, but effective. When we were inside our row of tents, the word was passed from tent to tent whenever the DI barked an order. It was usually, "Platoon 136. Fall in on the double." When we heard it, we passed it on while running out to fall in, grabbing caps as we went. Sometimes there were other messages, for individuals. Say Pvt. Smith had fucked up during the day and although he got a brief dressing down right then and there, maybe the DI was bored that evening and wanted to harass him some more. At night while we sat on our buckets studying the Marine Corps manual for enlisted men or cleaning rifles, we would hear the DI call out, "Private Smith report to the DI's tent, at once." By the time this was repeated down the line of tents, Smith was already on his way and we could hear him running by and stopping at the closed door flaps of the DI's tent, wondering what was in store for him.

The boot went through the ritual. He stood at attention and said, "Pvt. Smith reporting as ordered, Sir." Naturally, the DI called out, "You are supposed to knock on the wooden strongback before you say that, you idiot." So the kid starts over, pounds on the tent fabric with a two by four frame underneath and makes his presence know as before. Then starts the I can't hear you routine over and over for 15 minutes. The kid pounds harder and harder each time while shouting, " Pvt. Smith reporting as ordered, Sir."

Finally, the DI hears him and yells, "Get your ass in hear Smith." Smith crawls through the flaps, whips off his cap which he stuffs under his right armpit and snaps to attention. The error that he had committed earlier in the day is reviewed and his punishment meted out. It might be so many laps around the parade ground wearing pack, helmet, rifle and all his gear. It might be so many pushups then and there. It could be standing at attention for four hours straight in the hot sun, or marching alone around the parade ground all day long. Then Smith is dismissed to do whatever he was ordered to do right away, or go back to his tent to do it tomorrow.

All of us had that little session at the DI's tent door or inside. It was just a matter of time before each boot fell victim. Every night as we went about our chores, we waited to see who would be next and dreaded the message with our name on it. Sometimes the whole show seemed to be the DI's main source of entertainment and we inside our tents were able to share in the fun as we listened to the game.

One night before taps, a boot with a personal problem (and a death wish) went to the DIs tent on his own. We could hear him asking for permission to speak and mumbling his name, while rapping his knuckles on the strong back. The duet between the DI and the boot went on for 15 minutes the DI yelling, "I can't hear you," to each of the boot's attempts to get his attention. Finally the boot got fed up and shouted to the DI as loud as he could, "Then how do you know I'm out here?" This was followed by the boot racing back to his tent while the DI popped out of his tent fuming about catching that wise ass tomorrow if he could just remember the name. It gave us all a much needed laugh before hitting the sack.

We were advised in no uncertain terms by the DI early on, that we were only permitted to smoke when the smoking lamp was lit. It was an old naval tradition going back to sailing vessels and there was no real lamp involved for us, it was just a figure of speech. For us, the smoking lamp was out until the DI said that it was lit, at which time we could light up. If any of us had the gall to light up when the lamp was not lit, we were in big trouble if we got caught. He didn't describe the punishment for this heinous crime, but told us he would rather wait to catch a boot at it and show us what would happen to the rest of us

Because we were never really given a chance to be alone, even when taking a crap, a leak, or a shower, there was little opportunity to sneak a smoke. I took the DI's word for it that violators would pay dearly if caught. So he knew that the only chance an addicted smoker had to catch a puff or two was on watch at his post in the middle of the night somewhere in the platoon area. And that's how he caught his first victim.

At about 0200 hours SSgt. Sicklick sneaked up behind a poor sucker on watch. The DI whirled around the fool as he was taking a long drag under his poncho. When the DI popped up in front of him, the kid almost pooped his pants and tried to swallow the lit cigarette. He knew that he was toast. The DI having some consideration for the sleeping platoon, decided to torment the smoker by telling him to relax and try to imagine the punishment he could expect sometime tomorrow. He reminded the boot that he had been warned about smoking without permission and that he would be used as an example with some well thought out penalty.

Nothing happened the next morning, but at formation we were told about the smoker being caught and that we were to stand by for a public display of innovative retribution before taps. The daily training routine went on until late in the evening to let the victim stew and hope that the DI had forgotten. Just before lights out the DI called out from his tent, "Pvt. Dunnegan, report to my tent pronto. Pass it on." And so the word was loudly passed on to the Pvt.'s tent.

Now we knew who it was as the victim tore out of his tent and knocked hard on the strongback and canvas, saying,"Pvt. Dunnegan reporting as ordered sir." This time the DI got right to it and came to the door to glare at the private. He said, "So Pvt. Dunnegan, do you like to smoke?" The scared boot said, "Yes sir." Then the two of them went through the duet of I can't hear you and the skinhead shouted his replies louder and louder.

The DI told him to get back to his tent and return immediately with his scrub bucket and poncho. He reappeared moments later, reporting back as ordered and standing at attention, quivering slightly. We heard the DI tell the boot that he was going to help him cure his smoking habit in just five minutes.

With this, the DI told him that since you like to smoke, I am ordering you right now to smoke and I will provide the cigarettes. By this time, a few heads poked out from each tent door to catch the action. The DI ignored the voyeurs, wanting them to tell the rest of the platoon. SSgt. Sicklick handed the boot a pack of cigarettes and a book of matches. He then said, "You are to smoke the entire pack right now in front of me. But first put your bucket on your head and then put the poncho over that. Then light up."

The kid did as he was told and then tore open the pack and lit up the first weed. Then the DI began to sing "Smoke gets in your eyes" keeping time by banging his night stick on the bucket. With all this racket every other boot had to take a look until after about the fifth cigarette, the private started to barf and threw off the bucket and poncho in a cloud of smoke. He was sent back to his tent for a few minutes to catch his breath and then recalled to clean up his puke.

I know for a fact that no other boot in our platoon was ever caught smoking again. Although I had smoked before, I decided to quit until I got out of boot camp. In order to keep the camp clean, we were taught to field strip a cigarette butt during the first time the smoking lamp was lit. When you were finished with the smoke, you first put it out, then opened it up with your nails if you had them, then scatter the remaining tobacco around on the ground. The paper was then rolled up into a tiny ball and put in your pocket for later disposal in a trash can. What about the filter tips? No one smoked cigarettes with those things except actors, tarts, pimps, and the like in those days. In fact we used to call them "pimp sticks" around Detroit.

The DI was a stickler for looking you over every day for any violation of the rules. Haircuts were not a problem because we all marched back to the barbers every two weeks for a touch up on the shaven pate. Our hair was allowed to grow out to a fuzz only. However, even peach fuzz was not tolerated on the face. So when the DI caught you with any facial fuzz, no matter how slight, the first offense was quickly dealt with.

The offender was told to fall out in front of the platoon with his safety razor and had to dry shave without benefit of a mirror as we all watched. This wasn't too bad, but the second time one was caught unshaven, he had to dry shave again in front of the platoon, but with only the double edged blade—no razor (blade holder), no mirror.

For the third offense, you had to dry shave another boot who was in the same boat, while he shaved you, with only the blades. This led to some pretty sloppy shaves and some not so nifty nicks. After the DI explained the progression in punishment for the fourth time a boot was unshaven, and so on, all hands had clean shaven kissers every morning. The threat was enough to make even the baby faced among us shave daily. The fourth time called for the individual boot offender to dry shave with only a blade and double time in place while doing it. The fifth time meant that both you and another victim had to get out in front of us all and shave each other with only a blade while both did stationary double time.

Needless to say that the DI got 100 percent compliance with the daily shave. My only other reflection on the shaving for boots at Parris Island was the fact that we were issued a tube or two of Barbasol, brush or brushless shaving cream. The makers of Barbasol must have thought they had a wonderful gimmick. By placing their product in the hands of thousands of boots, who will become so used to it they would continue to buy it the rest of their lives. Not so with this former boot. I came to associate the smell of Barbasol with being forced to shave every day and all the other negative things that were an affront to our civilian sensibilities. This feeling for Barbasol lasted for years. I simply refused to buy it or use it. If it happened to be the only shaving cream available, I preferred to use my shaving brush on a bar of soap.

Now, 48 years after boot camp, I purchased my first Barbasol cream (in a can) but have yet to use it. It was on sale and I'm saving it for when I'm out of other shaving cream and out of soap. In the dark recesses of my mind I must be afraid to use this can of Barbasol because, like Aladdin's lamp if I shake the can, press the button on top, or start to smooth the foam onto my stubble, sure as hell, SSgt. Sicklick will appear in front of me as the duty genie. I'm sure he will give me all kinds of grief before I figure out how to get rid of him.

By explaining how the DI's punishment worked, by quick and innovative public humiliation among one's peers, you can see how some threats could be so dire that the punishment was never needed. Everyone was so sure that the DI was willing to do anything to us that we firmly believed he would and could carry out the wildest threat.

Our DI could not stand to see fingernails bitten down to the quick. I wonder how many guys came into the Corps with this problem and how many acquired it in nervous response to the machinations of this sadist DI. SSgt. Sicklick's cure for nail biters in Platoon 136 was to first select a sacrificial victim. He picked one poor sucker from the ranks during an inspection of our appearance. He hauled the boot out in front of us as we stood at attention and made him hold up his hands. Of course we had to take his word for it, because the victim was too far away for us to see his nails. SSgt., Sicklick said, "I'm feeling lenient right now and will not inflict the cure on this nail biter today. But this is how it will work for him or any other boot who bites his nails. You will be placed in front of the platoon and told to drop your pants and skivvies. Because we do everything by the numbers here, when I give the signal, you will put one hand in your mouth and the other in the crack of your ass. Then when I say switch, you will switch hands. We will keep this up until you decide to stop biting your nails. Is this understood, by all of you?"

Naturally he got a resounding "Yes Sir!" from all of us. He certainly heard us the first time. This threat was so real that to my knowledge it never had to be used. In spite of continuing personal inspections, the nail biting stopped quickly. Because I still have a sense of humor and am somewhat crass, I have offered this treatment advice to friends with kids who bite their nails. When I explained how it works, the husband (if he was a veteran) usually laughed while the wife sighed and just glared at me. I haven't bitten my nails since PI.

I found out that our DI wasn't kidding when he said he was not allowed to lay a hand on us, because he had other ways. One day he was not satisfied about some of the close-order drill movements and our proper response to his commands. We were getting ready for our first inspection by an officer from the Training Command and if we didn't look sharp, it would reflect badly on the DI. He thought that most of us could use some improvement in doing the about face—wherein you spin smartly around and face in the opposite direction. He sat on his folding chair in front of his tent while we came up one at a time in front of him and executed this maneuver

He had replaced his nightstick with a broom handle, for the reach, I guess. Now I had never had trouble doing this movement, but was at the end of the line and came up last so I couldn't see what he was doing. By the time I arrived in front of him, 70 other boots had already spun around in front of him in the same spot several times each. I failed to do it precisely because the other boots had twisted a hole in the warm tarmac causing my heels to become misaligned when I completed the turn.

As a result I had to execute this movement about 20 times and the first 12 times, the DI whacked me with the broomstick on either the shins or the calves as hard as he could until he was satisfied on the final turn. The next morning I could hardly walk when I fell in for morning muster. There were bumps all up and down my shins and bruises and welts all over my calves. I could not, nor would not complain to anyone. This was just part of the drill and you took your lumps as they came, no matter how unfairly you think you are treated.

Ask anyone who has been in the service what was the most important event of the week and he or she will always say it was mail call. This is especially so for those in boot camp who were already homesick and longed for some connection to their former civilian life. However, after going through three or four mail calls administered by the Marquis de Sadelick, boots were frantically writing home to tell their loved ones what not to put on the envelopes or in the packages they sent us. Some boots even told their folks and friends not to write at all unless it was an emergency, without explaining why.

For the 72 boots in our platoon, mail call might take two hours, which seemed like four if it was raining. The mail was not distributed to us. We had to go through a drill to get each envelope. SSgt. Sicklick made the announcement, "Mail Call." It was always after dusk as we fell into formation and waited eagerly for the letters. The street was not well lit, so the DI stood in the doorway of a tent facing us and used the light over his shoulder to read the names off one at a time.

When he read your name on the envelope, you had to move out of the formation and run fast around its perimeter. As you passed the DI at full clip, he would drop the letter and you had to catch it on the wing. If you were lucky you caught it the first time. If not, you had to tear around again, pick it up from the ground, hand it to him and repeat the lap until you caught it. Sometimes a boot would fall and we suspected that he was tripped by the DI.

The guys who made out were the ones who received no letters or only a few. The ones who suffered were the ones who received love letters adorned with lip(stick) imprints on the back flap or SWAK (Sealed With A Kiss) printed there. The DI rode these guys without mercy and especially so if the envelope was perfumed. Now one can see why no boot wanted to receive a lot of letters, especially the lover type who had earlier told every girl in his high school senior class to write to him twice a week—and they did.

Receiving a package was another experience. It can be compared to the system used for screening what a poojie goes through in a prison. There were certain items that boots were forbidden to have. One was shaving lotion, I suppose because we might drink it for the alcohol content. Another was excessive amounts of pogey bait, except homemade cookies, cake and the like. After all, they weren't out to completely sever your ties with home.

When a package arrived for you, the DI ordered you up to his tent at night and only then did you learn the good news. While he sat in his chair he handed you the package and told you to open it, which you did on the floor. He then poked around in the contents with his swagger stick. If there were smaller packages within, he instructed you to open them also. If there were cookies or cake, or some other kind of pogey bait, he would ask for a sample and who had the nerve to deny him his choice. I think that the types of contraband he was looking for were sidearms, ammo, knives, liquor, dope, prescription drugs, patent medicines, and God knows what else.

When dismissed, you scurried back to your tent with whatever was left and shared it with your tent mates with the tacit understanding that they in turn would share their goodies when they came in. The DI usually only confiscated some pogey bait for himself and the other DIs, leaving enough for the others in your tent.

Receiving mail was one thing, having to send it was something else. The DI informed us that we must write a letter home at least once a month, because if we didn't write at all, some angry parents would contact the Red Cross. The Red Cross would get in touch with the Commander of the USMC Recruit Depot, PI and want to know what has happened to little Johnny. "He hasn't written since he left home." The base CO would raise hell down the chain of command and then the DI would catch it. So he covered his cheeks by making us write home often. I suppose in reality that some who preferred not to write, were merely waiting for something good to happen to them before they wrote a letter. To others the only good thing to happen to them in boot camp was graduation day and getting the hell off "Devil's Island." I'm speaking of myself, of course.

THIS IS MY RIFLE

Every Marine is basically an infantry rifleman, no matter where he may end up serving in the vast world of the Corps. Until I arrived in Korea, I had no idea that there were lines of work in the USMC, aside from being a ground pounding grunt. So to get you off on the right foot, you were issued your very own rifle on the first day in boot camp. It was to become a part of you and you were to learn to care for it, love it, and get to know its inner parts and all their names. You were to memorize all of the technical details as to weight, chamber pressure, muzzle velocity, accuracy and range, and everything to do with its operation and function. This piece of weaponry might save your life one day and it had to be looked after with great care. Some boots loved their rifles so much they ended up sleeping with them, although not by choice.

The M-1 Garand is a 30 cal. rifle issued as the basic weapon to all Marines who served in the FMF and most other units of the Corps at that time. From day one, we were advised by the DI to refer to it as a rifle and no other terminology was tolerated. If you goofed and called it a gun, that was doggie (soldier) talk. After a few days of learning to live with our rifles, one boot was being grilled by the DI while in formation and he referred to his piece as a gun. When SSgt. Sicklick heard that his eyes lit up and he started to fume. " What in hell did you just say skinhead?" he roared in his face. The boot tried to lean away from the DI's red face, and squeaked, "My gun, sir."

The DI turned and stomped out of the formation to his usual place in front saying, " So its a gun is it. You shit head. Where were you the other day when we said that this M-1 was always to be called a rifle, because it has lands and grooves in the barrel, you idiot. You're among the ten percent who never get the word. Get your ass out in front of the platoon pronto." The victim of the day came to port arms and ran out to the front and came to attention facing us. The DI ordered the rest of us to parade rest and gave his instructions to the offender, "Buckass private when I give the order to commence the drill you will grab your rifle mid stock with your right hand and then grab your pecker with your left. You will then raise the rifle up as high as you can shouting as loud as you can, "This is my rifle, then squeeze your pecker and yell this is my gun. Then shake the rifle saying this is for shooting and squeeze your pecker shouting this is for fun."

So the kid stood there while the rest of us tried to control our smirks and smiles, because if we got caught we would join him. He continued for 20 minutes, "This is my rifle. This is my gun. This is for shooting. This is for fun." After that session, the message had sunk in and we never heard that song again.

Rifle inspections were held regularly as part of our conditioning, because they would be with us throughout our enlistments. At first these inspections were held by the DI himself with his buck sergeant or corporal at his side. Normally, besides the personal inspection of each boot and his uniform, we were asked all kinds of questions and we were expected to know the answers or else. Some of the questions were:

Who is the Commandant of the USMC?

What is the name of the Secretary of Defense?

Who is the Secretary of the Navy?

What is the name of the Commander in Chief of US Forces?

What is your serial number?

What is your rifle serial number?

Can you recite the General Orders? or

What is General Order Number three?, seven?, ten?

What is the name and rank of your drill instructor?

What are the three most important actions in administering first aid to a wounded man on the battlefield?

Why is this weapon called a rifle?

What is the chamber pressure of the M-1?

What is the muzzle velocity?

What do you know about ballistics and trajectory?

The DI and the officers, usually lieutenants, who conducted most of the rifle inspections did so with practiced efficiency and flourish. When the inspector stopped facing the man next to you, you prepared yourself for your role in the drill. As he stepped in front of you, you brought your rifle from order arms to port arms smartly slapping the taut sling and slapping your right hand on the grip. Your left hand comes around the other side of the rifle and you pull the bolt back with your thumb into the locked position. At the same time that you complete this movement, you nod slightly checking for a clip in the receiver or a round in the chamber. You immediately snap your head back to look straight ahead and into the inspector's eyes or nose. At this time you are ready to let go of the rifle the instant you see his right hand swing up and grasp it firmly away from you. Your hands drop to your sides and you watch him fling it around this way and that like a baton twirler.

He examines every inch, nook and cranny of the rifle looking for any trace of rust, a speck of dirt or dust. All the time you are wondering how it could have gotten dirty since you cleaned it last night and again this morning, field stripping it, wiping it down, brushing it and then applying a light coat of oil. Now he has thrown the butt up in the air and holding the rifle with both hands, carefully examines the bore. He is nearing the finish and spins the rifle so that it comes back to you in the port arms position. You then reach up and slap the sling with your left hand as he releases it and grab the grip with your right hand.

If he has any questions he asks you now. If he finds something wrong with you, your dress, person, or rifle, he tells the DI to note your name and your gigs for the day. As the officer goes to the next man you press down on the clip spring in the receiver and allow the bolt to slide closed. Next you come to order arms and the DI is now facing you and just glaring and communicating by visual darts to let you know that your errors will be paid for later on.

In preparing for rifle inspections we were very careful in cleaning our weapons just before the event. We used clean cloths, bore brush and patches on the end of the cleaning rod or the leather thong inside the butt plate, toothbrush, and small paint brush with fine bristles. A pipe cleaner was handy for cleaning small crevices and corners.

Dropping one's rifle within the sight or hearing of the DI always brought on delayed retribution. We were warned on the first day that, "Thou shalt not drop thy rifle!" After all, the rifle was a finely tooled piece of equipment and if your life depended on it in the future, it would not do to have either the front or rear sight out of line when you needed your weapon most. The punishment was put off until night time when you had to sleep with your M-1 right next to you under the sheets. That compact arrangement of cold steel and wood made it very difficult to get a good night's sleep. The sharp bolt handle found its way into your back, side, or arms.

I'm sure that you have seen the pictures of troops in the old days in their bivouac area with tents all in a row and rifles stacked in a tripod in front of the tents. There were no rifle racks in the boondocks, so they were stacked to keep them out of the dirt. Each M-1 had a stacking swivel high up between the muzzle and the top sling mount. It is similar to a sling mount, but it has a small open space in the steel for engaging one of the other stacking swivels on the other two rifles to be stacked.

The first time we were learning to stack arms, it was pretty tricky getting the hang of it. If the stack collapsed and one of the DIs could tell that one boot was responsible, the victim had to sleep with all three rifles, otherwise each boot involved got to sleep with his alone. The only variation with this penalty was that more nights might be added for one offense.

We had one poor boot who muffed the stacking twice within one month. SSgt. Sicklick decided that maybe this guy was a bit odd and actually liked sleeping with three rifles for several nights so he upped the fine the next time. He decided to wreak his vengeance right on the spot. He ordered the boot out and had him stand there facing us in formation with his arms out straight in front of him. The DI went up and laid this guy's rifle across his arms. Then he ordered every boot in the first rank to trail arms and file past the guy and lay each rifle across his arms piling them up.

Each rifle weighed more than nine pounds, so when the 5th was put on, his elbows bent. With the 6th, his knees began to buckle. With the 7th, he was on his knees and leaning forward. All this time he is being hectored by the DI with jibes and digs. Finally, with the 8th rifle, the boot tipped over and the rifles all fell in the dirt with a clatter. The guy was so flustered that he wanted to lay there face down until dark, but the DI ordered him up with the toe of his shoe and then royally chewed him out.

The DI closed the show by telling the victim that he would sleep tonight with every rifle that he had dropped. He then instructed each boot who had a rifle dropped by this clown to report to the boot's tent at taps and leave his rifle on his sack. He advised the victim that he could arrange the rifles any way he liked as long as all eight were in his sack, between the sheets. The DI said that during the night he would be in to check on him and he had better be in there with all the M-1s as assigned.

About halfway through boot camp we had no more problems with dropped rifles and we had become very proficient at stacking arms. I guess our DI was really being lenient, because it could have been worse. He could have made the poor klutz sleep with his rifle with the un-sheathed bayonet attached. We should be thankful for the little breaks that we got. The rest of us had gotten the message, however. By the way, when some DI or senior NCO told you that he was going to grab you by the stacking swivel as a threat to straighten you out, he meant he would grab you by the throat. If he said he was going to bust you one in the snot locker that meant he was going to use his fist on your nose.

In boot camp, the running of the platoon is left entirely to the DI and we boots hardly ever saw an officer, although we knew they were around somewhere. Their presence at rifle inspections, junk on the bunk and camp inspections was part of their training for future assignments in other Marine units. Even after boot camp I had little to do with offic-ers and I was perfectly happy to have it that way. I saw officers only when they appeared at formations, parades, inspections, and on payday. Other than that I don't know where they were or what they were doing the rest of the time. I noticed that they were the only ones who could sign forms and documents so maybe that is what they did all day, besides sitting on courts martial.

One day shortly before graduating the DI told me to report to his tent. Right away I start wondering what I had done. When I reported as ordered he said, "The colonel in charge of the Training Command wants you in his office at 0900. Put on your khakis, field scarf, dress shoes, piss cutter, and emblems and show up here before you go so I can look you over and give you directions to his office. What I want to know is what did you do this time?"

I told him I didn't know. He asked me that again after I had dressed and we rehearsed my reporting to the colonel. Sgt.Sicklick said that he had never heard of a boot being told to see the CO unless it was for a court martial. He added that I had better not fuck up this meeting and I was to report to him as soon as I got back.

Before I shoved off, he asked, "Are you sure that you are not related to someone important?" Now he was worried if he may have crossed the line in correcting my errant ways. I wanted to say that, since he was always calling us bastards, maybe I was the illegitimate son of some general or congressman, but I bit my tongue. I assured him that I was related to no one of importance.

When I arrived at the HQ building a master sergeant showed me into the colonel's office. I uncovered, stood at attention and said, "Pvt. Ginnelly reporting as ordered sir." He kept me at attention and said, "Do you realize lad, that your enlistment in the USMC is fraudulent?" He was looking at some papers while I replied, "No sir?" I had no idea what he was talking about.

He then said, "It says here that you enlisted in the Corps on 6 Feb 1951 while you were still in the U.S. Naval Reserve. Is that correct?" I said it was. He continued, "Don't you know that it is against military regulations to be enlisted in two separate branches of the service at the same time?" I said that I was not aware of it. He gave me a long lecture on propriety and informed me that my short record showed that I was doing well in boot camp and if I kept my nose clean I would be a good Marine. Then he said that he would recommend no punishment and that he would see that I was granted a General Discharge, under honorable circumstances from the U.S. Naval Reserve. I was dismissed and told to explain our meeting to Sgt. Sicklick, who told me I was a nut case, but seemed as relieved as I was. I'm still trying to figure out why I was in the wrong when the Army was going to take me without a thought to my Naval Reserve status.

It is a good thing the colonel didn't know that this kind of enlistment ran in the family. During WWII my brother John ran away to join the Navy at 16, by lying about his age (he claimed to be 17) and signing my mother's and father's signatures to the enlistment papers giving their approval. He broke into the local drugstore and used the druggists Notary Seal and signed the Notary's name on the document. Now to me that was a big fraud where mine was kind of minor, but he went off to war so it was no big deal. By the time the Navy found out, he had turned 18 and they didn't care.

Every morning at first muster, when roll call was held, the DI asked if anyone had to go to sick call. The DI made it clear that if you went to sick bay during sick call, you had better have a good reason for the visit. He would not tolerate malingerers and the corpsmen could tell the truly ill from the goldbricks. I don't remember anyone going to sick call, although they may have gone for some emergency, perhaps brought on by the intensity of training.

In boot camp, we were never given the opportunity to mingle with or talk to any other boots outside our platoon. This may have been done to prevent the boots who had been there longer from scaring us to death with rumors. However, some of us had talked to former Marines before we joined up and they had some of their own tales to scare us with. One dealt with getting shots. I'm sure this one goes way back in the services and had to do with getting some mysterious injection with a dull square needle in the left nut. Ouch!

When we went for our many immunizations, the corpsmen didn't fool around. We lined up and were fed through a gauntlet of five corpsmen on each side. We were given five shots in each arm. The huge boot behind me was about 6' - 5" and he must have had a thing about shots. As soon as he got the first two shots, he folded on the guy behind me taking him down. The corpsmen hauled the giant off on a litter. I suppose the doctor told the corpsmen that this boot was merely afraid of shots after checking him over for allergic symptoms. He was given the rest of the series in his sick bay sack. This way, he was already supine if he passed out from seeing the next needle closing in.

In order to get rid of the aches and pains which can follow multiple shots given at the same time, the DI marched us back for a workout with our rifles, i.e. physical drill under arms. He thought that all this activity for an hour with your rifle would work the drugs away from the injection site and alleviate the soreness. It must have worked, because I heard no complaints, except from the big guy when he came back from sick bay. He had missed the workout.

In the beginning, the DI wanted us to look the part of boots as much as possible. The signs of the new boots are obvious to others who have been there longer. For one thing, our dungarees were brand new and shiny light green. Our caps came down to our ears and were shapeless. We had only one black Marine and he fell into one formation early on with a somewhat blocked out, squared away cap. The DI saw it and told him loudly to get that dip out of his cap, pronto. He wasn't picking on him necessarily, he was making sure that we all looked the same. I never heard the DI bother him again and although he didn't single him out for harassment, he did make this boot the platoon guide, simply because he looked sharper that the rest of us. I think his last name was Perry.

I never really understood the purpose of the platoon guide, I guess that the rest of us just followed him when marching. The guide stood in the first rank to the right of the rest of us in formation. When we right faced to march off, he then moved to the front of the far right column. He also carried the guidon, or red pennant bearing 136 our platoon number.

THE HEAD AND WATER WALKING

Our area head (platoon toilet facilities and showers) was in a good sized Butler building. The showers would hold about 40 men at a time and there were about 20 sinks and mirrors for shaving and washing. The urinal was a sheet metal affair running the length of one wall with a constant stream of water to carry away the yellow stuff. On the opposite wall were the crappers, which were but a slight improvement on the ones back on the farm (i.e. they were indoors) and there was a flume of running water to remove the turdy effluvia. The crapper was about a 20 holer and was built up so that you had to go up a step to sit down on the wood seats resting your boondockers on the step. It was my first view of a multihole throne.

All this business of showering, defecating and peeing in public came as a shock to some of the boots who led a sheltered life back home with Mommy and Daddy. If you were used to bathing and evacuating your bladder and colon in relaxed privacy, it took some doing to adjust to having to carry out these bodily functions en masse with complete strangers. I'm sure that there was some degree of constipation among the sensitive boots at first, but because we were only allowed to relieve ourselves at organized head calls, you could not afford to be squeamish about it.

Now one might think that in spite of the public toilet facilities, at least it was a kind of refuge away from harassment by authority or anyone else. There had to be a shelter somewhere and we innocently assumed that it would be during head call. Here the torment was by the boots who had been here longer than we greenies. They had figured a way to burn your ass without being blamed. I guess none of us FNGs (fucking new guys) ever wondered why the downstream holes were not occupied except by the skinheads who have just arrived.

The saltier boots, knowing the drill, always tried to sit as far upstream as possible. The crapper was built over slow flowing water which carried it to the sewer. While the innocent sat downstream trying to imagine they were not in a circus, but back home in their private bathroom, the guy farthest upstream is wadding up a loose ball of toilet paper, which he sets on fire as he drops it into the stream and bolts for the exit. Like puppets, the boots jump up by the numbers howling and wondering what just singed the hair off their bungholes and seared their dangling scrota and other equipment. For me this was good conditioning for my future outfit, because I quickly learned what "Fire in the Hole" really meant. And when I heard that alarm, I really moved my butt to cover. More about that later. The flaming flume must have given rise to that old military expression to snap shit, or to tighten the pucker string while defecating.

Even when you knew the score, it wasn't always safe to sit upstream because, if you didn't check over the wooden seat beforehand, you just might suffer a chemical burn on your cheeks from some freshly applied creosote. That phenolic compound was used by the head cleaning detail to sterilize the wooden seats so we would be safe from germs. This strong antiseptic would plague you wherever you went in the Corps if the field head was the outhouse type with wooden seats.

My Irish mother used to tell me all the time that cleanliness was next to Godliness. The USMC took this concept to extremes, at least the cleanliness part. I don't think they ever thought about the relationship to Diety. Every week, on some day chosen by the DI, we had an area field day. We had to police up (pick up) around the platoon sector following the same drill as other services. As we turned to, the DI would shout, " All I want to see are assholes and elbows. If it moves, salute it. If it doesn't move, pick it up. If you can't pick it up, paint it." Just like the Army.

When we got through with the outdoor clean up, we turned to the tents. We rolled up the side flaps, took our sacks and everything else outside and scrubbed the wooden deck. Sometimes this coincided with laundry day when we turned in our sheets for clean ones. If we finished early enough we put all our gear back in the tent, made up the sacks and headed for the wash racks nearby. We pummeled our clothes with the bar of GI soap and scrubbed away with our brushes. We had to wring them out by hand and when rinsed and wrung again, they were hung on the clotheslines for the guy on that duty to watch them dry. I guess that is why it is called standing the clothesline watch.

Several times during my stay in boot camp, the DI would call for a sand field day. This meant that in addition to the usual deck cleaning, we had to use sand along with our scrub brushes and GI soap. First some of us had to go fill our buckets with sand from a nearby drum, maybe it was the fire control sand. The rest went for water. Then we rolled up our dungaree legs and got down with our bare knees in the soapy, wet sand and scrubbed away while the DIs watched. When we were through we had to reclaim the sand and return all of it to the barrel. Then we rinsed the floor. That is the best way to clean a floor, but not too good for the knees. The DI said that it was similar to using the old holystone on the wooden decks of ships in the old days and into very recent times on battle wagons and cruisers..

The cadence rang out from the senior DI as we were marching back to the platoon area from noon chow call, "won hup reep por yer leup hup reep." Five minutes earlier while in formation after chow, he read us the riot act for someone screwing up that morning and he was mad as hell about it. He marched us around trying to figure out some punishment when he decided to test our nerve and see just how far we would go in following orders, in this case marching orders. After 15 minutes of troop and stomp without rifles, which had been secured in the tents during chow call, he marched us toward the brackish water that surrounds the base.

The group thought it would soon hear, "To the rear, 'arch" to reverse the column away from the water. But he didn't and we marched into the water and kept going until the front ranks were tiptoeing and up to their necks. I'm sure that there was panic in the hearts of those boots who could not really swim, but when most of the platoon was well soaked, we gave a sigh of relief when the DI ordered, "To the rear, 'arch." We didn't break ranks except for the few stretching their necks to stay afloat in water that would soon be over their heads. Although many were scared silly, the DI was satisfied that we would follow his orders to the death if need be.

About ten years later, there was an incident where a salty DI at PI, did the same thing to his platoon with the result that several boots drowned. The shit hit the fan at USMC HQ and in congress. The DI was court martialed and reduced in rank from sergeant to private. His problem may have been that his boots might have been loaded down with packs, helmets, and rifles, whereas our platoon was not so laden when we took our wet walk.

Right after that incident, thousands of former Marines wrote or sent telegrams to congress and to the USMC Commandant, explaining that they had all been through the same wrenching experience, without harm. These veteran Marines further informed Washington that this was a necessary part of boot training and if a boot could not swim, he should not be in a largely amphibious branch of the service. Two years later, that former DI was named Marine of the Year for exemplary behavior and service to the Corps and was quickly back up to sergeant.

There was one other incident earlier, where our platoon was being punished immediately after noon chow by having to run several miles on full stomachs. Quite a few guys had to fall out with barfing fits. Most were not bothered, although it was certainly very uncomfortable. There was no way I was going to lose any food that day.

Because most of us boots would later have something to do with ships, we had to practice jumping into water from an equivalent height of a warship's deck. In preparation for the jump, we spent some time in a large swimming pool, learning how to rescue someone and rendering first aid to the drowning. On the first day of this aquatic grabass, there were a few boots who could not swim and were afraid of the water. With the typical soft touch and caring attitude of the USMC, these guys were simply thrown off the platform into the water to get them used to it. There was some cajoling as they held back while the rest of us swimmers made the jumps, but the DIs helped them overcome their fears. Good swimmers were always waiting for these boots when they hit the water to help them to the edge of the pool and allay their panic. Having grown up in Michigan and Ohio and always living near a lake, I was a very good swimmer, so had no trouble with the jumps. I stayed on for a day to learn life saving skills.

We spent several days now and then running the obstacle course which involved, climbing over, under and through various types of barriers. If a boot skirted the shallow, muddy pond when he thought the DI wasn't looking, he'd make that boot run into it and slide through on his belly four or five times while riding him with, "What? Don't you think there is any mud in Korea? Get used to it. You'll be up to your ass in mud over there." Crawling under an array of barbed wire stretched only 20 inches above the ground, while a gunner fired a 30 cal. machine gun over our heads was interesting, especially because he was using live ammo.

Climbing over walls, and all that, came naturally to me from running from the cops in my neighborhood. Because of my tree work using ropes, I was especially adept at climbing up the 2 inch diameter manila rope. I could zip up and down the thirty foot climb without using my legs, and do it faster than anyone else in the platoon. I think the DI finally found a use for me in the future. If a rope climb is involved out on a patrol, send the thin man up first. Say what? He said he was going to recommend that I be assigned to a recon outfit after boot camp. He thought I would make a good scout since I was stealthy and made a small target.

During our 11 week stint at PI we were allowed to visit the base PX only three times. We marched up to the building in formation and stood at parade rest in front while the DI went in and instructed the PX Manager as to what we were allowed to purchase. Usually this was limited only to letter size writing pads, envelopes, razors, blades, shaving cream, and soap. Absolutely no snack food, no pogey bait and certainly no ice cream, which was provided often as dessert at the mess.

However, one hot day when Sgt. Sicklick was in good spirits he announced to the platoon as we stood in front of the PX, that we would be allowed to buy one pint of ice cream as a reward for the progress we were making as boots. As usual we were only allowed in the PX in small groups and had to hurry with our purchase. We were all smiles as we fell in to the formation clutching our cold treat in one hand and the small wooden spoon in the other. As might be expected, someone had goofed up in the PX, so we were called to attention and the DI started ranting about the screw up. We were to be punished, but we hoped it wold be after we ate the ice cream.

The DI finished his tirade and ordered us to, "Uncover.......To." We snapped our caps off and deftly tucked them under the right armpit. He then said, "All right you fuckups, now place your carton of ice cream on your head and recover." We put the stuff on our heads and covered it with our caps. He followed with, "Now, you clowns wanted ice cream and there it is. As it melts standing here in the hot sun, you may lick it off your kisser if able. You will remain here at attention until it melts and runs all over you. Meantime, we will be watching you for any movement. Remember, you are at attention and you may not move any part of your body except in this case, your tongue."

So we stood there while the precious purchase melted and ran down our faces and necks. Because it was a really hot and we were there for 45 minutes. The guy in front of me who had chosen Neapolitan had three colors flowing down his neck, others were displaying strawberry, some vanilla, and lots of chocolate faces and necks. All the time we stood there we were wondering exactly who screwed up and what he did. The goofball probably backed into the DI at the counter in the PX and either knocked his ice cream to the deck or else stepped on his highly polished dress shoes. I wasn't mad at the screw up for this. After all, he could have punched me out over the illegal shower I had taken way back the first night at PI. We were a sorry sight as we marched back to the tent area to clean ourselves up. Ted K. says that this serving of ice cream on the head drill happened one other time just before mail call.

We were becoming highly practiced at standing at attention in information. It was really an exercise in self discipline. We were admonished not to move any part of our body when at attention and to look only straight ahead. Just try this sometime while there is some loud distraction in front of the platoon like when some sap is catching hell. You want to look but if you get caught, the DI is suddenly in your face with, "What the hell are you looking at skinhead?" You are afraid to say anything now, so he steps up the shouting so you have to answer him. He then asks, "Are you in love with me, you cunt?" You manage to shout out, "No Sir!" He retorts, "Then why in hell are you looking at me boy?" After much shouting he finally accepts your lame, "I don't know sir." He usually ended the routine by pulling your cap down over your face with a snap.

Parris Island was not only home base for the training command and the boots but an annoying little pest you could not really see. All skinheads believed that the sand fleas of PI were imported by veteran Marines from the South Pacific for the express purpose of torturing boots. They were always at their very worst when we were at attention in formation and when one or two started to work on your face, they eventually drew blood which would trickle down your skin until the little beasty left and the tiny puncture would clot.

Often when you felt a sand flea gnawing at your epiderm, you would try to locate the DI with one eye and if he wasn't looking your way, you'd take a calculated swipe at the critter on your face. It was a practiced and forbidden move. They say that the hand is faster than the eye. Whoever came up with that never had to deal with a DI. When the DI caught the movement, he would raise hell with the scratcher.

The DI knew what the trouble was because he was being bitten too, the sand fleas were equal opportunity feeders and all ranks were fair game. When the DI caught sight of the sneaky movement he would sometimes let you off with the comment, "Come on you pansies, you ate chow this morning, now let the sand fleas eat." Another time he might say, "If you candy asses think one or two sand flea bites a day are bad, just wait until two of them crawl into your ear while you're at attention and they start screwing." Pleased with himself, he would let out a guffaw.

Sometime near the last few weeks of boot camp, we had photos taken. One head shot for your USMC identity card and finally a group photo of the survivors of Platoon 136. I still have a copy of the head shot wearing a green piss cutter. I look like a cross between a poojie and a survivor from the Bataan death march. When the DI passed out our copies of the entire platoon, he had this comment. "When you leave here you will spend a couple of months in advanced infantry training and then be shipped to Korea in a replacement draft. Later on when I review the casualty lists in Leatherneck Magazine, as I come across your name, I will place an X across the face of the killed in action (KIA) and a circle around the head of the wounded. If you are reported to be missing in action (MIA), a question mark will suffice. If you become a deserter, I'll just blot you out. That is how I'll remember you." What a cheerful bastard he was.

Ted Kilberg has reminded me that we had stood at attention on the seats of a free standing bleacher section for the group photos. When the photo had been taken, SSgt. Sicklick simply turned around and ordered us to, "Right face. Foward 'arch." We did so and marched off the seats, Ted and I were on the next one to the top and had a step of about 8' to the ground. For some reason, this style of dismount didn't surprise us.

Looking at that group photo, I notice that it says Honor Platoon for platoon 136. No one ever explained what that meant at the time. Perhaps it meant that it was an honor for us who survived.

There is a saying, "Once a Marine, always a Marine." In other words, try as you might, you cannot separate yourself later from your training and life in the Corps. It is with you until you are called to a higher duty—to guard the streets of heaven according to the Marine Corps Hymn. In retrospect, I now understand that any living veteran of the Corps is referred to as a former Marine, whereas any dead Marine is called an ex-Marine. This drill must have originated with the practice of DIs inscribing the X across your mug shot in the platoon photo, hence making you into an ex-Marine upon news of your death. Morbidity lives on.

THE RIFLE RANGE

In order to fulfill your role as the complete Marine before leaving boot camp, you had to become proficient with handling the M-1. This included a thorough understanding of its workings, how to clean and maintain it, how to use it in close quarters, i.e. for bashing the enemy with the butt and use of the bayonet. In addition each Marine is expected to qualify in firing on the rifle range. To this end, two whole weeks were spent at the range.

To most of us skinheads, this was the best two weeks of boot camp. The routine harassment and chickenshit of daily drill was put aside to concentrate entirely on the firing range. The rifle instructors were in charge of us during daylight hours and they were technical people who were only interested in their trade, the skills of shooting. The DIs were lurking in the background for any emergency discipline problems and took over the platoon again at dusk. Once or twice SSgt. Sicklick went on liberty while we were at the range and would come back half-bagged to visit the Quonset hut area where we slept. At two AM he would run along the huts dragging the end of his night stick against the corrugated metal waking all the boots. Just to let us know he hadn't forgotten about us.

The first week at the range was spent in what is known as "snapping in" or dry firing. We spent all day, every day, learning how to hold the rifle and to use the sling for steadying support and to get into the various positions required, i.e. standing (offhand), kneeling, sitting and prone. All of these positions required the intricate use of the leather sling. Some of the time was spent in learning to respond to the commands of the range master and learning how to work in the butts, pulling and marking targets when it was our turn. Safety precautions were discussed every day.

When we moved into the second week we were issued clips and live ammunition on the first day and began firing in the different positions, first offhand from 50 yards, kneeling and sitting from 100 and 200 yards, and prone from 500 yards. As we arrived early each morning after breakfast, we noted that the red flag was flying high over the range to advise anyone approaching that live firing was going on.

The first day of live firing was devoted to zeroing in our rifles and trying to acquire a tight group of ten shots. The M-1 clip only held eight rounds, so we fired two from one clip and then eight from a full clip. The pause gave the boot a chance to learn how to handle and load a full clip from the cartridge belt around his waist. The rifle coach assigned to several boots when firing, advised on elevation and windage changes and gave other advice on stance, grip, breathing, sighting, and sometimes helped you to improve your sitting, kneeling or prone position for maximum effect.

As shooters prepared to aim at their target and assumed the correct position, the range master would call out the ammo to be used, "Two rounds lock and load." and we would shove a clip with two rounds into the receiver, let the bolt slide forward to chamber one round and to check that the safety was on. Then he would call out, "Ready on the right, ready on the left. All ready on the firing line. Commence firing." We would then release the safety, take aim and slowly squeeze the trigger after lining up both sights on the bulls eye.

When we took our turn in the target pits, we worked in teams of two boots to one target. The large, heavy paper targets were backed with cardboard and mounted on wooden and steel frames which we pulled down to mark when a firing series was over. One guy pulled the target down and the other noted the bullet holes in the rings, in the bull's-eye, or elsewhere on the target in the white. So the spotter could see the hits, we had small discs about two inches in diameter mounted on pointed pegs. We pushed the white discs onto the holes in the black and the black discs covering the holes in the white. Then we ran the target back up to be scored by the instructor who scanned the target with a spotting scope.and signaled the shooter's score by raising 12 inch disks on poles in front of the target and holding it in front of the places where the bullets had hit the target.

This gave the instructor a confirmation. If there was a complete miss, we waved a red flag up in front of the target, for all on the range to see. If the shooter fired ten rounds in the series, and we could only account for nine, we waved "Maggie's Drawers." The red flag could be seen up and down the firing line and was the ultimate humiliation for a boot.

Sometimes we would find 11 or 12 bullet holes in a target, where the shooter only had ten rounds to fire. Usually this meant that the goofball shooting at the next target garnered two flourishes of Maggie's Drawers by firing two of his rounds into the neighboring target by mistake. With the scoring recorded, we pulled the target back down to patch it for the next series of shots. We quickly covered the holes with paste and tape.

Working the butts was a bit unnerving at first as we heard the bullets snap overhead and through the target. However, it was safe as long as we remained down behind the dirt and concrete barrier in our trench. Sometimes a bullet would hit and splinter the wooden frame of the target but to my knowledge no one pulling butts was ever injured by the rifle fire while I was there. However, I read recently of a young boot being killed by a ricocheting round back in the forties. His father was a VIP in Washington, D.C. and there was hell to pay in the Corps for a couple of years. But for us this job was another welcome escape from the routine of the regular training schedule and any possible danger didn't bother us.

Any problems with rifle malfunctions were taken up with one of the many armorers on duty. They could quickly correct any problem that came up with a rifle and if necessary issue you another one that had been reconditioned. The new M-1 had to be zeroed in before you could start firing again for qualification. At the end of each day's firing we spent an hour or so cleaning our rifles for the inspections that sure to follow after evening chow. We had to use a special bore cleaner to remove the residue from firing live rounds through the barrel. Some swore that the bore cleaner was really made from the urn coffee left over at the mess hall.

The goal of live firing was to prepare the boot for his future primary duty as a rifleman. The DI insisted that every boot in Platoon 136 must qualify, i.e shoot above a minimum score (I've forgotten what that score was) to be certified as a marksman. If the score was higher by so many points, the shooter was designated either a sharpshooter, or the highest rank of expert. Each rank of qualification enabled the skilled shooter to wear a badge denoting his expertise to be worn with his campaign ribbons when he won them. Until then, the badge was worn alone above the left breast pocket on one's uniform.

Our drill instructor Sgt. Sicklick made so many dire threats about what he would do to anyone who had the gall not to qualify on the range, thereby bringing shame on the platoon, that it affected my own shooting. I was one of only three out of 72 boots who didn't qualify on the last day of shooting. The DI read the list to us in formation just as we left the range. He was looking daggers at me when he came to my score, which was only a point or two below the minimum. This was not pitching horse shoes, however. He reminded me that close shots, i.e. near misses would not do in Korea.

He said, "I'll deal with you three fuckups as soon as we get back to quarters at mainside tonight, but first I'm making arrangements for you twits to qualify the first thing next week. And you will stay at the range until you do qualify, if it takes all year. I do not believe that your fellow Marines waiting for you in Korea should be saddled with piss-poor shots. You're a menace to anyone in combat except the North Koreans and the Chinese we are fighting. In WWII, we gave your type a weapon they could not miss with, a flamethrower. Do you know what is the life expectancy of a flame thrower operator? About five minutes in combat if, he is lucky."

The hike from the range back to camp took about two hours. Although we marched in silence, except for cadence counting now and then, the mood of the platoon was good. Another milestone had been reached and we were that much closer to graduating. However, I was somewhat glum about facing my punishment that night and was ready to redeem myself the following Monday back at the range. It would be easier then, because Sgt. Sicklick would not be there to harass me and I felt that the range coaches would be a lot of help since any failure to qualify reflected on their ability to train boots.

After evening chow we fell out for mail call and dicked around with that routine for an hour. Just before we were dismissed, he called me and the other two non qualifiers to the front of the formation for our punishment. We stood there with our backs to the platoon and facing him like we were waiting for communion. In fact, he sort of ended up doing something like that. He had a huge jar of some pickled stuff in one hand and fished out a couple of those things that I thought were smelt. He handed me a couple and told me to eat them and get back in ranks. I saw that they were hot pickled peppers about seven inches long and one inch in diameter. Knowing this was bad stuff for a guy who grew up on bland American food, I squeezed the juice out of them as I ran around the platoon to get back in ranks.

That bastard did have eyes in the back of his head. It was dark and I was moving away from him as I squeezed the hot pickle juice out so I could eat them. He called me back up there saying, "None of that getting rid of the juice. I saw you do that, you shitbird. Get back here, chew those up and you'll get three more. My mother went to a lot of trouble to pickle these hot peppers and you will not waste this good stuff. I'm sacrificing my own stash of the kind of food I love on you jerks."

So I stood there chewing away on the first ones he'd given me. My eyes began to water and my nose was running. When I swallowed those with some difficulty, he told me to open up and he pulled out three more, one at a time and put them in my mouth, juice and all. As I started chewing the first one to make room for the second Sgt.Sicklick was muttering something I didn't understand. It was foreign, probably in Polish, but it sounded more like the priest intoning, "Dominus vobiscum."

I managed to get each one of these down my gullet, but was now sweating like mad along with the tears and nasal drip. I imagined my cheeks were flaming red from the heat inside.

As he dismissed us to return to ranks, he said to me and the other two fuckups, "You have my permission to drink all the water you want and visit the head any time you need to tonight. If you think that this stuff is burning your mouth and your gut right now, just wait until you have to take a dump tomorrow and the next day." Not having any experience 'til now with hot spicy foods, I didn't know what he meant. I got no help from my tent mates who were either from Boston or Detroit and weren't too familiar with ethnic foods.

I suffered pretty much all night with a roiling gut and I took his advice and drank a lot of water at the scuttlebutt. It turns out that this was the worst thing you could do to quell the fire in your innards. Water compounds the problem. The next day and the day following as my alimentary canal settled down to normal, I thought I was home free until I had a bowel movement. Then the burning started all over again at the other end as I evacuated the peppery stool. At first I looked upstream to see if anyone was sending the flaming toilet paper down to me. No one else moved. I was the only one with fire in the hole and I was in pain.

It took several days to get over the hot pepper episode, which by the way would not bother me at all now that I love hot spicy food. The peppery punishment had an immediate effect, because I returned to the range a few days later and qualified with the M-1 on the first day. I should mention that a few days after this episode, one of the other boots showed me the spot in the daylight where I had squeezed out the juice from the peppers that night while returning to ranks. There was a trail of holes burned into the tarmac from that vile pickling fluid.

GRADUATION

As we neared the end of our training, we had become very proficient at troop and stomp and looked a lot sharper at it than when we first came to PI. We marched in parades to the rythym of the drum and bugle corps or the marching band.

We no longer had the appearance of new skinhead boots. Our dungarees had lost their sheen through frequent scrubbing and we tried to look salty for the new arrivals as we marched smartly by their struggling formations. We were now functioning as an integrated unit, which was one of the aims of the intense training.

Several days before our graduation parade and ceremony, we were given our private first class (PFC) stripes to sew on our uniforms, red ones for the greens and dark green for the khakis. We were also provided with a full set of emblems (Globe and Anchor, the symbol of the USMC) for the caps and shirt collars. The stripe was stenciled on our dungaree shirts.

On graduation day, the parade and inspection was followed by a brief ceremony in which the CO of the training command told us what was expected of us from now on as we dispersed to further training and other assignments. He then handed out our warrants, which were the official record of our promotion to PFC.

After noon chow on graduation day, we were marched to the base travel office with our newly issued orders for travel from PI to our home towns and back to PI. We entered the travel office a dozen at a time to make our reservations on buses, planes, or trains. This was the first time

Top, left to right: Bob Goodell, Unknown; Bottom., left to right: Gerald Ginnelly, Ted Kilberg. Photo: USMC

we had seen any women since we arrived at PI. The office was staffed entirely with young women, all civilians. We noticed that SSgt. Sicklick had bellied up to the counter trying to make time with some of the girls, but in his usual crass manner, he was slamming his night stick into his other hand. Looking a little closer at his billy club, he had rolled a condom up the end of it as far as it would go. If he did it to get attention from the chicks, all he got were snickers as far as I could tell.

Early the next morning we held our last muster and formation and heard the parting words of our DI, who had stopped calling us foul names all of a sudden. One of the things he told us was that people would be calling us Marines by other names, such as leatherneck, gyrene, jarhead, etc. They were just jealous. Those names didn't trouble him, but he had a special retort for a soldier or sailor who hailed you by calling you a sea going bell hop. He shut them up by saying, "Hey, the last belle I hopped was your sister." This type of interservice banter usually came to blows.

He wished us well, especially the bulk of us who were destined for Korea. The day before we had stowed everything in our seabags and turned in our 782 gear and rifle to the supply shed. Now we turned in our linen and blankets and stood one more formation before being dismissed from boot camp for good. What a glorious feeling of liberation.

S. Sgt. G. Sicklick, Senior DI
Platoon 136, 5th Recruit Battalion, USMCRD, PI, SC
Photo: USMC

63

We had been allowed to go the PX to buy a small hand bag to carry a change of clothes and shaving kit for the trip home. Our seabags would be stored at PI for us until we returned in ten days for reassignment.

At this late date, I have no idea how I got home from PI for the leave. It was the third week in April and the snow and ice in Detroit had been replaced by green trees, grass, and flowers. It was great to be back home with the family and to see my friends. Most of the guys had gone into the service and I did get to see a few of them home from Army basic training or Navy boot camp. Naturally we compared notes and it seemed to me that they had a picnic, but I didn't rub it in. I didn't see much of Ted Kilberg who came back to Detroit with me because he went on to the Upper Peninsula of Michigan to see his family.

The only friend that I know of who went into the Marines was Elmer (Sonny) Bushaw from the old neighborhood so he can vouch for what I say about my cruise through the Corps. My best friend Paul Bergman joined the Army and volunteered for the Airborne. It was a good choice, because he was a tough kid and like to fight. When I saw him again after we both left the service, he was sporting a long scar across his neck. It seems that he'd gotten into an altercation, while still in the Army, with some Marines and one of them attacked Paul with a broken bottle, slashing his throat.

While I was in Detroit I decided to rectify a problem with the khaki uniform. Our summer uniform was cotton trousers and shirt which was cool enough but the cloth wrinkled so much we had to starch it before ironing. I'm not much on wearing starched anything, one reason being that the starch made the uniform warmer. I went to a uniform supply store and bought a shirt and pair of trousers made from a fine khaki colored material like gabardine, which didn't wrinkle and needed no starch. I could never wear this fine looking outfit around the base, but it was great for Detroit. Now I could adopt that famous saying of some, then in the military, who sported tailor-made uniforms, " I may not be regulation, but I sure am sharp."

For those who went through a different kind of basic training in other branches of the service, I reiterate that we led very spartan lives. During boot camp we were never allowed off the base or to wander about the base at anytime on our own. If more than two guys had to go somewhere, like the dentist, they had to march there smartly. We were never allowed to go to a movie, unless it was a training film. There was no recreation, unless you can call a couple of hours of organized grabass on the weekend recreation. There was to be no chatting between boots, except in your tent from evening chow to taps and from reveille to morning formation and at chow time. We had no access to reading material that wasn't official training stuff and whatever you received in the mail.

We were not allowed to go to the PX except in formation for those items approved by the DI. We were certainly never allowed to go to the slopchute or to the snack bar if they existed.

Many boots hated their DI so much for all the grief they were put through at PI, that they expressed a desire to do him in at the first opportunity. I never harbored these feelings myself, because my mother was tougher than the DI. She had put me through my paces from the day I reported for duty, on the day I was born. I was preconditioned for boot camp. There was nothing the DI could do to me that I hadn't already been through in the way of discipline. When my brother Tom came home from three years in the Pacific, my mother confronted him with a letter he had written at a point when he didn't think he would come home alive. She asked what he meant by this sentence and showed him the two year old letter. He had written, "The US government should send you over here (Philippine Islands) to teach the Japs how to fight dirty." He too had been well prepared for a tour in the military.

Once out of boot camp, I doubt that this animosity towards the DI lasted very long, even among those who were extremely bitter. After all, thousands of men had gone through this same training over the years. The DI was just doing his job and I think he did it well. I can imagine that if a DI turned up in a line outfit in Korea, he would be welcomed by his former boots as a good NCO to have around in a pinch. All thoughts of knocking him off in a fire fight would be quickly forgotten. In Vietnam, this kind of thinking led some enlisted types in the land forces to "frag" their superior NCOs and officers. That expression came from the use of fragmentation grenades which were rolled into the tent, bunker or hooch of the target.

ADVANCED INTANTRY TRAINING, CAMP PENDLETON

Before I left Detroit to return to PI, I knew that I would be going to Korea as soon as I completed nine weeks of advanced infantry training at Camp Pendleton, so I said goodbye to friends and family. My Dad had been in combat in WWI in France and Belgium and I asked him if he had any advice for my coming tour in Korea. He thought for a while and said that if at all possible, you and your outfit must keep civilians well away from you in a combat area. He did not elaborate and I did not press him about it. I was concerned about this problem, but it turned out that the USMC had as much good sense as my Dad. The US military could have used Dad's wise advice in prosecuting the Vietnam war.

Back at PI, it was a great feeling to be a liberated PVC instead of a new boot. All of us from Platoon 136 gathered there in a casual company, a sort of limbo for military personnel waiting for transfers to new billets. The Army calls them replacement depots or RepoDepos. The NCOs in charge found creative ways for us to occupy ourselves while we waited for our new orders. We learned where the prison chasers, head cleaning and police details, mess duty types came from—the casual company.

It was a great feeling to be able to go over to the PX and buy ice cream that we didn't have to wear on the head. We still had to form up and march to the mess hall for meals, but that was only to maintain some degree of military decorum for the boots now going through their training.

It was fun to watch the new skinheads trooping and stomping. The three DIs circling the platoon like hawks, watched for fuckups and poked the laggards with their swagger sticks, waiting to pounce on the guy with two left feet. Meanwhile, the head DI continued to call cadence," Wun, hup reep, por yur leup, yur leup," with occasional shouts like, "Lean back, dig those heels in, swing those arms, six inches to the front, three to the rear. Wun hup reep, por yur leup." We didn't think of kibitzing the new boots. It might get us 30 days on mess duty and we could miss the train to Camp Pendleton with connections in San Diego for the Far East.

The day we boarded the troop train in Beaufort, SC, we were cheered by the rumor that a PFC had seen an open semitrailer stake bed piled to the top with our seabags. It was on its way from the base to our baggage car at the train siding. SSgt. Sicklick was seen riding on top of the seabags. We assumed that he was being transferred along with us and on his way to Korea. Maybe while he was sacked out in the staff NCO quarters, he was mistaken for a seabag and loaded on the trailer by a couple of Gomer Pyle types on that detail.

The accommodations on the train were spartan. Each car for about 30 men had no shower or bath, only a small head with a toilet and sink. The trip took five days and nights, so although we tried to wash up completely in that tiny head, we were pretty gamey by the time we reached California. We practiced taking a bath out of a small basin. We would need that skill later in Korea when we took a "whore's bath" from our helmet inside a bunker or tent in weather that reached -30° and -40°F.

We ate box lunches and a few prepared meals on the train for the whole trip. The reason it took five days for trip from coast to coast, was that a troop train had the lowest priority on the main east-west tracks. Our train often pulled off onto a siding and we sat there for hours waiting for a freight or passenger train to fly by. That really made us feel great to know that freight took precedence over a load of troops on their way to a war. At least we hoped that the westbound freights carried ordnance and supplies for us to use in Korea.

On trains as on ships and everywhere Marines serve, we had to stand two hour fire watches. This was OK with us, because it relieved the boredom and we were allowed to smoke as much as we wanted. Our only really important charge during a watch, was to go to the rear of the assigned car whenever the train stopped. We were ordered to stop any Marine from getting off the train while it was on a siding or any other time. There was never any problem during the daytime, but by the time we got to Camp Pendleton, five Marines were missing from our train. In some cases, it was the guy on fire watch who got off and disappeared into the night. Once it happened near Texarkana. The Marine was probably from that area and wanted to go home. As we came closer to the final leg of the trip to Korea, some apparently were having doubts about going into combat.

Most of our time was spent in reading and playing cards, but no gambling with money of course, so we used matches for chips. The talk centered on the usual things discussed by troops: women, what we could expect to be doing at Camp Pendleton, rumors about what was going on in Korea. There was the usual banter between us Yankees and the Rebels from the south. We rode them and they teased us, mostly about our ways of speaking. As we drew nearer to California, talk focused on how much liberty we would be given and wondering what the girls were like in Southern California.

There were a few officers and staff NCOs aboard as the troop command, but we saw little of them, except for one passing through each car for a head count every day. Once or twice we halted at a whistle stop for some reason and the Skipper had us fall in on the platform for a roll call. It was a form of entertainment for the local yokels and a chance for us to stretch our limbs.

All of us were from the eastern US and took a great interest in crossing the Mississippi River and in the changing landscape from there to the coast. The west looked pretty desolate to me and I wondered how people could live out there without many trees and very few lakes. Most of the rivers we crossed west of Texas were only dry beds of rocks and sand.

After we went through Los Angeles, the track turned southwest then due south at the seashore and ran between the Pacific and the coast highway. I had never seen an ocean before—even at PI we never saw the Atlantic itself. The Pacific was beautiful and we knew that our destiny lay over the horizon thousands of miles to the west in Korea.

After we had left the suburbs of Los Angeles, the word was passed through the train to pack our gear and be ready to disembark at Camp Pendleton. The train slowed through some small towns and crept along finally coming to a stop at the station in the town of Oceanside. We formed up on the platform for a head count, then filed off to the waiting buses. It was very civilized, not like our nasty reception at the station outside of PI where the DIs came at us like storm troopers.

The buses entered the main gate and tooled through mainside, past the buildings around the Base HQ and a large number of barracks. We were surprised that we didn't stop and off load at one of them, but continued east into the boonies. Once in a while we caught a glimpse of a large group of Marines involved in what seemed to be a field problem, i.e. learning tactical combat skills such as patrolling.

After a long drive through barren hills, we pulled up at an area where bulldozers and graders were still leveling the terrain for our new quarters—Tent Camp Three, inland from San Clemente on the coast. The timing was great. The site was level and the tents were just being unloaded. As soon as we got off the bus we were put to work erecting pyramidal tents in long rows. Then we formed up for a roll call and received tent and training unit assignments.

These tents didn't have the wooden frame (strongback) and had only dirt floors. The tents were spaced about a yard apart and tied together by ropes where the sides met the edge of the roof. In front of every third or fourth tent was a 55 gallon drum full of water, a couple of steel buckets and a machete hanging from a pole by a thong. This was our fire fighting equipment. In boot camp I came to look on a steel bucket as a stool. Here it was the basic tool of the bucket brigade. The waterproofing material impregnated into the tent canvas would burn like crazy and was a hazard. The machete was for cutting the ropes between tents to stop a fire from spreading. Luckily we had no fires in our tents while I was there. As the tents went up, the engineers came along and built us a field head, mess and galley.

The next few days were spent at the supply sheds for issue of rifles, bayonets, web gear, helmets, etc. Once again we had to clean goopy cosmoline off the M-1s. This time however, every fourth man in each platoon was issued a Browning Automatic Rifle (BAR). We were also issued canvas folding cots, blankets and a small pillow.

Our technical training was taken more seriously by us PFCs because it was more interesting than boot camp and because we were getting closer to Korea. Another improvement was that the lectures and everything else were conducted out of doors in nice (May) southern California weather so there were very few nodding off. Attention was rapt. The long stick was not needed this time because our lives depended on what we learned here.

As usual the military sorted people alphabetically. Thus I ended up in a squad made up mostly of Italian Americans from the East Coast. My compadres were Paul Gallo, Henry Ferrini, Jack Giamati, and Salvatore diStasi. We called ourselves the Italian Fire Team plus one, even though

I explained to them that Ginnelly was an Irish name derived from McGinley in County Mayo. They ignored my background and said that to them I was simply Giannelli, a paisano—a Mediterranean Irishman.

I could not have asked for a better group of guys to train with. Italians are a happy lot and very easy to get along with. Serving with them made the training course a little more pleasant. No matter how bad things got, they never complained, or did so in a cheerful manner. We even went on liberty together. Since they spoke only Joisey (English with a New Jersey accent) and Italian, I went along as the interpreter. Other names I can still connect to familiar faces way back then are Good, Goodell (from Keene, NH), Gallant, and Sonny Gabriel. from Pennsylvania.

Since the outbreak of the Korean war, ten replacement drafts had already shipped out to Korea from here. Each draft was made up of thousands of Marines. Our training company was part of the eleventh replacement draft bound for Korea. The first few drafts were of reservists, most of whom had served in WWII in the Pacific. Then the drafts were made up with active duty Marines from all kinds of posts and later from new PFCs. like us just out of advanced infantry training. When we left this training command we would qualify for the infantry in Military Occupation Specialty (MOS) designation of 0143.

Where the main emphasis on physical training in boot camp was on troop and stomp and basic skills, the advanced infantry training had a different emphasis. We learned the theory and practice of combat skills in tactical and strategic maneuvering. To this end we spent a lot of time, day and night, in field problems, known to grunts as, "pooping and snooping in the boondocks." We spent a lot of time crawling through the dirt, humping over the dusty hills of Pendleton, and creeping up

The Italian Fire Team: Rear, L-R, Salvatore DiStasi, Paul Gallo, Henry Ferrini; Front, L-R, Gerald Ginnelly, Jack Giamati at Camp Pendleton days before shipping out. July 1951.

the dirt, humping over the dusty hills of Pendleton, and creeping up on the enemy (the snooping). If you could not learn to shit between your boondockers (the pooping), then you would not do too well in Korea.

Before we went out on field problems we had lectures and practice sessions in the following:

Patrolling and reconnaissance activities.

Map reading and orienteering with compass

Familiarization with light and heavy weapons

Working with heavy weapons crews, artillery, close air support and tanks

Unloading from an APA onto small landing craft, or Amtracs and hitting the beach.

First Aid, dealing with the wounded and field sanitation.

Learning communications systems.

Laying mines and clearing mine fields

Digging in, dealing with various types of barbed wire defenses, etc.

Hand to hand combat and bayonet practice.

All of this stuff was very useful and good preparation for Korea. The only thing I can remember of interest was how to answer this question put to us by the instructors, "What would you do if you were in skirmish line left and the enemy decided to do such and such?" We learned that every answer to a tactical problem should be framed with these words first, "Well, it all depends on the situation and the terrain." The rest of your reply didn't seem to matter as long as you included the buzz words. Also this phrase gave you some time to think over your reply. I found years later, that this phrase did not cut it when answering questions put to me by my university professors. They probably wondered why they heard that phrase only from veterans.

The Marine infantry squad of 12 was made up of three fire teams of four men each. Three carried rifles and one the Browning Automatic rifle (BAR). One of the others acted as the BAR man's assistant and carried extra ammo for the BAR. In training we took turns carrying the BAR to get everyone used to its weight and size. The BAR weighed 16 pounds and the extra magazines were heavy enough to require an ammo belt that had shoulder straps to ease the load. I was easily the thinnest man in training and knew that in combat, the smallest or lightest guy carried the BAR. The BAR was a formidable weapon and most looked forward to being assigned to use it in a fire fight.

Two things stick in my mind through all that field training. We were continually admonished to stay off the ridge line when patrolling. At certain times of day this would prevent your silhouette from attracting the attention of the enemy. Ever since then, when out hiking, hunting, or on field work as a Game and Fish Ranger, I found myself staying below the skyline from habit. I didn't want wild animals or poachers to see me outlined with the sky as the backdrop while hunting or on patrol.

When out in the field at Pendleton, we were constantly told not to bunch up. This was good conditioning for Korea where a close group could easily be taken out with one artillery or mortar round, or a burst of machine gun fire. We heard this so much during training and whenever we were on a field problem, that it stuck with us.

I'm sure that "don't bunch up" is still an important part of Marine training and I wonder why politicians are able to override this precept. I refer to the situation in Beirut on Oct. 23, 1985 when 240 Marines and their corpsmen were killed by a huge truck bomb placed outside their barracks by local militants. I'm sure that the colonel in charge of that small force from the US Sixth Fleet knew better than to place his men in jeopardy by piling them all into one building. Those Marines could have been just as effective by staying aboard their ships just off the coast. Whatever happened to the tried and true, "Don't bunch up men. Spread out." Even though a similar bomb was set off outside the American and French Embassies just weeks before, why did the authorities above the colonel in command on site, insist that he put his men in a building? On top of those blasts, it is obvious that no extraordinary precautions were taken to prevent such an attack on our Marines. The colonel was a good Marine and did what he was told. His men were put in danger for political motives only. I think it is time for the USMC to consider some means of handling direct orders from civilian politicians. US Army troops were also put in danger by unthinking politicians in Somalia causing the unnecessary death and maiming of several of our soldiers.

A monument now stands inside the gate at Camp Lejeune with the names of all those Marines and corpsmen killed in Beirut. The memorial is a fine symbol for those murdered with no chance to defend themselves and should serve as a monument to the more thoughtful deployment of our troops in hostile country. How odd that it had to be paid for from private donations. This monument needs a sign on top of it in huge letters reminding Marines, "DON'T BUNCH UP!"

Every one of our instructors at Pendleton was a veteran of combat in either Korea or in the South Pacific in WWII. We were warned about the various kinds of booby traps used by the Japanese, North Koreans, and Chinese. Among those that they had run across already in Korea, were devices left in the path of our advancing forces. Every kind of item left behind by the enemy in the way of bodies, wounded, and their equipment was suspect. Our troops after souvenirs had to be wary.

We were also cautioned in our training about things like an already prepared, but unlit pile of leaves, limbs, and other wood, as though the enemy had fled before lighting their fire. The reds expected us to take a rest break there and had prepared the pile with grenades or other explosives at the bottom. The first reaction of some might be to sit down and touch a match to the tinder, then gather around to warm their hands and heat water for coffee. The resulting explosion would take out a few guys for good. Another ploy was for the reds to tie a fragmentation grenade to a limb up out of sight in a tree over the track they expected your column to follow. A string or wire was then tied to the pin and then to a lower limb hanging down where someone passing might reach up and grab that limb and tug on it. The exploding grenade might not get him too badly, but it would get the next few guys behind him.

When it came to barbed wire we practiced setting up the apron type array, which was an arrangement two to four feet high and spread four to six feet on both sides sloping slightly from the peak in the middle. This would slow down infiltrators if they got past the mine field and trip flares. We were told that the Chinese had a way to get over this wire without having to cut it, so naturally we had to try that method ourselves. The first man rushing to the wire held his M-1 down on top of the wire and then laid on it in the prone position while the rest of his squad stepped on his butt or back to get over the wire. This would only work if the wire arrangement was relatively parallel with the ground. We took turns being the fall guy and keeping the rifle bolt down, other wise it would press into the gut.

Concertina wire was difficult to work with, stretching it out while trying to avoid too many cuts and scratches from the barbs. But it was better than the apron type, as it is quite difficult for anyone to get through. Our forces used bangalore torpedoes to blow holes in the enemy's barbed wire. These are long pipe bombs designed for this purpose. I don't know if the enemy had them or not. They probably used a volunteer to crawl under the wire and blow himself up with a satchel charge.

Looking back at the US experience in the Vietnam War, I found one of the things we were taught here at Pendleton quite silly. We were told never to fire a rifle at an airplane, even if it is attacking your position. Now this turned out to be a moot point for us, as our own Air Forces (USAF, Navy and USMC) had control of the skies over the lines in Korea from 1951-53. Now that I have read many books about the war in Vietnam, especially concerning air operations, I find that many of our own aircraft of all types were brought down by enemy small arms fire.

During part of the Vietnam War (1968-71) I was stationed between three USAF bases in NE Thailand. Combat missions were flown from all three to strike targets in North Vietnam and Laos. I knew Colonel Glass the base commander of the Royal Thai/USAF base at Udorn and had access to the surplus materials in their junkyard. While I was scrounging through military equipment for things I could use on my project, my nine year old son would climb into the cockpits of various wrecked planes to pretend he was flying the Phantoms, Thunderchiefs, A-7s, etc.

When I started to examine some of these wrecks out of curiosity, I was amazed to see all the damage a single bullet could do to all of the intricate wiring and tubing hidden just under the thin skin of the fuse-lage. These bundles of wiring and fine tubing go to the servomechanisms that operate the plane. If just one round rips through the bundles of wires or clips a tube or two, the pilot loses control and either limps to an airfield or the aircraft crashes. Redundant systems are supposed to help prevent the crippling of the plane, but don't always work.

There are documented cases from Laos and Vietnam, where an American pilot actually saw a farmer (or a guy in black pajamas) firing a rifle at his low flying plane and bringing it down. It seems highly ironic that one man with a rifle can wreck a sophisticated plane worth millions of dollars and cause the death of the highly skilled pilot. I have an idea how a man on the ground might feel with a plane diving on him. While working out in the field in southern Arizona, I became a target for two bored pilots practicing their attack skills. Once I was approached on several mock strafing passes by a low flying A-7 jet, while changing a tire on my truck in the high desert. Another time while taking water samples in the middle of lake near Fort Huachuca, I was the subject of several close dives by a twin-prop Mohawk. It must have been a US Customs pilot on a boring patrol trying to make me take to the water.

I was luckier than a Game and Fish Development crew which had prior USAF permission to work on water catchments on the Barry Goldwater bombing range south of Gila Bend. A USAF jet shot their truck and trailer up with nonexploding cannon ammo while the crew took refuge under the vehicle. Their equipment was ruined, but the crew was unhurt, except for some trouble controlling their pucker strings for months afterward. The USAF and Game and Fish had this hushed up for years although the offending pilots from some base outside of Arizona were disciplined for not clearing their training flights. They had mistaken AG&F vehicles for the many old junker vehicles left out there for legitimate targets.

One of the things we had to contend with at Pendelton, which we didn't even think about at PI, was rattlesnakes. There were lots of them and we killed quite a few around camp, just for something to do. When we saw our first rattler, we decided that maybe wearing the canvas leggings was not such a bad idea after all. So whenever we were out in the boonies we left our pant legs outside the leggings, instead of tucking them is as we were supposed to wear them. We figured that if a snake struck he would get his fangs hung up on the loose pant leg and the fangs might not penetrate the heavy canvas of the leggings. When we slept on the ground while pooping and snooping, snakes and scorpions were a worry. We had to check our boondockers every morning before putting them on, even in the tents. Blankets were shaken out before sleeping and again in the morning just in case.

I note that both American and British troops wore leggings in WWI, but they called them puttees. The men of the American Expeditionary Force (AEF) wore the wrap around type, which went round and round your ankle and calf like a bandage roll. Some soldiers of the British Expeditionary Force (BEF) wore a straight cut type, made of leather that was held on with a clasp arrangement. The leggings that we Marines had to wear, were lace up jobs with a strap under the arch of your boondocker.

No one ever explained to me the purpose of wearing leggings and I'm glad they sort of disappeared during my tour in Korea. Perhaps they were designed to keep dirt and stones out of our high cut boondockers. I have noticed that sailors in our Navy wore white lace up leggings when they were on shore patrol or guard duty. They tucked their bell bottoms into the leggings and bloused them over the tops.

While we were in Korea leggings were sort of forgotten during the winter because we had to wear thermal boots or shoepacs both of which rendered leggings useless. From our point of view, leggings were a throwback to the past. It was a pain just putting them on and keeping them clean. They just faded away and no one mourned their passing. However, the Chinese remembered them well. During the fighting between the Chinese and Marines in late 1950 and summer of 1951, the leggings, along with the camouflaged helmet cover, were the way to identify Marines. The Chinese soldiers referred to us as, "Those yellow legged devils."

We walked all over Camp Pendleton and I felt that if its terrain was flattened, it would be bigger than California. Two of our platoon leaders (2nd lieutenants) were race walkers. They carried the same packs and equipment as the rest of us, except they were issued M-1 carbines, but they never seemed to flag. We were many miles from the gate at San Clemente and when we went on liberty we took the bus. Not for our platoon leaders. They loved to walk so much that they even used shank's mare on Saturday to get to the gate. They also walked back to camp when returning on Sunday night. They spent their free time conditioning their legs by running and race walking on the sand at the nearby beaches. They were fine officers and our men had great confidence in them, especially one named Lt. Partridge.

LIBERTY AND LIFE ON THE BASE

One could not ask for a better place for liberty than coastal Southern California. It wasn't bad in the towns close to the base and up and down Hwy. 101. But to get away from sailors and other Marines we had go all the way up to Los Angeles and get lost in the crowd. There was liberty almost every weekend if we didn't have some guard duty or a field problem on the base. Liberty call was from 1700 hours on Friday night to 0700 on Monday. What's more, we could wear civvies if we had them.

We were warned about going to Tijuana, Baja California, Mexico. If a Marine got into trouble there and ended up in a Mexican jail, there was little the USMC or anyone else could do about it. The Mexican police simply locked you up and threw away the key. I took this advice to heart and decided never to go there and to stay away from San Diego as well. There were too many sailors there as well as staff Marines from the boot camp at the San Diego, USMC Recruit Depot (MCRD). Who wants to run into someone else's DI on liberty?

My first forays into the liberty scene along the coast were in the company of the Italian Fire Team. We went to the public beaches like Huntington Beach, Seal Beach, and all the way up to Santa Monica Beach. More than anything else our attention was focused on watching the chicks frolic on the beach and sizing up the situation and the terrain.

One weekend I went to Long Beach with Sonny Gabriel to visit a civilian couple from his home town in Pennsylvania. I later visited this civilian couple quite a few times. They took me around to see all the sights in the area including Knotts Berry Farm. The rest of the Fire Team had decided to focus on chasing girls in the greater Los Angeles area, but I didn't want to travel that far. On that first trip to Long Beach I stayed in a hotel downtown. When I filled the tub to take a bath, the odor of rotten eggs (hydrogen sulfide) filled the room. The smell came from the tap water. It must have come from the oil fields under and surrounding the city. I don't see how the people could drink water that would gag a maggot, to use an old Corps phrase.

The City of Long Beach had an amusement park right on the beach called the Pike, which had plenty of young women parading up and down followed by salivating Marines and panting sailors in civvies scouting them out. I didn't know it at the time, but my future wife was then living in a house on the beach near the Pike.

Some of the cruder type of roughnecks said that they always went to Hollywood on the weekend to pick up some free cash. The rubes, like me, wanted to know how to do that. The tough guys said they trolled for queers. They would hang around certain bars and restaurants where they would be picked up by a homosexual, who took them home for

75

some entertainment. After a few drinks and some banter, when things started to get sticky, the jarhead would then beat up the host and rob him of his cash and whatever and take off.

Not knowing anything about queers, I thought this was a pretty nutty and stupid thing to do, so I asked them if they weren't afraid of being arrested for that. They said no, their victims were afraid to go to the cops, because they would just be harassed again by them. Needless to say, I stayed away from these guys when I went on liberty.

I didn't know any Marine who had a car at Pendleton. Some took the bus to get from the gate at Pendleton to whatever town chosen for the weekend. There was no restriction on hitchhiking, so many of us went that route. It was easier to get a ride if you wore your uniform, so we carried a tote bag for our civvies. However, hitchhiking on Hwy. 101 did have its risks.

The first time I decided to thumb my way to Long Beach, I was on the highway shoulder just outside the San Clemente Gate, when I saw a USMC Jimmy (GMC) 6X6 headed right for me. Hey, I thought, they're going to give me a ride. As the truck came to a halt just past me, a staff NCO jumped down from the cab and told me to get into the back. I started towards the back of the truck asking if he was going as far as Long Beach. The NCO only laughed as he boosted me over the tailgate. I was greeted with hoots and howls from other PFCs. who had already been picked up.

I asked them how many guys were getting off at Long Beach, which really made them roar. One finally said, "'Welcome aboard shithead. This ain't no liberty bus and we ain't a goin' to Long Beach. Yer liberty has been cancelled for COG reasons." The guy next to the redneck added, " We're headed back into the middle of Camp Pendleton as soon as we change into dungarees." I sat on one of the benches and asked, "What's COG and why are we going back?"

I was told that COG stands for anything the USMC does to you for the convenience of the government. In this case, it seems that we were being summarily rounded up, wherever they could find warm bodies, to put out a rather large brush fire on the base. I asked, " Why should we have to do it?" Someone volunteered, "You dope, remember what you were doing all week?" By this time I recognized a couple of guys in my outfit, and motioning to them I said, "I was out with them for four days with our unit on a field problem. We were training with artillery and heavy weapons teams and air support." In unison they said, "And what were they firing?" I replied, "Well, the Corsairs were dropping bombs and firing rockets ahead of us and the artillery and mortars were firing HE (high explosive) and WP. (white phosphorus) and stuff like that." "Ijit, we started the fires so now we have to go back to put them out," I was told. I realized I'd just been shanghaied.

The truck dropped us off at our tents where we changed into work clothes, filled canteens and waited to be picked up by another truck. When all the available warm bodies were assembled we loaded up picks, shovels, rakes, hoes, whatever tools we could find and were driven off to the front. It wasn't hard to find, with smoke drifting away from the burning shrubs and grass. There were a few tanker trucks from the base fire department and from nearby towns hosing down the flames they could reach. Huge military type tankers of the semitrailer type were hauling in water for the fire trucks.

As we unloaded close to the fire line, but safely on the already charred side, an officer and a gunny directed us to our work site. There were hundreds of Marines already there. We were told to get on the other side of the fire and try to snuff it out with dirt and our tools. We formed one long line on slopes where the fire trucks could not reach and concentrated on fires burning down slope, which burned slower. It was very difficult to control a fire burning on the up slope, because it could sweep quickly up hill.

Camp Pendleton, like most of southern California is very dry in summer. This was June and it probably hadn't rained since February. The vegetation was primarily wild grasses, weedy stuff, and shrubs called chapparal, which made good fuel for wildfires. Santa Ana winds and winds from the ocean added to the problem. When you first see the outback of Pendleton, you are struck by the sight of mile after mile of firebreaks running over the ridge lines in an attempt to prevent wildfires from spreading. These 40 foot wide lanes of upturned bare earth are created with bulldozers and maintained with huge disc plows to stop vegetation from encroaching. Our walking lieutenants liked to make us hike up and over these firebreaks to toughen up our legs in the soft soil. No GI likes to hike any distance across plowed soil. It's hard going.

The problem this weekend was due to gusty winds carrying burning embers across the fire lanes and spreading fires over hundreds of acres. From past experience, the base fire chief had learned that when it gets out of his team's grasp, call in the Marines. If you put enough manpower out there, the fire will be contained. From our point of view, this was the ultimate shit detail. Being pulled off liberty to slave away in all that heat, smoke, and soot, while whacking away at the fire was not this city boy's idea of a good time. This experience gave me a healthy respect for fire fighters from then on.

Around noon a truck showed up with hot chow and lots of cold drinks (purple stuff) and coffee. By sundown we had the fire licked and some guys volunteered to stay out there to search out and smother embers. I opted to return to our tent city for a hot meal, a shower, and to sack out. The next day we were on standby in case the fire was rekindled and we were not allowed off the base.

From the above experience, I learned to bug out on Friday evening to get clear of the base. If you hitchhiked you were vulnerable until you got about 20 miles north of the base. Anyone who waited until Saturday morning to go on liberty was SOL (shit out of luck) if a fire had started from tracers or larger ordnance. Before we shipped out, I was stuck a couple of more times in this fire line grabass. I fell victim then because either liberty was restricted just in case a small fire got out of hand, or I was too broke to go off the base.

The one negative aspect of going on liberty was the fact that California had a law that required one to be 21 years old to buy alcoholic beverages. For a time, some bartenders and liquor store owners were sympathetic and allowed purchases without questioning the youthful Marines. However, there were so many instances of public disturbances involving drunken Marines, that the local authorities demanded that the Marine Corps do something about under aged drinking off base. After we shipped out for Korea, the USMC began to print MINOR in large red letters across the front of a Marine's ID card if he was under 21. This reduced the problem to a manageable level.

Even back in Michigan, this question of allowing servicemen under 21 to buy alcohol was in dispute. The State insisted that the law be strictly enforced. My mother thought it was a rotten deal for those in the service. She told me that if I ever got into trouble with the law over this issue, she would go to court herself. She would tell the judge that it if young man is old enough to be killed in a war, he should be able to have a drink. Why did the government want to draft young men under the age of 21, knowing that they would certainly like to have a drink now and then.

I can't recall exactly how much I was paid, but it was something like ninety dollars a month, probably less. Because I wasn't much of a boozer, or a gambler, and had no girlfriend out here, I could usually manage my money to last the whole month. Many guys on the base had a real problem trying to make their pay stretch and were already broke two weeks after payday. Although for Marines to loan money to other Marines at usurious rates was probably against regulations, it was always going on at every installation. It was the same for all branches of the military.

If you didn't have a watch, you were always asking someone for the time. Sometimes the sailor or Marine you asked would roll up his sleeve to look and he might have six watches on his arm—and maybe six more on the other. The first time you see this, you want to ask if he is the official timekeeper for the base or ship.

He sees you gawking and says, "Oh these? Each one is collateral for a loan to some guy until payday." That's how you find out who the loan shark is. On payday the debtors can redeem their watches for the cash loaned to them plus interest. Either these guys were the sons of pawn-brokers or they were snapping in for that profession when they got out.

The chow was not bad at Camp Pendleton. We ate all of our meals from our mess kit, to get us used to it, I suppose. As you left the mess area you arranged your mess kit lid, knife fork and spoon by stringing them onto the handle of your skillet. That was the serious part of the kit, because it held the most food. After eating you dipped your kit into the 30 gallon can full of hot soapy water heated by an immersion burner and scrubbed it with a long handled brush. Another dip into the rinse drum, and by the time you got back to your tent, the kit was dry.

The skillet part could also be used to fry up any food you could scrounge. When out on extended field problems, a chuck wagon brought out hot food and coffee once in a while. In this case we cleaned our mess kits with sand when we finished. Otherwise we ate C Rations to get us used to that stuff before we got to Korea. We were sure a lot of these rations were left over from WWII.

A good walk from our camp was a field shower put up by the engineers. It was very rustic, having only a wooden deck and plumbing to the shower heads. It would accommodate 50 - 75 troops at a time. Because it was far from mainside, in the middle of nowhere (another name for inner Camp Pendleton) the unit had no walls at all and no roof. I can recall only two incidents there.

When hundreds of troops go to the shower, there is much milling around on the periphery looking for a place to park your clothes on the ground. Once I found this spot close to the facility and stripped, leaving all my duds there folded so that my name was plainly visible on my jacket. Remember, we all wore the same uniforms. When I returned after to towel up and dress, I no sooner got all of my uniform back on when I felt fire in my crotch. I stripped to my skin in about five seconds, clothes flying in every direction. I had not noticed the tiny hole leading into a red ant nest and as a result attracted a lot of attention with my dancing and scratching. No wonder that spot was reserved for me, a fool from the east. Any westerner could tell you that when you see a bald spot in the vegetation, look for sand grains and any other sign of an ant nest before you sit down or make your camp on it. I was learning.

One day while we were showering off the crud from an extended hump over the dusty hills, we spotted a shiny black sedan stopped on the road a couple of hundred yards away. The sharp eyed said they could see women inside and a red plate on the front bumper with a gold star. We guessed that it was a general's car and his wife was using it to let friends from her bridge club catch a glimpse of a stable full of young studs bare naked, or in varying stages of undress. To me there was only one thing worse than a brown bagger, and that was the bored wife of a brown bagger. The higher the rank of the brown bagger and the older he was, the greater degree of ennui in the wife.

This whole thing was bizarre because we had never before seen a car in the six weeks we had been out there. After about ten minutes of their gawking, the car took off in a cloud of dust. The scuttlebutt later was that they would have lingered if they hadn't been spotted and a whole row of bathers at the edge facing the women suddenly decided to offer a salute by mooning them ensemble. A corporal was leading the movement by calling out, "Rear rank, stand by to moon roving observation post." At which point the guys at the edge turned to face inboard. He then called out, "Ready. Aim. Moon." The rank then grabbed their ankles and wiggled their bums for their admirers.

Even if a general had been present in the car, there is no way he could have disciplined the guilty. Can you imagine the Base Provost Marshal ordering a lineup of hundreds of PFC bare buns so that the brown baggers' wives who were offended could identify the perpetrators? Even if they identified them, what could the CO do to them? Send them to Korea? It is unseemly to threaten the damned, in any case.

While on the subject of discipline, there are two situations that need explaining. One deals with my own view of my position in the USMC at this point. I thought that once I was out of boot camp, the chickenshit routine and harassing discipline would stop. Although discipline was still tight and I could handle that, the inane harassment we suffered in boot camp was gone. The emphasis now was on learning survival and team work skills and toughening up each Marine .

For anyone who screwed up, the training cadre had a remedy in the form of physical conditioning. Tent Camp Three had a few high hills surrounding it and when we first arrived there we noticed a large wooden cross on the top of the highest one. We thought it might have some religious significance until we noted from time to time that it was gone. Then it would reappear in the same spot. The mystery was cleared up when a guy in our platoon was late coming off liberty. He tried to sneak into the morning muster and roll call just as we were being dismissed.

We were called back into formation to witness the meting out of his fate. He was told to fetch his rifle, cartridge belt, and pack, with entrenching tool. There was a large cross made from 8" X 8" timber lying in front of us. It was about ten feet long with a cross piece a couple of feet down from the top. Our gunny got the victim out in front of us and asked him if he had a good time last night in town. The Sad Sack allowed that he did. The gunny said that he looked like he didn't get any sleep either and he said that he didn't. Then the gunny pointed to a trail snaking up that hill and told the Sad Sack to take the cross up to the crest and plant it so we can all see it from here. He picked it up and marched and plant it so we can all see it from here. He picked it up and marched off with his load. His M-1 slung on his right shoulder and the huge cross on his left. He also had to fill his pack with wet sand before he left camp.

It was a long way up there in the heat and this trip usually cured those who would flaunt the rules. The next victim would of course have to bring it down to camp and if he was really in trouble he might have to make a round trip. This punishment drew extra attention from the troops because it was normally carried out in conjunction with the loss of weekend liberty. In other words, you had to do it on your own time, so you would not miss any training.

It began to get hot and very dry in June. With the endless humping over the hills and up and down mountains, digging in, and pooping and snooping day and night; I was beginning to flag. It was getting to me physically and mentally. All the time we were at Pendleton, we were practicing water discipline. This was OK in May but when it warmed up to over 100° F. in June, it was a problem trying to get by on one or two canteens per day. Often we had to use even some of that water to shave, wash up, or rinse out our socks.

We were told that the water rationing was to condition us for having to go without water for long periods of time in Korea. In fact we were led to believe that during the summer, drinking water was in very short supply in Korea. But, later during the first few days of August in Pusan, I thought that I was going to drown, right in the RepoDepo. I never saw so much rain and mud in my life. I guess that the instructors were really talking about the troops on the lines, usually on mountain crests. Every drop of drinking water had to be carried up there by grunts, or Korean conscript laborers.

At Pendleton in June, we were always thirsty in the field. Marching over those dry hills made it worse. When the water trailer showed up, or some Jerry cans were humped up the hill to our position, it was always hot from being in the sun all day. The only thing worse than drinking hot water in the heat of the day at over 100° F. in the shade (what shade?), was having no water at all. I tried keeping a small pebble in my mouth to stimulate saliva flow to keep it from drying out. It works.

I also learned to keep my canteen inside of a GI wool sock and wet that down when I filled it up. For a little while at least, the evaporating moisture cooled off the canteen somewhat. We also learned how to locate underground water in the bottoms of dry washes by digging down to it. In the high country, one might come across a spring fed stock tank, The water directly from the spring was OK, but any other water coaxed from a tiny stream or a pond had to be treated with the chorine tablets we carried. This was necessary because of the possibility of a dead animal in the water upstream, or in Korea it might be a dead body. The treated water tasted like a mild clorox solution. Ugh!

Some outfits were more Gung Ho than ours. We heard that earlier, the guys going into Col. Chesty Puller's outfit had to empty their canteens in the morning formation before setting out to poop and snoop for the day. I don't know how they did it. They must have tried to store up on it like a camel at morning chow. One time at a medical lecture on sanitation and hygiene in the field our corpsman told us that when we had been out trudging through the bush on a hot day, he didn't want to see us scarfing up quarts of cold water at the scuttlebutt when we came in to camp. It was not healthy to do so, i.e. drowning a hot body with gobs of iced cold water. He said that we should get our drinking water at ambient temperature from the water trailer, Lister bag or the tap at the shaving area. I finally got on to his reasoning when I saw the same corpsman sucking up the cold water at the scuttlebutt as soon as we came back from a day long hike in the sun. I guess he had a different kind of internal biological system than the rest of us. In reality, I think he told us that BS so he could be the first guy at the cold water and not have to stand in line. This must have occurred while we were in the barracks just before shipping out because there was no cold water out at Tent Camp Three. Out there we drew our water from a Lister bag, a large canvas container with taps at the bottom, that was suspended from a tripod of poles.

At one point I decided that I had it with all of the USMC crap and was going to bug out. Since we were allowed to have some civilian clothes at camp, I thought I would simply stash a set of civvies in my pack when we went out on a field problem and during the night while orienteering or while every one was sacked out after midnight, I would head for the Hwy through the boonies. When I got to the fence I would drop the pack and uniform, don the civvies, hitchhike to the Canadian border and disappear into the woods. It was a stupid idea, because it would be a lot easier to do it while on liberty and just keep going and not come back.

Looking back on it now, I must have been hallucinating from the effects of dehydration. I must have been pretty daffy to even think of such a caper. The reason I never did go over the hill, was that I often thought about my Dad. He had enlisted in the Army while in college in 1917 and ended up fighting in France and Belgium with the 37th Buckeye Div. of Ohio. He was a Battalion Sgt, Major in the 145 Infantry Regt. and was in several large battles, winning the French Croix de Guerre in one of them. To me he was a hero. Sometimes I wondered, what would the old man have done in this or that predicament.

Then I thought about Tom and John, my two older brothers. Tom, the oldest was in a B-25 outfit in the Pacific and saw a lot of combat over three years. Once he was blown off a ship in the invasion of Leyte, when it was hit by a Kamakazi plane. Many men from the ground section of the squadron were killed in that hit. John was in the Navy for ten years, including the last three years of WWII. When I thought about what they went through in two nasty wars, I wondered how I could do such a stupid thing as to go AWOL. The thought of being wounded or killed in Korea never entered my mind in this process of wanting out. When you are young, you look death in the face with a sneer. I thought that nothing would happen to me in Korea. Even my DI had given me some assurance when he said that I was too skinny to become a casualty. He told me, "When the shooting starts just turn sideways kid."

So after reflecting on the shame I would bring on my family and what my father and brothers would think of me for shirking my duty, I gave up any crazy thoughts of ever going over the hill no matter how bad things were. I also thought of the oath I had taken when I enlisted, and about letting the other Marines down by bugging out and all that. I decided to tough it out and did. It was a turning point in my life.

People these days don't understand what drove American GIs to fight as hard as they did during WWI, and WWII. This also applied to the British in the world wars. There were few men shirking their duty once they went into the service. This was due to the fact that in those days many units were made up of men from the same village, town, city, or county. Some were related and many others knew each other or knew their families back home. Each man was aware that the others were watching him and expected him to do his job and do it well. If a guy cringed at every situation and hid when things got tough, the whole neighborhood would soon hear about it back home and he would bring shame on himself and his family.

As a case in point, my Dad's Battalion was part of a National Guard unit, the 37th Division. Nearly all the men who enlisted in it 1917 were from the Northern Ohio counties, including Cleveland. If they didn't know each other, they knew someone from their home town. My Dad told me that when he became a sergeant, he was able to control the trouble makers in his company, because he had known most of them at home.

STANDING BY AND SHIPPING OUT

When the commanders are dealing with troops who are just about ready to shove off into war, they have to be careful how they handle them just before shipping out. The commanders want them to be full of fight and ready to take on the world, but not their world, only to focus on the enemy. The general mood of the troops sort of deteriorates, the closer the date of departure nears. After having to deal with ten replace-ments drafts, the Camp Pendleton brass finally figured out how to pro-tect civilians and the base from the depredations of marauding drunks.

It seems that in the past year, the guys in the replacement drafts would ravage the local off base drinking places on their last liberty. The few married guys were pissed because they would be away from their families for a year. Their testosterone was already raging at the thought of that dreaded disease, lacko'nookie. That means lack of nookie to you civilians. The bulk of the troops were bachelors and were just pissed in general, figuring that they were facing the big unknown and had noth-ing to lose in raising hell.

So some of the troops didn't give a rat's ass for anything they did while on that last liberty. If one got into trouble, what could they do to you that was worse that going off to a line company in Korea? For the first few drafts there may not have been any problem. They were all reservists or regulars with some rank and too old for that last minute drunken grabass routine. But when the drafts were made up of 18 to 20 year olds, the fights began with civilians, sailors, and other Marines and the destruction of property in all the liberty towns near Pendleton.

At first the Base Commander solved that problem by banning any off base liberty within a week of the date of shipping out. So the troops had to spend their last bit of free time boozing it up in the drinking establishments on base, known fondly as the slopchutes. This worked for a little while, at least in diminishing the threat to civilian life and limb in town. After the ninth and tenth drafts were involved in a demolition derby inside the area slopchutes, which resulted in major damage to government property, something else had to be done to provide the guys with some fun and to protect one and all.

The solution was typically Marine. Most Marines serve some extended tour of duty with the Fleet Marine Force (FMF), i.e the amphibious units. In the process, one spends a lot of time either hitting the beach or wait-ing to be taken off of it. Where else to have a big drunken party, where Marines could not harm any civilians or destroy any structures? The beach. The USMC owned and controlled miles of beach front property on the Pacific at Pendleton.

Just before we were due to ship out, the word was passed that there would be no liberty or leave granted. The area slop chutes would be closed and we would be confined to quarters. The gorillas in this draft were to be penned up and under control. The final ceremonies marking the completion of the advanced infantry course included a final inspec-tion and a parade in combat gear. On the reviewing stand stood a lot of brass, including a general, saluting as we passed in review with eyes right . I wondered about the only woman there, standing behind the general. Was she this senior brown bagger's wife? Did she ever tell him about using his official car for their sneak for a peek at the showers? Does she recognize any of us?

The final predeparture ritual also included a big party for the entire draft, broken down into our training units. The party was at San Onofre beach, now a mecca for the best surfing in CONUS (Continental US). We went to the beach in buses just before noon. There was lots of organized grabass, i.e., games for you civilians. We played scrub football with tackling allowed in the sand. There were also softball games, badminton, volleyball (a must in California), and pitching horseshoes.

Back at the base our mess was closed for the rest of the day because our cooks came out with all the fixings for a huge barbecue. Only a couple of guys on fire watch were allowed to stay back at our quarters. They were nonparty types, teetotalers who volunteered not to take part in the official departure blast for moral or religious reasons. The whole shindig was sponsored by the USMC, perhaps with grateful contributions from the local communities who were in reality paying for protection. Hey, just like back in Detroit and Chicago with the Mafia. You pay us and we make sure your business isn't trashed by our boys.

The BBQ grub for lunch featured hot dogs, burgers, and the usual trimmings, plus french fries, salads, fruit,etc. Lunch also featured some BBQ kielbasas and bratwurst for those from German and Polish households. At dinner we had BBQ ribs, steaks, chicken, and probably some road kill du jour, i.e., deer or javelina right off Hwy 101 for the guys too drunk to tell the difference. There were various types of pies, cakes, cookies, and ice cream for dessert at both meals and all the pogey bait you could eat—for the condemned in the last meal before shipping out.

As for the libations we had split halves of 55 gallon drums containing ice, canned beer, cokes, and other soft drinks. There were also gallons of hot coffee, iced tea, and milk (for those who knew they would not see fresh milk for a year). The beer was available in all you can drink quantities in two California brands. One wasn't bad and the other must have been made by adding brackish water to dehydrated weasel urine. It was called A-1 and it was anything but. Any GI would quickly mark it as "Numbah Ten." The procurement type who bought a carload of A-1 was either :1) bribed by the so-called brewer, or 2) or had it donated by the North Korean Army or, 3) he was a Mormon or 7th Day Adventist who didn't know what beer was supposed to taste like.

I've later figured it out. The Base Chaplain or the Psychological Warfare Officer on the FMF staff figured if the beer tasted like cold weasel piss, maybe the troops would not drink so much. He was right, except for the many Marines who would drink anything without regard to taste.

As the day wore on, there was also a lot of sobering up by swimming in the surf, if you can call that swimming. I had never seen the ocean before we came in on the train, now was my chance to swim in it. The surf was up and the first time I waded in up to my armpits, I was stunned by something crashing into my legs and feet as I walked. It was like strolling down a busy bowling alley barefooted in the dark. The waves were carrying in stones and rocks along the bottom with each surge and rolling them toward the shore. I swam out to the beach, checked the bruises and other damage to my feet and legs and put some A-1 beer on the barked shins. It was probably near beer and very low in alcohol content so useless as an antiseptic. When I reentered the surf this time, I swam out and thrashed around keeping my feet away from the bottom. According to surfers, this is what makes San Onefre Beach so great for their sport.

I'm surprised that there were no drownings among the many drunks. I had noticed an amphibious truck (a Duck) at each end of our party area, with a two man crew for fetching any drunks who floated out to sea. There were also a couple of lifeguard crews manning the lookout platforms. Maybe they were really watching for some wayward Marine making a last minute decision to swim or walk off the base beach and go over the hill to avoid the coming excursion and sight seeing trip to Korea. In California, no one would bat an eye at a hitchhiker in a bathing suit on the Coast Highway.

We had dinner about dusk. Afterward there were several bonfires for effect and for singing drinking songs around. Before we secured the party detail, we had one last ceremony to perform. Each platoon got to throw their leader (a lieutenant) into the surf. But we were not allowed to hold him under. I'm sure that if SSgt. Sicklick had been here, there would have been a contest to see how long he could hold his breath in the Pacific under a bunch of his former boots.

I'm sure that there was a platoon of MPs lurking somewhere out of sight, just in case things got out of hand. The platoon leaders and the XO got to throw the company commander, a captain, into the drink. By the time the captains went looking for the battalion XO, a major, and the battalion CO, a colonel, they were SOL. The dignified officers of scrambled egg rank, were long gone to the officers' club for some hard liquor and fine cigars in the company of their own kind. They probably got one taste of that A-1 beer and remembered what it was like to be a peon. Besides they knew what was coming after dark and bugged out before the captains could find them

All in all, the party had been a success. The Marines got fed and soused and that relieved some of their frustrations and tensions related to shipping out. The USMC benefitted by not having to rebuild trashed slopchutes on base and not having to pay for damages to civilian property ruined in town. Although the civilians off the base lost all that revenue in the last minute spending spree, they were spared bodily harm and general mayhem and no green tornado damage to their property. What is more important, their womenfolk were safe until the next replacement draft graduated.

During the last week we were to spend stateside we were moved into a barracks mainside for some administrative matters. Actually the few days that we spent in those barracks, was the only time I was to live in a building for my first 19 months in the Corps. All the rest of the time was spent living in tents, aboard ship, or camping on the beach.

We were tying up loose ends such as taking care of mail, calling home, making out wills, getting haircuts, getting paid, and so on. Some of the horny types wanted to know why were getting paid, when they couldn't get off the base to get laid. It seemed rather pointless to be paying us when there was no place to spend the money, except for some last minute things at the PX. What the Corps knew, but the troops didn't, was that we would need some cash for purchases in the small stores locker on ship and for playing cards enroute. We would also need some cash for a possible port of call in Japan before we got to Korea. The military didn't condone gambling on their facilities, even at sea, but at the same time they knew that it was going on. To keep them off your back you had to hide the cash and play with chips, or matches. Wins and losses were settled up in private later.

On the day for my haircut, I had the barber, another Marine in our unit, give me a Mohawk cut, figuring no one would complain where we were going. I was left with a two-inch wide strip of short hair running from the front and tapering down to a point on my neck. Other guys got some screwy cuts also. One was left with just a topknot. One had a tonsure like you would find on a monk. There was a circle of hair around the edge with a bald spot in the center and all shaved around the sides. There were also a few more Mohawks.

Because we were about to ship out, I didn't give another thought to my new haircut. It was an attempt to establish an identity apart from all the guys in the same uniform all around me. When I heard the word for pay call, I got in line on the veranda of the barracks—in alphabetical order of course. The pay master (PM) was seated at a table along with a gunny who handled the paper work. The PM was a captain who wore a duty belt with loaded Colt .45 in his holster. The table was just inside a foyer, which meant it was indoors, so you had to uncover when you got in there.

When my name was called, I stepped forward, whipped off my cap and bent over to sign the payroll sheet and pick up my month's pay in cash. Neither the captain nor the gunny looked at me. They were busy with counting the cash and checking the signature, etc. I did an about face, took a step toward the veranda and replaced my cap. Then I walked away as fast as I could go. But not fast enough. I heard the captain shout,

"Stop that man!" I kept on moving, until I heard the gunny give him my name off the payroll. He then shouted, "Giannelli, get back here." I guess he had looked up just as I replaced my cap as I left and saw the tapered tail of the Mohawk trailing down my to my neck. Pretty important stuff for a captain to hold up the pay process for a bit of fuzz.

Once he called my name, I knew that I was screwed so I bolted back to the table, whipping off my cap and stood at attention, saying, "Yes sir?" The captain looked at my noggin and asked, "What is the matter with your head?" I replied, "Nothing, sir." "Then what kind of a haircut do you call that?" he asked. I said, "A Mohawk Sir." Then he asked me., "Do you think that there are no barbers in Korea?" I didn't see what that had to do with anything, but replied, "I wouldn't know sir." Meanwhile, everyone from G to Z standing behind me in the pay line was snickering and gawking for a look at the fuckup. He talked to the gunny and then turning back to me said, "You go back to that barber right now and have him straighten that up so the Mohawk is not noticeable. You are dismissed."

I did as I was told and was soon a skinhead once again. I was to see only one more paymaster from then until I returned a year later. I failed to explain to the captain that I wanted a Mohawk so the Koreans and Chinese would recognize me for an American when I got over there.

THE TROOP SHIP

Although we knew we were going to Korea, we were never told the exact date of shipping out. This seemed to be a holdover from WWII, during which, the troops and often the ship's crew were never told their route, destination, or date of sailing. I remember the posters from WWII. One said, "A slip of the lip, will sink a ship." But civilians up and down the coast, such as cab drivers, tarts, bartenders, etc., could tell us the name of the ship we were leaving on and the date and hour it would sail. They also usually knew what ports we might stop at enroute and the final destination. So much for security.

We knew we were getting close to shipping out when our seabags were collected and transported to the ship in San Diego harbor. The next day we fell in for the last muster at Pendleton. An NCO checked our names off as we boarded buses with only our web gear, full packs, and rifles.

The buses took us to the ship at the Naval base in San Diego. Although there was some cheering as we passed through the front gate at Oceanside, the troops were mostly silent as we drove down the Coast Highway. We were drinking in every detail of our last glimpse of America and the coastal California scene was enough to lift our spirits. The surfers were out, along with the sunbathers, swimmers, musclemen (probably draft dodgers or flat-footed 4-Fers), and a few pleasure craft moving farther out past the surf. In San Diego harbor the warships of the fleet dwarfed the sailboats flitting by. These were precious images we could store away for later recall in attempts to escape the dreariness of wartime Korea.

We unloaded on the dock and formed up for the last time on US soil. As we filed onto the gangplank to enter the ship through a side hatch, our names were checked off once more by a clerk. I remember looking around and saw a few families and wives who came down to see off the brown baggers, probably mostly ship's company, i.e sailors. We assumed that some of the better lookers there, who did not have kids hanging on them, were the wives or girl friends of officers.

We filed into the bowels of the ship, up and down narrow ladders being careful to look down and step over the high sills of hatches, trying to make some headway with all our bulky gear. As we entered the troop holding compartments we were taken aback somewhat by the arrangement of stacks of bunks made from pipes, slung five-high on chains and higher in some spaces. The troop load master had us fill up the farthest compartments first, to cut down on the congestion in the narrow passages between the racks.

When we got to our section in a compartment, we tried to make what little selection there was in choice of bunk. Then the gunny shouted, "Come on, just put your pack on a rack and climb in with it to clear the passage. You can sort out who sleeps where in your stack later after we're all aboard. Move it!"

Landlubbers and sailors who never had to spend weeks at sea in the troop compartment, don't know what it is like to be crammed into a swaying and pitching metal box with hundreds of others for a whole month. If you thought you would be safer in the bottom bunk, merely because there was a bit of room beneath it to stow some gear, think again. If any one of the many guys above you got seasick, their barf just might dribble down on you while you're trying to sleep.

The only advantage to having the lowest rack was that it was somewhat cooler.On a bottom rack you were in all the traffic and guys liked to sit on them to bullshit and play cards when it was too windy and rainy topside. The top racks were OK but were warmer because there was no air conditioning. I found the middle rack to be the best for me.

When we laid claim to a sack we tied our packs, rifles and other gear to the chains The racks consisted of a stout piece of canvas tied with a small line through grommets to the pipe frame. They were comfortable enough, and although I don't remember any mattress or linen, there was a blanket. By now I had learned to wad up some clothing for a pillow.

We were told to stand by our sacks and wait for the next word to come down from topside. After an hour or so waiting for the rest of the Marines to find a sack in their assigned compartment, we followed the gunny topside for a meeting on the fantail—the aft most part of the ship to landlubbers.

After we got into a group the gunny started to pass the word. First we were each issued a Navy type life jacket and put it on to get used to it. He explained how the ship was laid out and said we could go almost anywhere we liked as long as we did not interfere with the working of the ship. The areas off limits to us were: officers' country, engine room, bridge, radio room, and a few other places.

We were assigned to various work details to break the monotony of a month at sea. In addition we attended lectures, physical workouts and rifle inspections topside. Each unit of Marines was assigned a spot on deck and specific hours for the meetings which, came to be known as cluster fucks. There would be no long hikes, no troop and stomp, and no pooping and snooping, because there were no boondocks for hundreds of miles in any direction.

Our ship was an APA (attack transport), one of a variety of vessel types used by Marine amphibious forces. They ranged from larger ships such as Landing Ship Tank (LST), Attack Cargo ships (AKAs), to the smaller craft like, Landing Craft Medium (LCMs) known as Mike boats and Landing Craft Vehicle and Personnel (LCVPs). The AKAs were designed as freighters and carried all of the cargo, i.e. ammo, rations, fuel, etc. needed by the landing force on the beach. The open decks were crammed with stacked landing craft used for putting the cargo ashore and some to be sent over to the APAs during the landing to haul troops into the beach.

The APAs were similar in construction to the AKAs, but were modified to transport troops to the landing site. Marines were crammed into the holds originally designed for cargo. The decks also carried many small landing craft. As on the AKAs, davits and cranes lifted off the small craft for the landing. Then cargo nets transferred equipment and supplies to them. Cargo nets were also slung down the ship's side for the troops to scramble down into the landing craft.

The day after boarding, a crowd of dependents gathered on the dock to listen to the Marine Band serenade us and wave goodbye to the troops. At this point I thought of my Dad boarding his ship on the East Coast in 1918 as the 37th Division band played Over There, Its a long Way to Tipperary, When Johnny Comes Marching Home Again, and those other songs popular back then. The Army band that day was told not to play Lili Marlene, not because it was a Hun song, but because it was just too melancholy for the moment. My Dad had said it was a sad time to be leaving, especially with no one to see him off. He was an orphan of Irish immigrants and had no relatives, save a younger brother, in the country he was going off to fight for.

As our ship was eased away from the berth, the deck was jammed with Marines and ship's crew for their last look at San Diego. A couple of tugs worked us into the harbor and fell away when the ship's engines took over. A submarine passed us coming in with its crew lined up on deck signal flags flying for our skipper. We assumed the flags said, "Good hunting", or some such words of parting. About a mile out a despatch boat removed the pilot and we were on our way.

We were all very quiet standing there on the fantail watching the San Diego skyline grow smaller. I suppose each of us wondered if we would ever see it again. The silence was broken by PFC Joe Gentile calling out in his Joisey accent, "OK. The joke is over. You on the bridge. You can take us back now." We all laughed at that and some began to wish that it was a joke. When the coastline had faded away, we turned to and settled into shipboard routine.

The Marines have several routines. There is daily routine wherever you are stationed. There is holiday routine on national holidays, when you can relax on the base or ship, if you were not on watch. Shipboard routine revolved around keeping us busy all day. The next day's routine started with a head call to shit, shower and shave.

Reveille was held as usual at 0530, but there was no immediate need to get up because of the crowded quarters. There was no room in the passageway and the head would only hold so many bodies. The guys who had to relieve themselves always got up first. The first time I went to the head, I was surprised to see a message stenciled in large letters on the bulkhead over the urinals, sinks, and in the showers: DO NOT VOMIT IN THE SINK, SHOWER, URINAL. Official government graffiti.

That was the warning to the queasy. I'm sure that sign was not displayed on regular Navy ships, nor in the heads reserved for ship's crew. Sailors learned this message in boot camp but Marines had to be housebroken, or rather ship broken. So that left me wondering what to do when we got into rough weather and pitching seas. Well, that left only the toilets, which were without the notice, or over the side where sensitive seafarers have been heaving since man first took to the seas. There was only one caution from the sailors, "If you are on deck and have to spit or barf, be sure to check the wind first. If not, you or someone else might get a face full of yuk." We didn't want to make enemies on a ship. There was no place to hide.

To condition us to shipboard life on extended cruises and perhaps for the water shortages we would encounter in Korea, we were introduced to water hours to conserve fresh water on the ship. This meant that we showered only at certain times with fresh water, with the time under the water strictly limited to a few minutes. Get the body wet,shut the water off and soap all over. Then a quick rinse to finish the job. We also learned to squeegee ourselves off as much as possible with our hands so there was less water to towel off. Our small towels didn't dry very well in the troop compartment and they began to take on an odor after a few showers.

The only alternative to the fresh water hours was to take a shower at any time if you didn't mind seawater. A salt water shower was better than no shower, as we were to learn in Korea, where we would have welcomed any kind of shower. The problem with the salt water shower was that ordinary soap wouldn't lather up for a proper wash. I believe that there were special bars of soap that the crew used when they used salt water on a ship, but the Marines didn't get any of that. Salt water is a little rough on the skin but we got used to it.

I can't remember just how we laundered our clothes aboard ship, although many of us tried to do it the old fashioned way from the days of sailing vessels. We tied a line around a set of dungarees and threw them into the wake. We were told to hold on to the end of the line and leave the duds in the turbulent water for only a few minutes. Some guys tied the end of the line to the railing and left their clothes in the wake for a half hour or more. When they remembered to pull them in, they were surprised to find the cloth well worn away. Seawater is not only hard on fabric, it also makes the fabric abrasive to the skin.

After morning head call, we organized our gear and bunk, and went topside to get into the chow line or to our unit spot for the latest word. The normal practice on a troop ship is to serve only two large meals per day, with coffee and some small snacks or sandwiches available during the night for those standing watches. On larger troop ships run by the Military Sea Transport Service (MSTS), some passengers found that the wise thing to do is to get into the PM chow line as soon as you finished your AM meal. Some chow hounds on our ship did just that when they could.

I heard few complaints about the food aboard ship. Because we were unfamiliar with the Navy, it was a surprise to find baked beans on the tray nearly every morning. Another dish that we Yankees (northerners) were unaccustomed to was grits, and I mean true grits as in ground hominy. This Yankee did not even know what hominy was until then. I thought hominy was the Charleston, S.C. pronunciation for ensemble singing as in barbershop style. For Southerners, grits sort of filled the place of oatmeal or other hot cereal that Yankees were used to. There was plenty of well prepared food served by our own cheerful Marines on mess duty. An old military standby was chipped beef on toast, known to American GIs everywhere as "shit on a shingle" (SOS). It was served several times a week.

After filing through the chow line, we ate at tables, which along with their benches, were bolted to the floor. The table held what condiments were available and the ever-present pitcher of either coffee or the duty cold drink. The latter was almost always some kind of purple stuff like Kool Aid. We thought it was prepared in the sick bay by the pharmacist mates, because whenever we went to any sick bay on ship or ashore, the duty medicine was always purple. If your visit to the corpsman was for a skin problem, it was painted with the purple goop, only more concentrated than the stuff on the mess table. If your ailment was internal, you might get your throat swabbed with the purple passion. Or the pills were purple. I believe that whatever the active ingredient was (probably gentian violet), the color purple was to make the ill think that it was something important and therefore promoted healing. In that way, the purple drink at chow, was a subterfuge to get us to think is was a healthy libation. I have steered clear of purple drinks ever since I left the Corps—unless they contain some alcohol to neutralize whatever the nefarious purple active ingredient might be.

The first few days were spent getting settled into quarters. It took a while for us landlubbers to get used to the ship's movement. It rolled from side to side, pitched down into troughs and plowed up out of them. The sailors scampered around the decks with ease, while we Marines kind of felt our way along like a wino coming off a drunk. We took halting steps, wondering when the deck would move up to the foot coming down and were always holding onto a railing, a stanchion or any solid object within reach. Some sailors told us not to worry about it because it took a week or so to acquire one's sea legs. Even for them it took a few days to get used to the moving deck after coming back aboard from a prolonged leave. I also noticed that months at sea gave one a strange gait when first walking ashore. One leg or the other was waiting for the deck to come up and meet the foot.

Because I was an outdoor type, I tried to spend as little time as possible below decks. I admit to being slightly claustrophobic so sought every chance to be topside. As guys were being assigned to work details, I was put on the one for chipping paint. The corrosive action of seawater constantly tries to turn every ship into a rust bucket and there is a continuous battle waged by the crew to thwart the oxidation process. Before treating spots of rust by covering them with coats of special marine paint, the oxides of iron had to be scraped, chipped, or ground away.

The ship's crew looked at painting as an art form that had to be done by skilled seamen. On the other hand, rust removal was a real shit detail for coolies and reserved for Marines whenever they were aboard. Personally, I didn't mind what I had to do to remain topside, so I happily chipped away with whatever tools they gave me. We usually used the typical paint scrapers, Model M-1, 1885, with handle, and cord to loop around the wrist. That kept it from going over the side if you dropped it. The most effective hand tool was a hammer with a chisel point edge at one end. At least the chief did not hang us over the side in a bosun's chair to do the sides of the hull. That was usually done by the crew when the ship was in port or at anchor. The sailors who worked along with us were using an air driven power chisel to whack away at the heavy rust.

The other type of work detail I recall for the Marines was mess duty. About the worst mess duty chore was the scullery, where the mess trays were cleaned after each meal. There was always plenty of hot water on a ship, so the scullery was like a sauna. I understand that this special detail was reserved for overweight seamen in the Navy when at sea. For us it was the throw of the dice, because there were no fat Marines on our ship. I learned later on that the scullery on a small ship like a destroyer or LST was a really lousy detail because the work space was about as big as a telephone booth.

We spent a lot of time gazing out to sea wondering where we were and watching the rolling of the other ships in our little convoy. It was always interesting when a ship appeared on the horizon and passed in the distance. From time to time we could watch flying fish soaring away from our bow wave and porpoises riding the pressure zone just off the bow and arcing out of the water to greet us. For a kid from Michigan, this was really fascinating. Perhaps that's why I went on to become an aquatic biologist years later.

The only real excitement on this cruise was of the negative sort. After two weeks at sea, we came to a stop somewhere in the middle of the Pacific. We sat there adrift for a day or so while the ship's engineering crew worked on a steering mechanism that was not working. After all, this ship was built in the early 1940s and probably carried troops in the amphibious assaults on the islands of the South Pacific. On the one hand, we wanted to get off the ship, so weren't pleased with the unscheduled delay. On the other hand, we were not exactly in a hurry to get to Korea. As far as I was concerned, the war could wait for us.

One thing going for us compared to my Dad's trip across the Atlantic was that we did not have to worry about enemy submarines. The summer of 1918, when he rode a troop transport to France, the threat of being torpedoed was quite real. In a six month period at least a dozen American freighters, oilers, and liners had been sunk in the Atlantic. In June, an American transport, the Lincoln was sunk by a sub and in August an armed US civilian tanker was sunk by a U-Boat's deck gun.

While watching for imaginary periscopes, I also thought about my oldest brother Tom's experience at the invasion of Leyte, Philippines in 1944. His unit was aboard a victory ship hauling troops and ammo. The troop accommodations were makeshift, wooden stairs going down into

the hold and wooden racks everywhere. While all the racket of the attack was going on among the ships and on the beach where the Japanese were putting up a stiff resistance, a bunch of guys from his squadron were crapped out on the deck between the edge of their hold and
the scuppers of the ship.

He remembers that he was passing by when one of them grabbed
his arm and tried to get him into their card game. He pulled away saying
he wasn' t in the mood and went down the ladder. He was sheltered by
the deck overhead when a Kamikaze pilot crashed his plane right into
the hold, setting fire to the wooden framework. Tom scampered up the
few dozen steps to the deck through the heat and smoke and there was
a blast from the hold as the plane's gasoline and ordnance exploded. A
dozen men from his unit, including the card players were plastered
against the bulkhead, killing most of them. Tom was laying on the deck
near the railing and seeing all of the carnage and devastation around
him on the deck, followed other survivors over the side.

Tom floated around wondering what had happened and was picked
up by a huge black GI driving a Duck. Tom was still in a state of shock
and buck naked. The Duck driver took him and another GI into the
beach and they waded ashore. When they found that this area had not
yet been secured by our troops, the driver took them down the shore-
line to a town near Tacloban. There he wandered around among all of
the GIs who had recently landed, trying to find some clothes. No one
could help him because they had come ashore with only their field packs.
They told Tom he looked pretty bad because his hair, eyebrows and
lashes were all singed off. They steered him to a field aid station where
the medics checked him over and helped him scrounge some clothes.

I once asked him what he remembers most about that hairy escape.
He said that of course he felt bad about losing everyone in his section,
but what really stays with him, was seeing that smiling black face in the
Duck when the GI pulled him out. He said that was the reason you
would never hear him say anything against black people, and I never
did.

He was told later that the elderly Skipper of the ship was seen helping to pass five-inch shells out of the after hold in spite of the heat from
the bulkhead. The Kamikaze had crashed into the adjacent hold. The
after hold contained five-inch shells and other ammunition and the Skipper was determined to salvage the lot at the risk of going up with his
ship and crew if the fire spread.

I also thought about my brother John who had served on a fleet
oiler. Now that is one ship you don't want to be aboard when it is shelled
or torpedoed. If you survive the explosions and fire aboard, the leaking

fuel also burns on the sea surface and the unburned fuel will mess you up make life miserable while you are in the drink. He must have been glad when his cruise on the tanker was up.

Besides our work details, physical training, rifle inspections, standing in the chow line, watch standing, and sleeping, we did have other things to occupy our time. There was an occasional movie shown on deck on calm evenings. The guys who had money gambled in card games and shooting craps, but did so discreetly.

The rest of us spent a lot of time cleaning our rifles, sharpening bayonets, etc. Those of us who had heard stories from Marines who had already returned from Korea took those tales to heart. There had been instances they said, where Chinese and North Korean infiltrators sneaked into Marine and Army positions in the winter time in the middle of the night and killed men while they slept. Weapons, particularly the M-1 and M-2 carbine, were prone to freezing up at -30° F. They also said that sometimes there was a problem with the old style sleeping bags. It seems that the moisture from your breath would condense on the zipper pull near your chin, freezing it to the track so you could not get out of the bag quickly. By the time I arrived the zippers had been modified so you could push the bag at the sides with your elbows and the zipper would separate.

The freezing of rifle bolts was not a problem if you chose to sleep with the rifle in your bag, but who would want to do that. So some guys acquired Marine fighting knives called Kabars, or personal sidearms that could be kept at the ready inside the sleeping bag. Because we were not allowed to have a personal sidearm enroute to Korea, we opted for the Kabar. We either bought or scrounged them before leaving Pendleton. The city boys, myself included, had a thing about knives and I had always carried one since I was a kid. By the time we got to Korea, some of the Kabars were so sharp that we could shave with them. After honing them on a whetstone we took to stropping them on the side of our boondockers. Another thing I noticed was that those of us with Kabars didn't waste time sharpening bayonets. If a bayonet was designed for thrusting into the chest of the enemy, all that mattered was the point. We wanted the enemy to get the point and the edges would take care of the rest of the job.

Sleeping accommodations on a troopship were spartan. There were hundreds of us crammed into a very small space, in a compartment that was originally designed to serve as a hold for cargo. Fresh air was fed into the space from forward facing funnels on deck. At least that is what we were told, but sometimes the air became a bit close from the respiration and gas passing of all those warm bodies.

I am a light sleeper and one of the things I couldn't abide in the troop compartment was the snoring that kept me awake. I had to ignore those noises farther away from my rack, but I tried to deal with those snorers within reach. When one of them was grunting and snorting nearby, I would hang on the vertical rack chains like a monkey searching for the offender. Then using my free hand, I would shut his mouth and nostrils at the same time to make him wake up or just stop the racket. If the log sawer was a little farther away I would prod him in the side with my foot to make him roll over to shut him up. You had to be careful doing this, because if you happened to be accosting a sleeper who was punchy or goosy, you might be nicked by a Kabar or a bayonet. Whenever I could get away with it, I would get out of my rack after taps and head for some secluded spot on deck to sleep in the open air.

Another thing we had to get used to was the PA system, which could be heard everywhere on the ship. The announcements were terse and always started with, "Now hear this." For example, every morning this message was standard: "Now hear this. Clean sweep down fore and aft. Throw all trash over the fantail." Or "Tonight's movie will be the Sands of Iwo Jima on the main deck between hatch covers to holds one and two. It starts at 2030 hours." Or " At 0336 tonight we will cross the international date line. There will be no ceremony." The most unwelcome announcement was for inspections. Now hear this "The (ship's) captain will inspect the troop compartments and heads starting at 0945 today. Fall to!"

The other routine announcements dealt with ship's operations and drills. There were drills and lifeboat drills and once or twice a call to general quarters (GQ). The latter must have been to keep the ship's company on their toes only, because I saw no naval guns at all on the ship. You would know that something was really serious if the message was, "Now hear this. This is not a drill, GQ, this is not a drill." But that never happened while we were aboard. I heard that later on another ship during a crisis. Thinking back on the lifeboat drills, I can't remember seeing any lifeboats on the APA but there must have been some. I do remember seeing stacks of heavy duty life rafts aside from the landing craft.

For three weeks at sea we heard rumors that we would stop in Japan for liberty, but no one was sure of that. We hoped it was true, because for most of us it would be our last liberty for a year. We did not like to think about it, but for some, it would be the last liberty forever. Korea was going to be a crap shoot and the losers would either be wounded or killed. The winners would come home unscathed, at least physically. So the attitude of all the Marines going ashore was to hell with everything. This might be the last fling so just go out and have a good time.

A few days out of Japan we were reunited with our seabags and told to unpack one complete set of khakis, dress shoes and socks for the two days of liberty in the port of Kobe. Because we would be in port only a few days, the ship's company was restricted to port and starboard liberty, which meant that only half of the Navy crew would be allowed ashore in one day. It would help reduce the crowd of fleet personnel ashore.

The Marines aboard, however, were going on to bigger and hairier things in Korea, so were allowed ashore en masse, with the usual condition that all enlisted men be back aboard ship by midnight. That is known as Cinderella liberty. Of course officers were considered to be gentlemen, so could be ashore until the ship sailed unless they had duty back aboard. Enlisted men were not considered to be gentlemen, but rather trained in organized mayhem and violence, so could not be trusted ashore past midnight.

Every Marine was topside at dawn to watch for the first view of Japan. We stayed there as one of the islands loomed slowly into view and we only left for chow. The word was passed for a muster at our station where the Marine captain told us what time to be on deck for pay call, etc. He also told us how long we would be in port and that we had to be on our good behavior so as not to discredit the Corps and our country. He knew how we felt about this last liberty thing and told us to be easy on the people we met or had to deal with. " And remember," he said, "That when you come aboard and leave this or any other naval vessel, you must salute the officer of the deck (OD) on the quarter deck and then toward the naval ensign (flag) on the fantail." He added, "When you come back aboard do not attempt to bring back any kind of alcohol with you. You may bring back small souvenirs, however. The OD and the Master at Arms (MA) will be on the quarterdeck to greet you and examine whatever you might bring aboard. Be forewarned!"

Kobe was a huge port and signs of bomb damage from WWII were still evident here and there. We stopped well outside the port to pick up a Japanese pilot who would guide us to the waiting tugs closer in. I was fascinated by all of the activity in the area, with fishing boats and other vessels large and small coming and going. I noticed that some of the smaller craft had some kind of one-cylinder engine that blew black smoke rings from the stack into the still air. The sailors called them one lungers.

As we pulled closer to the pier, the tugs pushed us abeam right up to the concrete and the bumpers. Only a slight jolt was noticeable as we stopped. It was 0800 and liberty would start at noon. Most of us took off to find an iron to press the wrinkled khakis, shine shoes, get in the pay line or go to chow. Since we did not know what to expect in the way of local food ashore, we'd better fill up on the kind of food we were used to eating.

I can't remember who I went ashore with, but you always hitch up with some other guys when going on liberty in a strange port. The dockside neighborhoods are usually full of unsavory characters in any port in the world. It might be safe traversing the seedy area during daylight hours, but you ought to have someone with you after dark, especially close to the Cinderella hour of midnight.

We hit a few bars to sample the local beer, which was quite good. We also went to local restaurants to taste the food, which wasn't bad either. To get rid of the accumulation of salt from so many seawater showers of course we had to have a Japanese bath. The water was very hot and the tubs deep, all we needed for a good soak. There were some female attendants there to wash our backs—and the rest of the body if we liked.

On the second morning the word was passed that when we left the ship, we had to show the OD how much money we had on us. If a Marine had less than ten dollars US, he was not allowed to go ashore. We assumed this was to prevent the crazy types from trying to rob a bank, or strong arm Japanese on the street for spending money.

With the devastation of WWII only six years behind us, American cigarettes were still a valued commodity in Far Eastern ports. At the end of WWII GIs found that a pack of American cigarettes would buy such things as a short time with a Japanese girl. Two or three packs would buy an all nighter, or so I was told by the old salts. Because we Marines were not allowed to carry anything the least bit bulky in our pockets, that left only our long dress socks as a place to stow things. Although we were permitted to take only two packs of cigarettes ashore per day, some guys would dare to take a ten packs ashore in their socks. Now and then, the OD would stop a liberty bound Marine on the quarterdeck and pull up his pant legs to see if he was carrying more than two packs ashore. If so, he had to forfeit the extra packs. At that time, cigarettes cost us only eight cents per pack at ship's stores.

While Marines and sailors were going ashore with socks filled with cigarettes, the Navy firemen (Snipes) were wheeling and dealing over the side with native refueling crews on lighters alongside. Cartons of cigarettes from the ship were sold for cash in US dollars. The traders from the bum boats were also there with the usual junk for sale.

When we went ashore the second day, we just walked all over town looking at everything and had a few beers. Most Japanese beer is made from rice and I took a liking to Asahi and to Kirin labels. At the time I did not care for sake, which is served warm—not something to slake one's thirst in midsummer.

I was with three other Marines walking back toward the ship, when a bunch of young women accosted us on the sidewalk. We could not communicate with them, but they kept badgering us to go with them as they pulled on our sleeves, some grabbing our arms. They obviously wanted us to go back to their place to help "lower our white count" and relieve us of whatever cash we had left. We were all broke, otherwise we would have stayed ashore until the Cinderella hour to be aboard. So we broke away from them and had started walking faster when one of them came running up from behind and planted one fist and then the other right in my back. She was screaming something at us and I figured she was saying, "Yankee Go Home." I guess some street walkers just have no sense of humor when GIs don't want to cooperate by having a little fun—and showing up in Korea later with a dose of the clap.

We returned to the ship just before sundown and passed the Pro Station on the pier. Those who had dipped their wicks in the local brothels had to go through the ritual of stopping any VD that may have been transmitted to them in the process. Even though they may have used a condom, which was issued free before liberty, they had to take the prophylactic treatment just in case. The ProKit offered in the Pro Station contained a small tube of medication that was squirted up the urethra. One then massaged the limp member slightly to move the ointment as far up as it would go. If it worked, the medicine that is, then hopefully the guy would be spared the curse of a case of VD. The ProStation was manned by a couple of Navy corpsman in case anyone had any questions or needed further instruction in using the ProKit.

Good thing we didn't need to stop there, because there was a long line of both sailors and Marines waiting for their turn for the treatment. We boarded the APA and changed into dungarees before going to evening chow for some familiar food. We then spent the evening on deck watching the lights and activity of the last real city we would see for another year.

Early next morning when the Skipper was reasonably sure that every man was aboard, we were pushed away from the pier by two tugs and a Japanese pilot took us out of the harbor. Any sailor or Marine who missed the ship would be in deep trouble and have a lot of explaining to do to the Provost Marshal in the Port. After a few days in the brig there, he would probably be flown over to Pusan and assigned directly to a line company if he was a Marine.

We saw plenty of the coasts of several islands as we threaded our way through the inland sea to the straits separating Kyushu Island on our port side from the southwestern tip of Honshu Island on the starboard side. As we left Japan in our wake with silent *sayonaras,* we crossed the Korean Strait toward the Port of Pusan in Korea. What the future held for us there was still on our minds.

PART TWO
FIRST MARINE DIVISION, FMF

PART TWO:
FIRST MARINE DIVISION, FMF

FIRST ENGINEER BATTALION

 I DON'T REMEMBER THE EXACT DATE, but it was the first week of August when our APA dropped anchor outside Pusan harbor waiting for a berth. It was hot and very humid. The ship's PA system boomed, "Now hear this. The anchor was dropped at exactly 0646 hours." Then the date was given. This was an important bit of information, because nearly everyone on the ship had put a buck into the anchor pool. The guy who had chosen the hour and minute closest to the time the anchor actually dropped, won the pot. The date wasn't included because too many sailors aboard would have inside skinny on our day of arrival. We studied the green hills and wondered what the rest of the country was like. Fighting was going on a couple of hundred miles north of Pusan.

The North Koreans started the war in June 1950 by invading South Korea and had pushed the Republic of Korea (ROK) Army and the small US advisory force, the Korean Military Advisory Group (KMAG) all the way from the 38th parallel to a line that arced around Pusan. It became known as the Pusan perimeter.

US troops were quickly bolstered by reinforcements from the USA and troops from other UN countries fighting under a unified command. Eventually they fought their way out of the perimeter and the US Army, 1st Provisional Marine Brigade, the British Brigade 27, and others pushed the enemy back to the north. The 1st Marine Division landed at Inchon in September to attack and secure Seoul. In November the Division landed at Wonsan and fought their way up to the Chosin Reservoir. The Chinese Reds suddenly attacked from the North with over 300,000 troops and forced the US Marines, Army and British units to evacuate from Hungnam on the North coast to the Port of Pusan.

Later that day a Korean pilot guided our ship into the harbor where two one-lunger tugs, coughing black smoke rings, maneuvered us into the pier. There was a mixed crowd of US military personnel and Koreans on the wharf waiting for us to tie up. Marine trucks pulled onto the pier and lined up alongside the godowns, as warehouses are known in the east. We went below to collect our gear and stand by to disembark by the numbers. A month confined to a ship was enough. We were eager to get ashore. No matter what lay ahead, not one Marine was sad to be leaving the ship. The ship's company was perfectly happy to be staying aboard. After all this was their home. In the next few days, the APA would take aboard Marines who had survived the hell of the past year and earned rotation back home to the land of the Big PX.

As we filed off the gangplank, we went directly to the trucks and climbed into the back. We were told that our seabags would be stored in a godown either in Pusan, or in Kobe, Japan, and we would be reunited with them on the way home. We hoped that they went to Japan, because that would give us a good chance of pulling liberty there in a year.

I noticed that the 6X6 trucks were all driven by Marines and wondered how I could get a cushy job like that. I couldn't imagine a job in the Corps where I didn't have to hump over the hills carrying all my gear, food and water, ammo, etc.. A driver always had a place to carry extra stuff for himself. What a racket, just pick up your trip ticket and drive these guys over there and wait for them. Then pick them up and bring them back later. Wow! What a life. Varoom! Varoom! I was already practicing double clutching and grabbing gears. Then I quickly forgot about that MOS because I probably had to know someone or go to school for that cushy slot.

We folded up the benches so we could stand up clutching our rifles and wearing field packs. This way we had a better view of the city as we drove from the port to the Replacement Camp (RepoDepo) on the outskirts of Pusan. Having never been anywhere outside of North America, the place looked like a dump to me. It was dusty and crowded with people riding rickety bikes, walking, and pushing carts loaded with stuff. Most guys were sizing up the women, but we didn't see many of them and they wore really frumpy clothes. There was a war on after all.

The thing that caught our attention right away was the strange odor, which we came to associate with night soil. The most popular type of fertilizer was human excreta. The locals did their business into a honey pot, known to us in years past as the thunder jug or chamber pot. When full, this piece of crockery was placed near the road and was picked up by the guy with the honey wagon. When his cart tank was full, he pulled it out of town to the fields where the smelly contents were dumped on the crops, usually rice. A very efficient system of recycling, but somewhat dangerous for foreigners who consumed vegetables without first washing them in Clorox.

We were taking it all in and I remember very little of what I saw with the exception of something that I will never forget because it pissed me off so much. We were pretty quiet on that trip through town, until we started to notice young Korean men of about our own age lolling about the streets as if they had nothing else to do. Some Marines started calling attention to these young Koreans and wondering aloud just why these guys were not in the Korean Army and off fighting the war. One voice shouted, "What in hell are we doing here fighting their war while these draft dodgers traipse around way back here in the rear." There was a lot of grumbling among the troops on our truck and it occurred again every time we saw some more of these young male civilians in Pusan.

We pulled into the RepoDepo outside of town where we would get some orientation on the situation and the big roll of the assignment dice by the HQ personnel types. This crap shoot would mete out our individual destinies. All we had been taught about the divisions of the Fleet Marine Force was that the First Marine Division was made up of the 1st, 5th, and 7th Infantry Regiments, plus an Air Wing, and the 11th Marines, the Artillery Regiment, Amtracs, Tanks, and others. We wondered which regiment we would be assigned to and what it would be like in the new unit. The 1stMarDiv was a component of X Corps under Eighth Army.

We were assigned to tents and put on work details while we waited for the wheels of HQ to turn. We were only there for a few days and I remember one date precisely—August 6, 1951. Here I was in Pusan, Korea, confined to the camp and standing guard duty on four hour shifts, when I should have been celebrating back in Detroit with my rowdy friends. The bartenders in Detroit were not amused when you came into their joint to celebrate your 21st birthday after you had been coming in there for the past three years with fake I.D. For me it was especially difficult on the midnight to 0400 watch where I had to stand at a certain spot for a half hour in the pissing down rain, then slog through the mud on patrol for a half hour. Yuk! If I was home, I'd just be coming in from a party by 0400.

One morning we gathered in a large formation to await our assignments to line companies. The PA system announced the major units first, then called the names of the victims, I mean Marines assigned to that unit. For example: "Now hear this. The following men will report to the First Marine Regiment. As your name is called, go to that section of the parade ground designated for your new unit." The process took a while as most guys were sent to the three infantry regiments, artillery outfit, tanks, force recon, amtracs, etc. . .

When they announced the First Engineer Battalion, they called a number of guys. When I heard my name, I said to myself, "What the hell is this? I've never heard of that outfit. What do they do? What can I possibly do there? I was trained for the infantry." I mentioned that to another guy as we walked over to the engineers' section. He told me to just shut up and remember, "Ours is not to wonder why, ours is just to do or die."

A lieutenant and a gunny were waiting to check our names off a list. There were about 50 of us and we followed the gunny to the trucks that would haul us up to the Division HQ. We didn't see very much on the way to our new outfit because of the dust on the road. My only impression of the countryside was the devastation and abject poverty everywhere. I didn't realize it at the time, but the Korean civilians we saw here and on the streets of Pusan were just about all we would see until we left Korea a year later. The odor of night soil was more pronounced out in the countryside.

The trip to the Division HQ took hours due to the narrow, windy, and poorly maintained roads. We arrived late in the afternoon and pulled into a huge compound crammed with greenish brown tents of all sizes—pyramidal, squad, and big mothers like those used for field hospitals. We ended up in the area of the First Engineer Battalion and stopped in front of the HQ and Service (H&S) Company. We jumped off, stretched our legs and waited for the next step. Another gunny came out and introduced himself, then directed us to follow a Marine to our tents, where we would spend the night. The guide showed us where the head and the mess tent were and what time to expect evening chow. He told us to be ready for a formation at 0800 after morning chow.

The next morning, we assembled in front of the HQ tent marked PERSONNEL where we were interviewed by clerks who dealt in Military Occupation Specialties (MOS). I was called in to a seat at a desk opposite a lieutenant who asked me a lot of questions about what I did in civilian life. He had my very thin Service Record Book (SRB), the USMC's personal record that went everywhere you served. He noted that I was a forestry technician with the City of Detroit. "Not much use for that here", he commented. Adding, "There are few trees in most of Korea. They have been blasted to smithereens by war, or this starving population has cut them down to heat their shacks and cook their food.'"

"Hmmm," he was mumbling to himself and chewing on the eraser. "Well now," he said, "What else did you do for the City of Detroit in connection with forestry work?" If I had thought about it, I would have told him that I knew all about working with ropes and cables, splicing and all that for repairing trees and winching logs. I didn't know until later that each engineer company had a couple of slots for riggers, who had to know about ropes, knots and cables, etc In fact I had to serve as a rigger several times to cope with problems later. Finally, I told him that twice a week, I had to drive a load of tree brush or logs to the city dump on a semi trailer or flat bed truck. "That's it, " he said, " We need truck drivers. Have you ever driven a ten wheeler dump truck? Never mind, a truck is a truck isn't it? That's settled." He wrote something on a piece of paper and stuck it into my file.

Then as an afterthought he asked, "What did you study in high school?" While I was listing the courses I had taken, he was looking at a list of specialties he was to look out for. I mentioned drafting and he said, "OK, forget about truck driving, anyone who drives can do that, but we have an urgent need for someone with training in drafting. You've got a slot right here in Battalion HQ. Here is the name of the lieutenant to report to in S-3. It's down the road on the left. Good luck!"

I walked over to the tent with the S-3 sign above the door. I found a bunch of desks and the lieutenant in charge of drafting and design. He took me to the drafting section and introduced me to the staff NCO in charge. I sat down and talked to him for a while and found that I would start out by drafting plans for such important things as: volley ball courts, horseshoe pitches, badminton courts, shithouses, etc. I was so surprised that I almost fell off my chair. I think maybe that they were just checking out my skills, but what it did was offend my sensibilities. If I had any skills at all along this line, I would love to be designing culverts, bridges, air fields, giant cribs for roads along cliffs, etc. But I had only taken a couple of drafting courses and although I had good grades in them, I quit school in the tenth grade to go to work.

The reason that I would be given these mundane drafting tasks, was that the First Marine Div. was now in reserve after having been on the lines for more than a year. The current drafting work was to provide the troops with some recreation. So I asked the guys in that section what happened when the Div. went back on the lines. They told me that I shouldn't worry about that because H&S Co. would be in the rear with the gear. We would have it made in the shade. The letter Companies Able, Baker, Charlie, and Dog would move up to just behind the lines to support the Marine regiments, i.e., to do any engineering work required. Each company was assigned to an infantry regiment and much of their work would be on the main line of resistance (MLR).

So I asked what life would be like in the Battalion HQ then. They told me life was good. However, there were lots of inspections and because we were close to the Divisional HQ, we had to live almost like we were back in the states. To me that meant a chickenshit life with strutting 2nd lieutenants right out of the Academy, or Quantico, lots of rules and regs to abide by, and all that crap. I said to myself, "Screw that. I didn't come over here to a war zone to live like I was back at some Marine Guard Barracks on a Naval base."

I hadn't been there a week when I told the sergeant that I wanted a transfer. He and every other guy in the section told me I was nuts. I was allowed to present my case to the lieutenant in charge and he understood, so he asked me where I wanted to be transferred. By this time he had my SRB and was reading what the personnel type had written about the interview. I said that I would like to join my friends in a line company (an infantry regiment), because that is what my Dad had done in WWI. He said that he couldn't go along with that, what else would I want. I then told him I would settle for tanks. He said that wasn't easily done as I had no training for tanks. The lieutenant told me quite bluntly that the colonel would not permit any transfers out of the battalion because we were already under strength. He asked me if I would settle for a transfer within this battalion to a letter company. If so, he would discuss it with our company commander and if he approved it was a done deal.

Several days later I found myself on a Dodge weapons carrier (WC) for the trip to Able (A) Co., First Engineer Battalion, where I was to be a truck driver or whatever else they wanted me to do. The latter was always couched in the words, "and any other duties and tasks as assigned." I had finally found a home for the next year, although a highly mobile one as I later learned. When I got out of the truck I noticed ABLE ENGINEERS painted on the side. It had been painted on there by the driver, Sgt. Thomas.

A Marine engineer letter company was made up of a headquarters platoon and three other platoons. Headquarters platoon contained the following sections: motor transport, heavy equipment, light and stationary equipment, administration, maintenance and repair, supply, food service. The three other platoons did all of the other work not involving the above. This may not be exact, but it is the way I remember it.

I went to meet my boss, a sergeant. named Powell, who was called Joey Chitwood by the rest of his drivers. He was from California where Joey Chitwood was some kind of hero on the stunt car circuit there and taught wildly defensive driving to the cops. Powell was the Motor Pool dispatcher. We reported to him every morning for work assignments. A staff NCO was in charge of the Motor Pool and we were all supervised by Lt. Zarzeka. He had an attitude, but we got along until he was rotated out many months later. As I was taken around the camp, I was introduced to many Marines, most of whom forgot your name in a few minutes. As with other new arrivals, I would be referred to as the fucking new guy (FNG) until I had been there long enough to be dubbed with a nickname. That marked your acceptance into the group

Sgt. Powell took me to my tent and introduced the me to my new roomies. They were a really salty lot. These Marines were older, had been through the meat grinder at Chosin reservoir and told me all about it. One salt, Jackson Thomas was from Auburn, Alabama and talked with such a drawl and so slow, it took him forever to tell a story. He was a nice guy and drove anything with wheels. Thomas was once a student at Auburn University and well educated. There was a redneck from the hills of Appalachia named Smitty, who carried a .38 Special revolver and was always fiddling with it. I had to sleep near him and thought he was slightly crazy so I slept with one eye open.

Smitty knew how to make his own booze. He was always fermenting something like raisins. When it was ready it was called Raisin Jack. The 1stMarDiv had an attitude about allowing enlisted men to have alcohol.

We were each supplied with eight cans of beer every six weeks The catch was that you were issued one can per day and you had to turn in the empty to get the next can another day. No saving up. This 8 beer ration was brought on by an incident on the lines earlier that year where a 12 can ration was given all at once. Some riflemen got soused and began firing towards enemy positions with no targets in sight.

There were always some nondrinkers who were very popular because they would give away their ration to the boozers. The Command decision was the strict rationing of beer for enlisted men. As gentlemen, the officers continued to received their normal liquor and beer ration each month. So what did the thirsty peons do for booze? Most just sipped their can a day when it was issued and were happy to get it. The hustlers were always able to find someone who knew a pilot who brought whiskey back on his plane from Japan. The going price to any of us was up to $50 per fifth. The creative, like Smitty, found ways to make their own out of whatever basic materials they could scrounge. The safest and purest way to go was to make friends with the corpsman, or a guy in medical supply for a small ration of absolute alcohol, also known as medical alcohol, or by its proof designation, 190. That stuff was too powerful to drink straight, so we learned that the best mixer available was canned grapefruit juice .

Another booze source was legitimate high quality Japanese whiskey labeled SunTory. Anyone with access to Korean civilians could buy bottles with famous labels from all over the world. However, usually what we got from the SunTory or famous brands bottle, was some form of toxic alcohol or just plain colored water. The wily Koreans bought the good stuff under an honorable label and drank it themselves. They made a small hole in the bottom of the bottle, remove the good stuff, replaced it with the bad, and sealed the hole. In this way the integrity of the seal on the cap was maintained to clinch the sale to the thirsty buyer.

If we had a source of illicit booze, we had to be careful in consuming it so as not to attract any attention from the officers, so there was little exuberance in enjoying your quaffing on the QT. When we had some extra booze we drank it, weather and security permitting, in a culvert outside the camp.

My Dad sent me a newspaper clipping from Detroit (in 1951) which reported about sixty GIs in Korea had either died or become blind from drinking antifreeze and other toxic forms of alcohol such as wood alcohol (methanol). Dad wrote that although it was against the law, he would send me a fifth of V.O. anytime I asked for it through the Fleet Post Office (FPO). He said he could pack the bottle in a large potato chip can full of popped popcorn. I knew that this was painful for him to do, because he was afraid that his three sons would succumb to the curse of the Irish. He believed strongly in the adage that, "Whiskey was invented to prevent the Irish from ruling the world ."

One time while Smitty was waiting for his five gallon can of Raisin Jack to ripen in a cache in the ground outside our tent, he had been drinking something else and was mumbling incoherently and staggering around in our tent. He decided to try to impress the FNG (yours truly) by showing me how to play Russian roulette. The trouble was, he started pointing his .38 Spec. at me and clicking the trigger each time after spinning the cylinder with a single round in it. I called the guys standing outside and they came in to help me subdue him and hide his pistol and all his cartridges.

One guy in our tent was explaining a way to extend the effect of one can of beer. He had heard that if you made a pin hole in the can and sucked out the contents, the alcohol's effect would be enhanced. Where he got that one is beyond me, but there were a lot of guys with sore lips for a week, all to null effect. Then Smitty heard that if he added shaving lotion to each beer, it would multiply the effect of the alcohol in the beer. We were all sitting in the tent when Smitty speculated then that if he did that, the FNG would be sticking his head in Smitty's sleeping bag at night just to get a whiff of perfumed farts. About then I was planning to play Russian roulette with him, only with an automatic pistol as soon as I acquired one. Screw that one round in the cylinder nonsense, lets get it over with.

When sergeant Powell rotated out, he was replaced by Bob Callahan as dispatcher. He had gone to High School at DeLasalle in Chicago, which had some famous alumni. Bob went down to an Army camp where he knew some old school friends in supply. He came back with cases of beer which we had to hide from the rest of our camp. One guy dug a hole in our tent to stash it in with the idea of covering the hole with boards the next day. During the evening we worked on the beer and hit the sack. In the wee hours someone got up to go out for a leak and accidently kicked the tent pole into the hole and the canvas came down on us. The ruckus and swearing woke up Chapin and the rest of us, but when we realized there was no crisis, we went back to sleep smelling tent fabric all night. In the morning we got some boards to cover the beer and put the tent back up. No one else in camp had seemed to notice.

I spent the next week learning the ropes in driving a 6X6 ten wheeler dump truck for construction work. It had a lot of gears and a double reduction gear box for hauling heavy loads slowly up hill. I already knew how to double clutch for shifting down the gears and had no trouble learning how to spread a load of dirt or gravel evenly on the new roads we were building. The dump trucks were made by International Harvester. The other 6X6s were GMCs called Jimmys, and also known as the deuce and a half (2 and a half ton). The small crew carriers and weapons carriers were Dodges, such as the Power Wagon. We also had a few Jeeps for the officers and the top sergeant to get around in. During the last week of August we got the order to move north. The Division was moving back onto the line to relieve an Army Division whose turn it was to go into strategic reserve.

As we moved north, I was a regular driver, replacing a guy who rotated home. We would stop at the end of the day and pull into an area that had been swept for mines for the past few days by one of our platoons. We made camp for the night and the officer of the day (OD) or the sergeant of the guard came around to tell us who had guard duty, the time of our shift, and the outpost or foot patrol. When we were moving we ate C-Rations unless we were in a spot for more than a few days, which gave the cook a chance to whip up a hot meal for all off us. Otherwise, on short hops, he made only coffee and sandwiches.

I can only recall two small incidents as we moved forward. At one point, the FNG, namely me, didn't check the barrel as I hand pumped fuel into one of my 20- gallon tanks. I suddenly realized that I was pumping diesel fuel into my truck, which burned only gasoline. I had to find a container and drain the diesel out of my tank, then refill it with gasoline. We transported our own fuel right along with us and when we ran low, a truck was sent back to the nearest fuel dump to fill the 55 gallon drums. They were plainly marked for diesel or gas and even a blind man could tell the difference by just loosening the bung. I was off to a good start. But I soon learned that other people had also screwed up during their on-the-job driver training.

One new driver had overheard others discussing how much oil their trucks burned and they were always adding more. He decided to fill his truck engine with oil to the top of the dipstick so he might never have to top up. After a few weeks of driving, the excess oil ruined the engine. Another new driver wasn't too familiar with the working of the transfer case and the power takeoff which operated the winch and the hydraulic dump lift. The local laborers from the Korean Service Corps always climbed on his truck for a ride out to the job site, because many other drivers had given them a bad time. One day he had a dozen of them in the truck bed when he accidentally tripped the dump lift. By the time he responded to their yelling, he found the dump bed raised all the way and the Koreans were hanging onto the tailgate. After that episode, they didn't want to ride with him either.

The other incident occurred one night while we were on the move, setting up at a new location every few days. The large force which was fighting along the eastern sector of the front was made up of the First Marine Div., the Korean Marine Regiment, a ROK Division on one of our flanks and a US Army Div. on the other. As they pushed the North Korean and Chinese armies back, we followed right behind them. When an Army or Corps advances rapidly forcing the enemy to give ground, there are always a number of enemy troops who remain undected in the sweeping movements. If these soldiers are not found by the time the new main line of resistance (MLR) is established, they form into small groups to harass us from the rear.

We had been warned to be on the lookout for these irregulars from the communist forces so security was tightened around our camp site and on our work details off in the boonies. We were also told that we didn't want to be taken by irregulars, because they would kill us outright. With no rations of their own they couldn't be burdened with a prisoner while on the run. This was somewhat disconcerting to the FNGs so I was a bit edgy for the first couple of nights in each new camp area, where everything was unfamiliar.

One night I was sleeping on the ground and woke up with a start about midnight when I heard a noise at the secured tent flap. Someone was working their way into the tent. I was already sitting up with my rifle in one hand and flashlight in the other. The beam lit up the face of an oriental in a khaki uniform wearing one of those caps with the fuzzy flaps turned up. I almost pooped my pants. I was lying right in front of him, so dropped the flashlight and aimed my rifle at him ready to shoot. Someone else in the tent woke up and shouted at me, "He's our interpreter. Let him in." Man, this punchy FNG was ready to drop the Korean. How was I to know he was working with us. The interpreter told us he was just coming off duty and was told by the top to bunk in with us.

Smitty was awake by then and chipped in with, " We're already asshole to elbow in this tent, but you guys on the ground can scrunch up some more to make room for Kim. Just what we need, a garlic snapper in our tent." Kim paid no attention to him, rolled out his sleeping bag and crawled in.

The next morning I was still irritated by the incident and wanted to know why no one told me that we had a company interpreter and why we were not informed before dark that he would be coming in late and bunking with us. I wondered how many other outfits wasted their interpreters, because some FNG wasn't told they had one.

The interpreter was only with us now and then when we were working with the Korean Marine Corps (KMC) regiment or we had a company of Korean labor conscripts doing some construction work nearby. I remember having only two conversations with Kim. After the incident in our tent, I asked him how we could tell a North Korean from a South Korean soldier. He told me that was easy, you can tell by the dialect they speak. A lot of good that did for us, since not one of us Americans knew more than a few words of Korean and that was bastardized Japanese pidgin English. I had heard from another Marine that the stitching on the quilted uniform jackets was horizontal on the North Korean ones and vertical on the South Koreans. That didn't make much sense to me. What about in the summer when they don't wear quilted uniforms?

We had little to do with the Korean Service Corps, which was only around our outfit a couple of times for a week or so. They stayed in large tents about 100 yards from ours. The poor guys were obviously not getting enough to eat, because they would carry off our garbage and eat whatever we threw away. We heard that poor Koreans existed on rice and fish heads for their diet. They were paid in local currency at probably 15 cents (US) per day, including meals and a place to sleep. ROK soldiers received 10 cents per day. The local currency was so badly devalued during the war that when a laborer drew his pay at the end of a month, he had to carry all the Korean Won (paper bills) in baskets or a wheelbarrow.

On payday they crowded into their tents and gambled night and day for several days arguing and fighting over the gaming. They would not fall out for work details until their money ended up in the hands of a few sharks. On a work detail, they had a way to use three men on a shovel. Two Koreans stood on each side of the sand pile to be moved and held one end of a rope tied to the shovel handle down by the blade. The senior laborer held the end of the handle to guide it into the sand. The guys on the ropes pulled the loaded shovel up to the edge of a truck with a swinging motion, where it was dumped. The operator pulled it back and the cycle began again. We round eyes called it the three-man shovel shuffle. I guess that's what you do when you're long on manpower and short on shovels.

My only other conversation with Kim was in answering some questions put to me from a bunch of Koreans in the labor unit. They wanted to know what I did before I was a Marine. Before I could answer, they wanted to know if I was any of the following kinds of persons: a cowboy, an Indian, a gangster, a cop, a rich man in a mansion, a dancer, a comedian, a playboy, and so forth. I was surprised by this line of questioning and asked Kim what was the scoop on these guys. He told me that they were simple farmers and not very sophisticated, like he was. In the past year they had been around many American military camps as workers. At night they were allowed to watch our outdoor movies showing old flicks from the states. We only had movies in the reserve area.

Their whole body of knowledge about Americans was gleaned from watching our actors and not understanding a word that was spoken. Therefore, every serviceman that was in Korea now, had to fit into one of these movie roles according to them. I told them that I was a truck driver and worked in the trees in civilian life. God only knows what Kim told them as I wandered off. They were all nodding and grinning, so it must have been good. Their other question was, " How many guns do you own in the states." I told them, " A hunting rifle and a shotgun."

Post USMC, I worked as a civilian for 17 years in six other countries. Although I was never asked what I did at home, I was always asked how many guns I owned. If you were an American, you were obviously a gunslinger. I sent a local student to study at a U.S. university in 1960 when I lived in Cambodia. I knew him quite well and he was always ragging me about gun ownership in the USA. He was against it. When he returned to Cambodia with his degree he was assigned to a marine fisheries post at Sihanoukville on the coast of the Gulf of Siam. The Khmer Rouge were working their way into this remote area to control Cambodia's only sea port and he was worried about protecting his wife and kids.

In 1970 I met this former student at an international fisheries meeting in Bangkok. He said that he was terrified by the Khmer Rouge and asked me if I had a gun he could have. Guns were not readily available there except to the Cambodian Army and the Khmer Rouge. He told me that he was ashamed to ask me for a weapon after all the things he had said about guns years before. I had a survival rifle at my home on an experiment station in NE Thailand, but couldn't get it to him before he went home the next day. I never was able to find a way to deliver it to him in Cambodia. However, even if I had gotten it to him, he would have been summarily executed by the Khmer Rouge if they found him with it. As it was he was placed in a forced labor camp and slowly starved to death by 1979 along with his parents, grandparents, wife, kids, and several brothers and sisters and their families.

Sleeping arrangements in Able Company were in constant flux. When I arrived there was a shortage of folding cots (canvas on a wooden frame) so the FNG had to sleep first on the ground and then on an air mattress when one became available. As the old salts rotated home, the FNG inherited a stretcher. I slept on one of those for weeks until I graduated to a cot. The folding cot was great because it gave you something to sit on and a place to stow your boondockers, helmet and personal gear underneath. Our pyramidal tent would accommodate four to six sleepers comfortably, but three to four more could squeeze in for a night or two.

Living in tents for 18 months was a spartan existence. The dirt floor made it easier because it only had to be swept. As Lee Marvin once said in an interview about his friend's house in the desert near Tucson Arizona, "It's the kind of place where I have to wipe my feet when I go outside." The homeowner was the widow of one of his Marine buddies from the Pacific and she kept injured or orphaned young wildlife for the Game and Fish Dept. The creatures had the run of her house. Our tents never got that bad, because we moved often. Aside from the stove in winter, the only other furnishings next to the cots, were small tables and desks made from the wooden crates our gift tobacco and sundries arrived in. If we were in one place more than a week, a wooden frame and a simple door were rigged up. A single bulb on the center tent pole provided light in the evenings.

As we moved forward our company was busy with routine engineering work. The platoons had mine clearing details every day as well as looking for and disarming booby traps. Our CO and XO, along with a couple of platoon leaders and some senior NCOs went a few miles forward every day looking for the best route to build a road and to size up a fairly secure place to camp when we moved up. I don't know for sure, because I had little to do with the officers, but it seemed that most of them were either civil engineers or had some other engineering training and experience.

The drivers were busy hauling the platoons out to their work sites or hauling aggregate material to improve the road. The bulldozers were always out in front blazing the trail. We followed up spreading gravel and dirt for the graders to level and pack it down.

Our heavy equipment included the IH-TD16 or 18 bulldozers, one or two D-6 or 7 Caterpillars, a Caterpillar grader (sometimes called the motor patrol), a pull grader which had to be pulled behind a truck, and one Allis Chalmers tracked front end or skip loader. The motor pool included all of the road vehicles in the company. Stationary equipment included several generators and flood light units, plus a large Le Roi (105 CFM) air compressor permanently mounted on a 6X6 truck. The maintenance section included vehicle as well as heavy equipment mechanics, two welders and their equipment for arc and gas welding. The admin. section included the usual suspects: the Skipper (a captain), the XO, the first sergeant (the top), the gunny (a technical sergeant), the company clerks, and a corpsmen for each platoon. The company HQ probably had a radio, a radio operator and an interpreter (as needed). The mess sergeant, cooks, supply sergeant and his men were also in HQ platoon.

The other three platoons were made up of squads which contained specialists in rigging, demolitions and mines, carpentry, plumbing, and pipe fitting, etc. Each squad also had a number of men without a particular specialty who did the hand labor. When extra hands were needed for the labor, any specialist could fill in if he had no other work to do. Whenever a platoon went to the field to work, a corpsman went along. If the platoon was split up and working in different places, the corpsman went with the squad with the most dangerous task, such as mine clearing. On very rare occasions when we needed lots of hands, a Korean labor company came in and camped nearby until the job was finished.

We made many of the road culverts out of heavy lumber. I was there with the LeRoi compressor using the huge air driven circular saw for trimming the planks. One of the Marines was driving huge spikes in the wood to hold the culvert together with a long handled small headed hammer. I asked him how he could be so accurate in driving those spikes home with one or two blows. He said that he was a gandy dancer in civilian life, working on the railroad driving steel spikes in newly replaced ties. This guy lucked out. He was right where he belonged in the engineers.

Driving one of the dump trucks was not bad during the summer because they were convertibles—a soft top truck. Because the cab only had a canvas roof, the dump bed was equipped with a large steel panel that came up and curved over the cab to protect the driver. This panel was called a headache, probably because that is what was avoided when rocks and dirt were being loaded. The trucks, like everything else, were painted Marine green. There was a large white star painted on each door, on the hood and a smaller one on the tailgate. This was to identify our vehicles to our own side, especially fighter bomber pilots.

The trucks had no windows, only a canvas and clear plastic panel that snapped onto the door and the roof for driving in the rain and for the winter months. If there was a heater, it must have been a manifold type like I had in my 1930 Model A Ford back home. Under certain conditions in warm weather, when the canvas top was removed, you could lower the windshield to the hood and clamp it down. We had to do this a couple of times later on so the Chinese forward observers would not pick up the reflection of the sun from the windshield in a place where the MLR of the opposing armies were miles apart. Each one of our vehicles had one or two metal rifle racks attached to the dash or somewhere close to hand. These racks were designed to securely hold one M-1 rifle or a carbine. These racks were also a part of every other piece of motorized equipment, such as the grader, bulldozers, front end loader, etc. We had to have a weapon close by at all times and it couldn't be bouncing around on a vehicle. All vehicles were equipped with a pioneer kit. This was a firmly fixed metal frame with a shovel, axe, and pickaxe strapped to it. These tools were indispensable when working out in the field.

COMPANY ORGANIZATION

The leader of each platoon was either a 1st, or 2nd lieutenant aided by the platoon sergeant, usually an staff sergeant. The platoon leaders reported directly to the Skipper and the staff NCO to the platoon leader, the gunny or the top. The platoon squads were led by a buck sergeant with each squad loosely organized into three fire teams. Each fire team was led by a corporal and one of the team carried a BAR and the other three carried M-1s. The word from division and battalion seeped down to us through the chain of command, we suspected that most of the time the word stopped at the lieutenant level and never reached us at the bottom of the heap.

Until late 1951, the officers and senior NCOs all carried either 45 cal. Colts for sidearms, or a 30 cal. carbine. The BARs were scattered through the platoons and the rest of us carried the M-1 Garand. We also had a 50 cal. heavy machine gun and a crew assigned to it for camp defense. There may have been some other types of weapons I didn't know about. The 1stMarDiv HQ had noted the difficulty with malfunctions with the 30 cal. carbine both M-1 and M-2 models during the winter of 1950-51. There were so many instances reported of the carbines bolt mechanism freezing up in extreme cold, that it was deemed to be a threat to those carrying it and those assigned a carbine had to turn it in to the armorer for the M-1 Garand as winter began in Nov. 1951.

The carbines were favored weapons among many because they were not as cumbersome and as heavy as the M-1 Garand. This was important for certain types of work such as radio operators, commo (communications) wire stringers, corpsmen, and operators of bulldozers and other types of equipment. I thought that the officers liked to carry the carbine because it served as a badge to separate them from us peons. The carbine replaced the swagger stick they would normally carry somewhere else outside Korea. It took some of the senior NCOs and officers a while to get used to carrying the M-1 rifle in place of the carbine.

Many of us acquired personal sidearms which were not part of the system but who would deny military personnel this privilege in a combat zone. Looking back at Smitty's carrying on, perhaps some guys should have been denied privately held sidearms. Early on I bought a 9mm Walther P-38 that was issued to officers in the German Army in WWII. I do recall that some bulldozer operators had Thompson submachine guns that were taken from captured Chinese soldiers. Where did the Chinese get them? From materiel supplied by the US to the Chinese Nationalist Army then captured later by the ChiCom Army in 1948-49.

We also had several 12 gauge pump shotguns assigned to our company—and probably every other company in the 1stMarDiv. We heard that the Chicoms were complaining to the UN about Marines using them on their troops while on patrols in no man's land. They insisted that shotguns with slugs or double aught (00) buckshot were banned by the Geneva convention, along with other undesirable weapons such as the wicked trench knife all troops had carried in WWI. I never could figure out exactly why some methods of killing are not acceptable by convention, while others are OK. We had the shotguns available for entirely unwarlike purposes which I explain later.

From the time I arrived in-country until winter came, it was muddy for days after a spell of rain. I was given a raincoat by a guy going home. It was an olive drab sort of Marine green and made of very fine material. It was nice because it was lined and it had a feature I had never seen before in a long coat. There were a pair of leggings made of the same waterproof cloth attached to the inside rear. When it was really sloppy outside, these leggings would unfold so that you could cover your legs down to your ankles when they were zipped up.

I wore it for a couple of weeks and I liked it so much I knew it couldn't last. A lieutenant stopped me one day and asked me why I was wearing that coat. I said, "Because someone gave it to me and it was better than a field jacket for keeping dry and warm." He asked, "Do you ever wonder why no one else is wearing one?" I said. "No, I never thought about it." "Well," he said, "It was an officer's issue." I wanted to say so what, but I asked him instead if he wanted it. He explained that officers had them, but didn't wear them this close to the lines. He added, "You know, we really don't want to stand out among the troops and you shouldn't either. Carry on then lad." I just couldn't see how a sniper could mistake a truck driver for an officer up here, but you never know. We had heard that us occidentals all look alike to orientals. I gave the coat to another guy and it changed owners a few more times before going back to supply.

Marine engineer units were something like the Navy SeaBees (US Naval Construction Battalions). We had the basic equipment and gear for rudimentary engineering in a combat zone. I note in the present day (1999), my other old outfit in the 2nd Marine Div. is now designated as the 2nd Combat Engineer Bn. at Camp LeJeune, N.C. I guess Army combat engineers are somewhat similar. However, the main force of the US Army engineers had much more equipment than we ever did and were able to undertake complicated projects like large steel bridges, and building permanent roads, etc.

Our company was forging new roads where there had only been paths and cart tracks before. As we moved up behind our infantry, the Army came along later and using Le Tourneau earth movers (Tournapulls), D-8 Caterpillar dozers, roller compactors, etc. and improved our primitive roads to a high degree. The Army also had large power shovels for loading larger dump trucks, rock crushers, cement mixers, cranes, drag lines, and pile drivers for working on the larger bridges. We had none of this type of equipment. Most of the work we did was strictly temporary and done quickly.

People don't believe me when I tell them now, that the only Koreans I saw in the year I was there, were on the streets of Pusan as we went through town, the labor gangs, and Korean Marines when they were running in formation past our camp in the winter. The only Korean I actually saw up close and talked to was our interpreter, twice. I never tasted Korean food until I went to a Korean restaurant in Cairo, Egypt in 1982. Even if Korean food had been available, we would not have been allowed to eat it due to the use of human waste directly on vegetable crops.

This lack of contact with Koreans became a sore point with me later, because I would get letters from friends asking me to send them souvenirs from Korea. They didn't understand that we had nothing to do with Koreans, especially civilians. There was no place to shop. We were given no R & R and no trips to any towns or cities. Well, they would write to me, "Jake so-and-so has just sent his girl friend a beautiful kimono, or some other souvenir from the orient." Jake was stationed at one of the US Air Force Bases like Kimpo, or some other guy they knew was stationed at a Naval or big Army base in Japan where you could buy all kinds of stuff. The only thing I could send them was fragments of mines that had been blown up or maybe worn out rock drilling bits. Maybe it would have shut them up.

So, they asked me, "Why not just go down to the PX and buy something there to send home?" Vietnam vets will not believe this, but there was no access for most Marines in Korea to a PX. Well, then where did you get your smokes and things that you needed for day to day living? We received care packages of a sort.

Once every month or so every Marine company received a number of wooden crates, each about the size of a small foot locker. Inside each crate were the things that made life easier for the troops. There were cartons of many brands of cigarettes, some cigars, chewing tobacco (plugs and leaf), tins of snuff, pipe tobacco, corncob pipes, boxes of all kinds of candy bars, chewing gum, life savers, shaving cream and brushes, safety razors, tooth paste and brushes, after shave lotion, talcum powder, and hand soap.

There were also a few nonconsumable items, such as pocket knives, combs, decks of cards, dice, a compass, and a few pocket books such as westerns and mysteries. All of this was purchased or donated by businesses back in the states. Under the cellophane wrapping on the cigarette cartons were business cards stating, "To the troops in Korea with the compliments of the Acme Chevrolet Dealer in Amarillo, Texas," for example. The donors were from all over the US.

118

I don't know if any of our troops in Korea ever thanked them. If not, I will do it now. Thank you donors for everything you sent us in Korea. We couldn't have survived without all the smokes and sundries you sent each month. Just opening that crate every time was like a little Christmas for us. Thanks a million from myself and the other ingrates who failed to acknowledge these gifts way back then. .

Even if we had access to buy something in a PX or civilian store, most of us had no money. The first month I was in country I drew my pay, not realizing that there was no place to spend it. When I worked in Detroit, I liked to see and feel my money on payday. In Korea we were not paid in dollars, but rather in military scrip. It was illegal to have US dollars in one's possession due to currency speculators.

However, the circling buzzards knew what to do with it. The vultures I refer to were the old salts, most of them crusty WWII veterans of the landings in the Pacific who had been called up from the reserves to serve in the first year of the Korean war.

When the old salts found out that this FNG had drawn his pay, they conned me into playing poker with them. For the first few nights, they let me win a lot. Then the next time I played they cleaned me out. I learned my lesson after that and let my pay ride so that it would accumulate. Then I could draw a lump sum when I went on a month's leave at home.

Those who drew pay received it in military scrip, sort of like Monopoly money. Use of scrip was intended to cut down on speculation in the ever fluctuating rate of exchange between the Korean won and the Yankee dollar. However, a black market continued to exist for changing scrip for either dollars or won. To control speculation in scrip, the US Military, on very short notice, set a time and day for everyone to turn in old scrip for new. The old scrip became worthless. For example, it would be announced at morning chow in every camp in Korea, that everyone with scrip will line up to turn it in for the new scrip at 0900 today. The camp was closed, so that no one was allowed to enter or leave it. All who had scrip waited in line to turn it in to a Marine finance officer. Everyone counted their old scrip (it was all in paper, no coins) and the finance officer placed it in a lock box and then counted out new scrip, which was another color or had some other mark to distinguish it from any other scrip previously issued in Korea. This exchange occurred several times during my tour in Korea.

I heard that changing the scrip without any prior notice, left many Korean, and some American servicemen, stuck with thousands of dollars of worthless scrip. Usually this was because their scrip was squirreled away somewhere in a can buried under a jar of Kimchi away from the military compound.

While we were in the Punchbowl, I heard of several instances where GIs were swiping parkas and selling them to the ROK soldiers. DurIng the first month of winter of 1951, we had ROK soldiers come to the entrance to our camp with a five gallon GI Jerry can scrounging gasoline. When it was learned that they were humping it through their lines to sell to the North Koreans and Chinese, we got the word from Divisional HQ to stop that practice. The ROK soldiers always claimed they needed the gas for fires to warm themselves. Gasoline is a dangerous fuel to use for that purpose anyway.

John Chapin recently reminded me that at one camp site on the road north, one of our cat skinners finally showed up with a big Caterpillar D-7 we got from the US Army. The poor guy had walked this bulldozer over 60 miles from the Army camp at the top speed of eight miles per hour. He was famished when he pulled into the compound and left the dozer idling while he went to the chuck wagon for some chow. The word hadn't got around yet about the new Cat but all the operators wanted to drive it because it was the top of the line compared to our small IH TD-16s and 18s. They never got the chance. One round of incoming mail exploded right on the Cat, destroying it. If there had been a crowd of men around checking it over, they would have been wiped out.

It was late September as we moved forward. I believe that the X Corps strategy was for the UN forces to advance as far north as possible and to establish the MLR as straight as possible all across the peninsula. The planners were looking for the most suitable place to do this before winter came. They had to have a front line that could be easily serviced from the rear in order to bring up supplies and to evacuate the sick and wounded. They also wanted a ridge with good height so our forward observers (FOs) could see what the enemy was up to.

THE PUNCHBOWL

A large volcanic crater known as the Punchbowl was fought over for months. The Chinese wanted it as a troop staging area for a drive to capture Seoul. UN Forces took it from the communists, then lost it and regained it by mid 1951. The Punchbowl was about five miles across from rim to rim. As the line regiments took the north rim and settled in making new fortified positions, we began to build a road up and over the south rim and then on into the crater's bottom across to the base of the north rim.

Our work up to the base of the south rim was mainly building the road and making box culverts where streams crossed the new road. I don't know where the materials came from for the culverts, mostly heavy lumber and semicircular corrugated steel sections, but they probably came from Army supply. One of our platoon leaders knew his aggregates and found suitable materials around our construction sites for building the roads and filling in around and over the culverts. I once asked this lieutenant if he could give me the definition of a landslide or avalanche and he gave me a long technical spiel. I told him I had a shorter one, "It's a mountain getting its rocks off."

Because we didn't have a large mechanized shovel for loading our trucks, we had to make do with the AC front-end loader or a huge loading structure. This device was built on the side of a hill of aggregate material and was a huge wooden and steel hopper with a chute. When ready to load up, we put a truck directly under the chute and left the cab for a safe place. The operator used his bulldozer to push a few cubic yards of aggregate into the hopper, where it crashed down into the truck bed filling it to the side boards. The steel headache kept the materials from munching the canvas top.

There had never been a good road into the Punchbowl, except a very steep one from the southeast, so we had to create one over the very rocky south ridge. This meant a lot of drilling and blasting to loosen the rock. Then the bulldozers would push the rubble over the side and down the steep slopes. The first priority was to make a one lane road all the way over the ridge so supplies could be moved up. About the time we arrived at the top of the ridge, it took several days for the engineers to figure out how to speed up the construction. They decided to send one bulldozer straight down the slope off to the side. The operator would then move over to a preselected spot and begin to make the road up from the bottom while we continued working down to meet him.

The slope was very steep. Because few people had lived in the area, there was still some good sized virgin timber, mostly pines. We had some tough cat skinners running the bulldozers and they all wanted to take their machine straight down that steep slope. The operator used the lowest gear possible, crept over the side and inched down the steep slope, edging around some huge boulders and big trees, but pushing the smaller ones over. Four men went going down with him riding shotgun, although some were on foot. When the dozer reached the floor of the crater—quite a feat, the crew camped at the bottom and moved the next morning to start making the road from that end.

About half of my time was spent driving and the other half in preventive maintenance (PM) or repair of my equipment. The really dull stuff was back and forth all day from the aggregate loading site (gravel pit), and dumping and spreading it on the road. I enjoyed the PM stuff because at least I was learning something.

Sgt. Powell AKA Joey Chitwood, was very helpful in teaching me driving and PM skills. The first thing he told me was that when driving, keep my thumbs out of the spokes of the steering wheel. Since there was no such thing as power steering in those days the steering wheels on trucks were very large to give the driver some leverage. When driving over rugged terrain, and especially over rock fill on a new road, the sudden wrenching of the steering wheel if one front wheel hit a big rock, would sprain one or both thumbs if they were in the wheel spokes.

Because we were mostly driving in the mountains, I had to remember the rule for using the trucks gears, i.e. always use the same gear going down hill that you had to use to get up the hill, or the next one lower. We constantly had trouble with the braking systems on our trucks, so we had to learn to use the transmission and transfer box as a brake in some situations.

When the roads were snow or ice covered we had to continue working. If you've ever had to put chains on your car or pickup tires, you can imagine what it is like to put them on all ten wheels of a large truck. On top of that, when it was below zero we were on the ground trying to do all this with mittens on. If the bad weather lasted, the abrasion from the road would start to wear on the chain links and a length of cross chain would break at one end.

Once I was hauling a load of fuel (diesel and gasoline in 55 gallon drums) over the south pass into the Punchbowl. I had just started on the down slope when I heard a slapping of metal on the front fender. I brought it to a stop, got out and inspected all the wheels. A cross chain on the front right wheel had broken and had severed the brake hose. Brake fluid was leaking out of the broken end of the line. I didn't want to stay on the ridge, so decided to put the truck in granny gear and creep down the mountain over snow and icy patches. It took longer to make it back to camp without brakes.

Another time I was hauling a truckload of full gasoline and diesel drums up the alternate road leading up to the southeast ridge of the Punchbowl. This road was fairly straight but very steep. Other drivers had complained that their fuel systems cut out when they drove up this grade even in low gear. Paddy Driscoll was riding shotgun with me and we were about halfway up the mountain. Because of the heavy load I had the truck in double reduction, i.e. granny, the lowest gear, when the engine sputtered and quit. Without the engine running, the booster for the brakes won't function and the truck began to roll backward gathering momentum. I tried to hold the shift lever in gear while looking in the mirror and tried to steer the truck into a large boulder to stop. If I had been on the other road I could have steered into the rock face along the road to slow it down, but where we were there was open flat space on both sides of the road.

As we picked up speed the steering wheel suddenly spun out of my hands from the momentum and moment forcing the truck over on its side with a crash. All of the fuel drums were flung out and there were weird sounds coming from the truck as its vital fluids began to gurgle out. Paddy had the sense to bail out soon after we started backward. I was momentarily stunned and could only think of a fire with 40 gallons of gasoline from my tanks seeping out and all those other drums laying nearby. I tried to climb out of the passenger side but my feet kept slipping off the steering wheel. I finally managed to scramble out safely— not injured, but a bit shook up.

John Chapin was following in a truck behind me. When my engine died, John had already pulled off at a right angle, stopped his truck and tried to stick a rock under my rear wheels. He told me later that when my truck went over the rock and picked up speed, they were shouting to Paddy Driscoll to jump. When Paddy did, he hit the ground rolling and his pistol went flying about 50 feet through the air. Chapin and Paddy came over to check on me and then drove back to camp for help.

A lieutenant arrived hours later with another truck and crew to salvage the fuel and right my truck. Another truck came to tow mine back to camp. This officer really had an attitude and started out with, "What did you do to cause this?" That really pissed me off. He never once asked me if I had been hurt. Paddy and Chapin told the lieutenant that I had tried to ride it out at considerable risk to myself. This kind of thing just added to my wariness of junior officers in general. He wasn't there when the accident happened and the three of us were, so he had no basis for blaming me for the accident.

It was very difficult to properly maintain vehicle engines under primitive conditions in Korea. We depended on a fuel supply system of 55 gallon drums and there was always crud and water in the fuel. Nearly every day we had to clean out both of the sediment bowls in the fuel line. These glass bowls trapped small bits of rubber and dirt, but mostly water. Under really bad conditions, the bowls had to be cleaned several times each day. The rubber bits came from the hose on the hand-cranked pump we used to transfer fuel from drums to the truck tanks. A large piece of crud could block the fuel line and never reach the sediment bowl.

I had only been in Korea a few months when it began getting colder. I had been issued a brand new woolen Army sweater and was wearing it one day while working alone with a bunch of Koreans laborers who were loading rocks in my truck by hand. When my truck was loaded they sat on their haunches like a row of birds watching the round eye trying to crank up his truck. I could tell that it was the fuel line and checked the bowls. Both were clean. No fuel was reaching that far. I took the line apart to blow it out. Whenever you do this you end up with some gasoline running onto your arms, hands, etc. This time it soaked the sleeve of my new sweater from wrist to elbow.

I stood up, took off the sweater and draped it over the open truck door to let it dry. I then went back under the truck to clear the gas line. After about 15 minutes, I put it all back together and got up to try the motor when I noticed my sweater missing. I was really pissed because the only people around for miles were the laborers. They spoke no English and I no Korean. However, my rifle spoke every language. I hauled it down checked that there was a round and full clip in it and pointed it at each of them motioning and miming removal of the sweater and where I left it on the door. I separated them and shook them down looking for it under their jackets, all the while brandishing the M-1.

Now I would never kill an unarmed person over a stolen sweater, so I told them I would be back with a Korean Marine to give them the 3rd degree. I might as well have been telling them to come to dinner in Detroit when the war was over. I didn't know any Korean Marines. I did know that at least one rotten thieving Korean was warm. After a while you come to realize that those people were so poor, they had to do anything to survive and we that had so much, wouldn't miss a little sweater. They just stared at me with blank expressions so I gave up and left for my run. This incident stuck in my craw until spring, because I was never allowed another sweater to replace it. For all the supply sergeant knew, I sold it to the civilians and would do it again with another. That was a mighty cold winter for me. Now I knew what the old salts meant when they said, it pays to make friends with both the mess and supply sergeant.

Joey Chitwood taught me about loading a truck. I had to remember to distribute the load and secure it to the truck. The driver is always responsible for the tying down of items he is hauling and placing really heavy stuff forward or over the rear wheels. On the dump trucks we had to watch our for overloading, i.e., having the weight of the load press the regular springs too far down on the helper springs. Also if the tires were not inflated properly, a heavy load would cause the bottoms of the tires on the duals to touch while driving, resulting in friction and burning tires.

When we were spreading gravel mixed with rocks on a road, a few rocks always end up getting stuck between the rear dual tires. When this first happened to me, I tried to pry them out with a pick axe and other tools. Cpl. Al Pinto, another driver showed me how to remove them easily. He told me to carry a length of hefty rope in my truck. He came over with his rope, looped it under the rock wedged between the tires, then tied it to the truck bed. With the engine idling, he pushed the lever raising the hydraulic lift and the bed up, pulling the rock out. I was learning. Cpl. Pinto was the very image of the Hollywood Marine. He was a swarthy, handsome dude and hailed from the Portuguese community of Hayward, Calif. He was known as Hollywood because he was the only guy in camp who wore sunglasses and a scarf, and because the dullards got Hollywood confused with Hayward.

Aside from the gasoline and diesel fuel we had to haul up from the battalion fuel dump, the only dangerous cargo we had to transport was explosives for our work. Most of the time we hauled it up in a small 6 X 6 personnel carrier because our platoon leader thought it was better than having the stuff rattling around in the bed of a rough riding dump truck. The only touchy stuff was the dynamite and the blasting caps, which were packed in tough cardboard cartons . The safer explosives were the plastic C-3 and the mines, which were in small crates. The drivers took turns bringing these loads up and we never had any problems. Our greatest concern was being shelled or hitting a mine while hauling either fuel or explosives.

We regularly serviced our own vehicles in changing oil and filters, changing flats, cleaning the oil bath air filter, cleaning and repacking wheel bearings, etc. When my truck was deadlined (not working), I drove another truck or helped the mechanics with the repair of my truck.

Every outfit in the military, no matter what their specialty, had a certain amount of work to be done that no one volunteered for—the shit details. In our outfit, there seemed to be few assigned to mess duty. Here a guy wanted to be on mess duty just to keep warm and because he had a chance for extra food, mostly hot. The mess detail seemed to be handled largely by the cooks and their assistants.

One of the worst jobs in our platoon was fixing flat tires. Repairing a flat tire on a large truck or a grader is not the same as fixing the tire on your sedan. The worst part is having to break the tire loose from the truck rim, which has to be done by someone pretty hefty. Because I was real skinny I wasn't put on that detail much. They put the biggest guys on it, but when I had to help them, I learned a trick for us lightweights. Most of the time, the tires were broken away from the rims by pounding on them with a heavy maul. However, in a pinch it could be done faster by slowly driving the front wheel of a truck on the side of the tire to break the seal to the rim.

I never went back to Battalion, except for a few medical trips, and trips to pick up or drop off vehicles for repair at their big shop, or a fuel run, or taking a truckload of guys back to the hot showers. On one trip when I had to pick up the Jimmy mounted LeRoi compressor, I was edgy. I was dropped off at the battalion maintenance shop in the morning and expected to drive the truck back before dark. However, it wasn't finished until after dark and I had been ordered to bring it back that day. It was about 9 PM when I hit the road going up the south rim of the Bowl. I had been able to drive fast on the level road up to this point so was not concerned about being stopped by any North Korean irregulars. We were not supposed to travel alone, but I had no choice. I suspect that my lieutenant thought that LeRoi and Jimmy were other Marines. Therefore, I was technically not alone.

This road was steep and the Jimmy very heavy, so I could only make the grade in granny. That meant I had to creep along at about five MPH all the way to the top. The Jimmy had no doors and anyone could easily have leaped on to the running board and into the cab. My loaded rifle was on the seat next to me, but it wouldn't do me much good if I had to struggle with a boarder while I was trying to control the truck. I did have my P-38 and had stopped the truck before I came up the grade and to make sure the magazine was full and there was a round in the chamber.

Although I was nervous all the way to the top of the ridge, I did feel safer with the P-38 in my lap. Anyone jumping on either side of the truck would have been blown away, friend or foe. If they pitched a grenade in with me, I would be SOL. I wasted little time coming down the ridge into the Punchbowl using only the blackout lights. I swore there would be no more night driving alone for me in this area. Because I am a needler at heart, and had seen no reason for hurrying back to camp that day, at 0030 hours I made a point of waking up the lieutenant who ordered me to do it, just so he would not worry about little old me getting back safely. He was pissed 'cause I woke him up, but he tried not to show it.

At about this time, I was given a new assignment. The operator of the LeRoi compressor was rotating home and Lt. Zarzeka was looking for someone to replace him. I didn't volunteer. One learns early on not to volunteer for anything, so the lieutenant told me to start snapping in with the compressor operator before he left. I'm always happy to learn something new, especially since driving a dump was pretty boring most of the time. When the operator left, I took over the Le Roi compressor, but still had to drive a dump or cargo flatbed, whenever there was no call for the compressor. Driving the compressor rig was great because it was so heavy. We became the Able Co. drill team, Bones, LeRoi, and Jimmy. There was even more PM involved with this rig, because the compressor engine and all the air driven tools had to be maintained as well as the Jimmy ten-wheeler. By now I had been in country a couple of months and was given the nickname Bones because I was tall and thin.

Much of the work on the one lane road over the ridge was accomplished by the bulldozers with continual use of the air drills and blasting. When drilling was required, I situated the rig as close as possible to the site and got out the air drills, shaft rods, and drill bits, then assembled everything. There were two air hose lines on reels at the back of the compressor. I paid them out to maximum length, then attached the drill machine to the coupling and then the bit and shaft were secured.

The actual drilling was done by the guys from the other platoons. I started the engine on the compressor and built up pressure in the tank.

When the drilling crew signaled that they were ready to start, I opened the valves and they began drilling into the rock. While they drilled, I was standing by at the compressor, working on other tools, or filling the oil reservoirs which were used on each hose line. These reservoirs provided lubrication to the piston in the drill (really a jackhammer). As the drilling went deeper into the rock, I would add another length of drill rod on each machine until the blasters decided the hole was deep enough to bring down the required tons of rock.

The drills made a racket, which was occasionally joined by the compressor engine when it revved up automatically to pump more air into the pressure tank. When we were working in an exposed position, where we could be seen from the Chinese forward observers' positions, the lieutenant told me to get up high and away from all of the noise to listen for incoming artillery rounds. If there was any incoming mail, the euphemism for incoming shell fire, I was to run down to warn the crew to take cover, then shut off the compressor. Fortunately, we never had to stop work as there was no incoming fire where we worked on that road, at least not while I was up there. John Chapin said that while he was sitting up there one day a sniper fired several shots at him, but he wasn't hit. He couldn't hear the shots because of the noise, but saw the rounds kicking up the dust.

An old salt told me that in 1950, they were working on a road when the lookout with their detail spotted a Chinese gun crew bore sighting on them from a nearby slope. It was a 76mm pack howitzer that they kept hidden in a cave until they found a target. They would wheel it out and having no sights, just opened the breech and sighted through the barrel. After firing a round or two, they would wheel it back in the cave to hide from any counter fire. The crew left their tools, piled in a truck and took off. The Skipper called for an infantry unit to take care of the problem. They arrived in short order and killed the gun crew. After towing away the howitzer, they collapsed the cave on the bodies with satchel charges.

Sometimes, the demolition guys would have the drillers make holes up high, which they had to do from the headache platform of a dump truck. The drillers were always covered with fine rock dust as the work progressed. After so many minutes of drilling, they would press a lever on the drill to blow air down through the shaft to clean debris from the hole. The fine rock dust ended up all over them by the end of the day. When the drilling was finished the demolition crew filled the holes with dynamite, shoving the sticks all the way in with a long pole.

One day when they had drilled a lot of holes up high and the crew packed them with explosives, I wondered how they were going to set them off. The head NCO said it would be the same way we drilled and packed them—from the top of the truck. This time they were using old fashioned fuses, which had to be lit. The head explosives man was known as Short Fuse Fred, which didn't reassure me when he told me to bring a dump truck alongside the rock face so he could use it for a platform.

When I positioned the truck where he indicated, Short Fuse got on top, yelled, "Fire in the hole," and began to light the fuses as I crept the truck along about 150 ft. to the end of the shoot. When he jumped down on the running board, I sped up and away from the area around several curves to where the rest of the guys were waiting. as we arrived several blasts rent the air, throwing rocks all over the place, but only a few small ones reached us. I wasn't sure that I wanted to do that too often. I don't know why they weren't using the hellbox to set the charges off. Probably because it wasn't as much fun as lighting fuses. The hellbox provided a jolt of electric current along wired charges in series to set them off. The blasting guys told me that in the old days, the mechanism from a crank telephone was used to set off charges.

As soon as we had cleared a fairly smooth road wide enough to accommodate one lane of traffic over the ridge, we moved our camp into the basin of the Punchbowl and gathered all of our equipment into the compound. From this base, we were able to send crews forward to work with the line companies up front and continue to widen the road from the south over the ridge. Our crews working with the KMC and USMC regiments along the lines, were primarily helping them to lay new mine fields and string various kinds of barbed wire in front of the MLR. Defensive positions were being strengthened for a long cold winter. We were also hauling small logs and timbers up there and helping the infantry to build strong bunkers to withstand enemy mortar and artillery fire.

The road north to the lines was also being improved to enable tanks to get up a point right behind the MLR for fire support. The crews I worked with continued to widen the south ridge road to accommodate those tanks, eight-inch self- propelled howitzers and supply trucks. It would take us two more months to blast loose tons of rock and then doze it all over the edge along miles of road.

When I think back at the amount of explosives we used and the number of mines planted by the men in the platoons, I am wondering exactly where all that stuff was stored in our camp. Hopefully it was in a bunker where a stray round might not set it all off. Maybe it's better that we didn't know or we would have lost more sleep fretting about it.

Some months after I began driving, the wheels thought I was good enough at it to be assigned the MOS of 3500, and I was also issued an official US Marine Corps driver's license. It was better than being back home. There was no written exam, no road test and best of all, I didn't have to stand in line for it. I guess the wheels figured that I was qualified if I didn't run over anyone or completely demolish a vehicle.

It's a good thing the Corps didn't find out how I came by my driver's license in civilian life. When I was 15 or 16, a buddy of mine, Paul Bergman, used to swipe his old man's '37 Ford when Dad was asleep. That is how we learned to drive. His Dad went off to Sweden to visit relatives for a couple of months and we drove his Ford all over Detroit every night. Paul had made his own key and when his Dad came home from Sweden, we still drove it late at night. We would push it down a block so he couldn't hear it start.

When I turned 18 I remembered to register for the draft but neglected to get a driver's license. I went to work for the city which required one to drive a truck now and then so you were expected to have a license when hired. However, this was never really explained to me. One day while I was out with a crew trimming trees, the foreman told me to take a load of brush and logs to the city dump. I did this about every ten days or so for about a year without a license and without incident.

One day I decided to stop on the way to the dump to eat lunch at the Finlander restaurant next to my house. When I left the place I pulled away from the curb without looking and tore up the side of a moving car in the street. The cops came and gave me tickets for pulling into traffic and for not having a driver's license. I drove the load out to the dump figuring I wouldn't be stopped again. I called the office to report the accident and drove slowly back to the job site. I was stalling for time to think over how I was going to explain this deal.

I figured that I would probably be fired for not having a license when I hired on, but it turned out that they never asked me when I was interviewed or after I went to work. Of course they never imagined that an employee of theirs would dare to drive a big truck without having a license. The city admin types were upset about it, but thought it was their fault for not making sure that I had a license when I came to work. One of my supervisors started to ask me about the other driver's report that he saw a young woman get out of my truck at the scene. Then he told me that he really didn't want to know. They made me go down to the MVD office and get a commercial driver's license right away. I guess that was about the time I thought I'd better start taking things seriously so it taught me a lesson.

Besides driving and maintaining the LeRoi rig, I had to replace the bits attached to the drill rods when they wore down. New bits and those that had been resharpened were sent up from Battalion supply when needed. The rig had compartments to hold all of the other equipment for the compressor. The compressor also ran jackhammers for breaking up rocks, using the same air tools that powered the drills. Other tools were for cutting wood and timber. There was a large air-powered circular saw and a chain saw (Disston) with three or four foot blade.

One of the advantages of working on the road over the south ridge was that we had to stop traffic on it when we were blasting. It usually took an hour or so for the dozers to push the blasted rock falls over the side. While they were working, our cumshaw patrol went on a scrounging detail to see what could be pilfered from the rear of the Army supply trucks. Sam Camarato from Cleveland was one of our regular ration raiders. We could only swipe stuff from those trucks where there was no guard on top, or from the last truck in line. If some of our guys could distract the drivers long enough, we could hit any truck. The only thing we were looking for was food. Sam was injured by rocks from one blast, and earlier had been wounded by enemy artillery while clearing a mine field.

The most sought after stuff was canned grapefruit or tomato, or any other kind of juice for mixing with the 190 proof alcohol. Sometimes we hit on a case of peas and carrots, or a case of other kinds of veggies. A real prize was a case of canned bacon. We never took very much, just a case of this and one of that and we split it up among the crew on the spot. We didn't see anything wrong with this practice. There was a war on. In any case, USMC units drew all of their rations and most of their supplies from the US Army X Corps Materiel Center. As I learned later studying biology, "A good parasite does not kill its host." In other words, we didn't want to ruin a good thing.

WINTER

When winter came on and the temperatures started to dip down below freezing, we had trouble keeping warm. At one point, another Marine went with me to an Army camp south of the Punchbowl and we showed the supply sergeant our sorry leather boondockers, which were not worth a shit in cold, wet weather. We looked like Willy and Joe, Bill Mauldin's cartoon characters from WWII, so he felt sorry for us and gave us each a good pair of shoepacs and some extra thick wool socks. Shoepacs have been worn for winter foot wear by generations of hunters in North America. The shoe part is made of rubber and the boot top is made of leather. I fit right in with the shoepacs, because all the Finns wore them in winter. In fact the main street (Woodrow Wilson) through the Finnish neighborhood where I lived in Detroit was known as "Shoepac Alley" or "Beer Boulevard." The shoepacs really helped and we wore them everyday for a couple of weeks until we were called to our own supply tent to be issued new thermal boots that just arrived.

The Marines were being issued modern cold weather boots well before the Army troops. That was a first. We were usually the last to get any new gear because our supplies came through the Army. There had been so many cases of frostbite among American troops during the winter of 1950-51, that a great effort went into developing a good, well insulated, waterproof boot. Our supply sergeant made us turn in our Army shoepacs when he issued us the thermals. The new boots were fantastic. They were black, had a good lining and were very warm because of an insulating layer of air between the rubber exterior and the lining. They were large and bulky, even when the fit was good, so we called them Mickey Mouse boots.

The scuttlebutt was that now that we had the new boots, getting frostbite was a court martial offense. The one odd drawback with the thermal boots was that they kept our feet warm at -35° F, but only if we were able to keep moving around and generating body heat. If our feet were a little sweaty, that seemed to add to the warmth. I found that when I had to spend the night on a perimeter outpost hunkered in a bunker for eight to ten hours at a stretch, my feet got very cold even in the Mickey Mouse boots because I couldn't move around at all. I finally decided to take my sleeping bag out with me just to keep my feet in it for the night to keep them warm. Two guys at a time were assigned to the outposts for one eight or ten hour shift. One guy slept while the other guy watched and listened for a two hour watch. We alternated throughout the night. It was very quiet most of the time, but now and then we could hear the crump of mortars, the crash of incoming artillery or small arms fire fights along the front line. Sometimes the sky on the lines just to the north of us was lit up by flares dropped from planes or fired by our artillery. Some star shells were lobbed in over enemy lines from the large guns on a cruiser or battle wagon near the coast.

One night I was on duty in the outpost with a guy I didn't know. In the middle of the night, while he was supposed to be on watch while I slept, I woke up and found him sound asleep. I was so mad I slammed into him to wake him up. "For God's sake", I growled," Do you want to get us killed? Don't you know that it's a court martial offense to be sleeping on post? You could get ten years breaking rocks at Portsmouth. I'm going to run you up to Captain's Mast first thing in the morning." I was already a corporal now and could do it, but I didn't. I just told him the next day that I would turn him in if it ever happened again and I warned anyone else who had to stand watch with him all night. This was a problem for all of us because we had to work all day every day, no matter how many hours we were awake on watch at night.

Another advantage of the thermal boot was some small protection from injury from certain types of antipersonnel mines. One mine in particular was small, but did enough damage to remove victims to the hospital unit and sometimes even from Korea. It was known as the Schu mine, perhaps developed in Germany. We had some of our guys step on the Schu mine which could blow off a foot or severely damage it. When it went off, it also threw stones and dirt straight up into your crotch, severely bruising or even lacerating your private parts and the skin on your inside thighs. They said that aching balls took the mind off more serious injuries.

According to our corpsmen, the new thick boots offered some degree of protection to the foot if we stepped on a Schu, mine. However, they offered little protection from the M-3 type antipersonnel mine. The docs noticed the difference in treating victims. However, the damage to the crotch was still devastating from a Schu mine. This reminds me of a story I heard at the restaurant where I used to hang out in Detroit. Most of the customers were Finlanders from Upper Michigan who had just been discharged from the service in 1945. One Finn I knew was just out and still in uniform wearing a Purple Heart among his other ribbons.

The well meaning waitress was staring at his decorations while he ordered a big ice cream sundae with all the trimmings. While her gaze was fixed on his chest, order pad in hand she asked, "Crushed nuts?" He looked at her eyeing his Purple Heart and said, "Hell no, shrapnel in the ass." I can't imagine anyone who stepped on a Schu mine finding this story funny, except maybe now. Now that I think about it, he may have had an encounter with a Schu mine. I recall reading about Lee Marvin talking about the wound he received from a Japanese sniper. Marvin was a rifleman in a Marine Raider Battalion in the Pacific Islands campaign. He was hit in the ass and it bothered him, because it is difficult to explain how that could happen. He is the only movie star I have ever considered as a tough guy in real life. I might add Steve McQueen to that.

I remember a couple of other small incidents while we were working on the ridge road over the south rim. It was so cold up there that we usually had to have a fire in a small drum going most of the time so the guys could warm up their hands. We used diesel fuel for this because it was safer. One day a guy had been cleaning some parts with gasoline and without thinking walked over and pitched the contents of a quart can of it on our fire. The flames leaped back to his can and then he spilled the rest on himself in a panic. We knocked him to the ground to roll him around trying to put out the flames on his clothes. He was thrashing around violently and almost threw himself off the road. If he had done that he would have been a goner, the slope was that steep and hundreds of feet to the bottom. We wrestled him back and proceeded to roll him over and over until the flames were out.

When it was really cold, I would sit on top of the compressor while it was running. If I sat with my legs around the vertical exhaust stack on the LeRoi, I was able to keep my legs and my hands warm. One day I watched the crews working from my warm perch. We were working in an area where there were a lot of trees just below our new road. The lieutenant decided that we could use some of the 15-inch pine logs for cribbing to hold up the side of the road in some bad spots. I watched as the guys from his platoon struggled to fell the trees with primer cord and naturally the logs always fell down hill. Then they had to hump them from there back up this steep slope to the road.

I told the lieutenant that I could speed things up if he would let me show them some tricks. He said OK and told one of his guys to get me the lengths of 1/4" and 1/2" ropes I asked for. When I worked for the city, we were not allowed to use ladders to climb trees, but used ropes, especially one called a swing line. In order to get into the tree we used a 1/4" throwing line. We made a small ball out of the rope and then using loosely held coils of line, threw the little bundle 50 or 60 feet with accuracy. When the bundle got over a limb and fell down the other side, it unraveled and the end came down to where we can reach it.

When the lieutenant selected a tree, I threw the line over a limb and let the it fall loose. One of his guys at the base of the tree attached the half inch line to my throw line and we pulled it back up over the limb and back to us. I got the other end of the half incher and made a running bowline on itself and had a guy near me pull it up so the noose tightened around the trunk up high. Meanwhile the demo guys at the base of the tree wrapped their primer cord around the trunk several times. We secured the half inch line to the back of a truck, took up the slack and signaled the demo types. They yelled, "Fire in the Hole" and let her rip. We heard the blast and pulled the top of the tree over to the edge of the road. Then the truck snaked it up to the road. The lieutenant asked me why a truck driver had to show his rigger how to do his job. I told him his rigger probably never trimmed trees. After that the rigger had it down pat and dozens of trees were blown over and hauled up that way.

The only other thing I remember about working on that road was a mean trick that the demo guys pulled on me, although they swear that it was a purely innocent oversight. After the crew finished drilling, I always put all of the equipment away or worked on maintenance of the pneumatic stuff while the demo crew loaded the holes with explosives, set the blasting caps and the fuses or wires. Then I pulled my rig around a few bends in the road where it wouldn't be hit with falling rocks. Sometimes I would walk back down to where they were working and BS with the NCO in charge.

One day I was on my way back to the compressor rig on foot from where they worked, when I had to take a dump. So I climbed up the side of the road angling away from the blast site and when I got to where I thought I was far enough away, I dropped my drawers and proceeded to relieve myself between my boondockers. I was squatting and reading an old copy of Stars and Stripes. Instead of toilet paper, I carried newspaper sports page clippings in my pockets, especially those articles explaining why the Red Wings lost a game. Those are what I called hockey tickets and I would end up cleaning my butt with them.

I was about half way through with my leisurely dump, when I heard someone yell, "Fire in the Hole!" For all I know they also added, " This one's for you Bones." Then came the blast and the ground shook, I didn't know which way to go, but I started away from the blast with my pants at half mast, when rocks started coming down all around. Fortunately, I was only pelted with some little stuff, dirt clods mostly and I had my helmet on as soon as I heard the shout. Now I know what that old Marine expression means when they say to snap shit. We had a big argument when I came down, but the only thing hurt was my feelings. I was constipated for a few days afterwards. For some reason or other, my pucker string was not functioning well at all.

During the middle of winter I was detailed to drive a dump truck down to Battalion on a shower run. I didn't mind because I had a rare chance to take a hot shower myself. On the way back it was late in the day and some of the snow melt had frozen in a thin sheet of ice all across the road for a few hundred feet. I had a lieutenant in the cab and about 20 guys in the back of the truck, including Sam Camarato and Jim Milliken.

I saw the black ice coming up so shifted into low as we crept downhill. I kept the truck as close to the mountain wall on my left to keep it away from the edge of the cliff. Because we had cut the road on a slight cant to drain water off to the side, the truck started sliding slowly sideways toward the cliff edge. The officer had everyone pile off and they stayed near the cutbank while I inched the thing off the ice. Then they crept down hugging the up slope rock face and reboarded the truck when it was safe. Nice guys they were, with no thought for the driver. We had to do that a few more times before reaching the bottom. We decided then that taking a shower wasn't worth the risk. We'd wait until spring thaw.

That reminds me of something the Finlanders used to say about the non Finns who lived around them in the Copper Country of Houghton and Keewenaw Counties in the northernmost part of Upper Michigan. The non Finns used to put their long johns on in September and never took them off until spring thaw. The Finns said that the non Finns would then just take off their outer clothes and stand in a good stiff wind in May to blow away the shreds of their rotten long johns. The Finns thought all these other people up there were genuine cruds. Even though the Finns only took a sauna bath once a week, even in the depth of winter, they were the cleanest people I've ever met. They couldn't believe how the other lumberjacks lived without bathing all winter.

Another driving problem was dense fog in the early morning hours, a daily occurrence in certain seasons. Much like the Thule fog in California, the Korean fog usually burned off by noon. In some cases where we had to work our men and equipment out in front of the lines or clearly visible to enemy FOs just behind our lines, the fog was a blessing. Fog also gave our infantry a chance to strengthen their fortifications on the MLR and in the various outposts. Naturally the enemy was able to do the same thing since they were protected from air attacks by the shroud of fog. In the early hours of daylight as viewed from the south rim, the Punchbowl resembled a huge bowl of white soup. Whenever we woke up to dense fog it was always eerily quiet. It made me think of the meaning of the word Korea, "The Land of The Morning Calm." Try to explain that to all those who served in Korea from June 1950 to July 1953. They don't believe it.

During that short period between the end of Korean winter and the beginning of spring, we began work on an emergency airstrip in the middle of the Punchbowl where the terrain was flat enough for a long stretch. The engineer officers had no geological maps to work from and nothing was known about the subsoil as we began to clear the area and haul in fill. The substrate behaved something like permafrost. When we began work in the early mornings dumping truck loads of aggregates and spreading them out and compacting the stuff with the graders and dozers everything looked great. On some days, however, when the sun warmed up the soil, the fill we put on the surface began to disappear, sinking into the subsoil. I remember only two planes landing there and one must have been in the morning hours.

We had all of our equipment out working on the strip one day when a plane came over and scared the hell out of us. We thought we were going to be strafed. It looked like a P-51 Mustang, but we saw only a circular red emblem on the wings and on the sides of the fuselage. That made us think it might be a communist plane. It made several low passes over us and the lieutenant decided it was a friendly one in trouble and the pilot wanted us to get our butts and our gear off the field so he could land.

We pulled everything off to the side of the strip and he came in landing with his wheels up in a controlled crash. The P-51 went off the end of the strip and through a few rice paddy dikes before coming to a stop. The pilot was spirited away by some of our Air Force types who materialized out of nowhere. We crowded around to get a look at the plane. The red emblem we had seen turned out to be a depiction of a Springbok in a red circle. It was an African gazelle, the symbol of the South African Air Force. Because Marines were loose in the area, the USAF sent out their own guards to watch over the damaged aircraft until it could be hauled away. It was a good thing, because some of our engineers were already eying the radio and fingering the machine guns.

The only other plane I saw on the strip was a crash-landed Marine Corsair F4U fighter used in close air support along the lines. It had also come in with its wheels up, probably because the strip looked unsafe from the air for the pilot to chance a wheels down landing.

Among some other things that I remembered happening in the Punchbowl included two instances of artillery units moving in on us without any advanced notice to us. For all I know, our Skipper was advised about the placement of these batteries and he probably told his platoon leaders, but nobody bothered to tell the troops. This was very typical of the military. Here we were, a bunch of peons in the middle of a war and nobody tells us a damn thing. We were never told where we were when we set up camp. We were never told why we were moving out, nor where we were headed. Forty five years later as I read about the Korean War or see documentary films about that war, I learn much more about the whole situation.

After I left the Corps I spent many years working for federal, state, county, city, and with many foreign governments. I came to appreciate an unauthorized patch I wore on one part of my Arizona Game and Fish uniform when I was in the field where my supervisor couldn't see it. It had a mushroom in the middle and around the periphery were the words "I must be a mushroom, all they do is keep me in the dark and feed me bullshit." It is very appropriate for government work.

In one case, we were working on a construction project in the middle of the Punchbowl, when we were surprised to see a Marine weapons carrier (WC) drive up towing a set of about 24 rocket launching tubes on a small trailer. They unhooked the trailer from the WC, loaded all of the tubes with 4.5-inch rockets while the gunner in charge aimed the unit to the north (at the Chinese front or maybe their rear?). They were doing all this some 50 yards away from us and we were fascinated, because we had never seen rockets used before. When they fired them off, the rockets swooshed away towards the enemy lines one row at a time, each rocket leaving a trail of smoke all the way from the launching tubes. We had stopped working to watch this whole thing unfold.

The crew chief of the rocket detail shouted, "Hey, you guys had better haul ass like we're going to do right now. The Koreans can figure out where these things came from by the trail of smoke and they'll fire back on this place. So clear out." With that, his voice was drowned out by a Marine Sikorsky chopper swooping in to hover over the launch tubes. The tube launcher trailer was hooked to a cable from the chopper, which lifted off and disappeared over the south rim. The rocket crew jumped into their WC and drove off south in a cloud of dust. We piled our tools into our truck and beat it back to camp. We heard later that there was some counter fire on the launch site area shortly after we pulled out.

One night I was sound asleep when a loud BLAM shook the ground, the tent, my sack and my teeth. We all jumped up wide awake, most of us saying, "What the fuck was that?" Then there were more blasts and some guys, especially the short timers, jammed their helmets on and were already into their holes just outside the tent. There were more blasts coming from across the road next to our camp. It wasn't incoming mail, it was outgoing. After we had gone to bed the night before, part of a Marine 105mm howitzer battery had set up there to carry out fire missions. We didn't know that they were there until they began to fire at about 0300 hours. I had never heard a cannon go off while I was right under the muzzle and it scared the crap out of me. I'm sure that the Skipper knew they were there, but no one told us. Our tents were close to the damn guns so we got the brunt of the racket.

Anyone who never had to drive or maintain a vehicle in subzero conditions, has missed a challenge. When you wake up in the morning living in a tent and have to go to work when the temperature outside might be hovering around 40 to 50 below zero, do you really think your truck will start? What about the diesel engines on the dozers, grader and tracked loader? Diesel fuel has a much lower flash point than gasoline. A chemical was added to diesel supplies at the battalion fuel dump to maintain proper viscosity. Diesel fuel can thicken to a gel below -25° below zero. As the weather proceeded to get colder day by day into the beginning of winter we had to learn the hard way. We found out that we had almost no antifreeze on hand when the freeze came in force. A typical military snafu. It took almost a month for us to receive a delivery of antifreeze from somewhere in the depths of X corps.

In the meantime, we tried several things to cope with the lack of antifreeze. We left the trucks and jeeps idling off and on all night, which can't be good for the engines. We tried the same thing with the diesels on the tractors and grader, although I understand that idling for many hours is not good for these high compression engines. Running the engines off and on all night long also required a guy on watch to start them up and shut them off every hour or so. Lt. Zarzeka had us drain the cat engines after work and put the water from the cooling system in the 40 gallon cans we used to wash our mess kits in after chow. These cans had immersion burners that burned kerosene, so the water could be kept from freezing in the mess tent. In the morning the water was cooled so it would not crack the blocks when returned to the engines. We also had immersion burners mounted on our water tank trailers to keep our drinking water from freezing.

When the antifreeze arrived, we still had problems with frozen gas lines and the 90 weight lubricating fluid thickening in the transmissions, transfer cases, and differentials. To solve this problem, the men on motor pool night watch had to move each vehicle back and forth every couple of hours to prevent the 90 weight from solidifying. Another reason for us to lose some sleep.

In the middle of winter we received a new gadget that promised to solve all our problems with starting up vehicles in the morning. It was a slave kit, a square metal box about as big as a desk. It contained a fuel tank, a firebox, a 2" flexible metal tube, and a dozen 12 volt batteries mounted in series to crank any but the biggest engines. Before this gizmo arrived, we had to pull every truck with whatever tractor was running and sometimes we used a truck to pull the Allis Chalmers tracked loader to get it started.

The slave kit could be carried in the back of a weapons carrier or a Jeep trailer and turned out to be very efficient in getting us on the road every day. The battery setup allowed us to crank all the vehicle motors. The heat from the firebox was applied from a blower through the flex tube to frozen fuel lines, fuel pumps, and carburetors to get the gas moving to the motor.

Usually the small gasoline pony engines on the big diesels were enough to get them going. If there was a problem, the slave kit was used on the pony. Otherwise we either used some starter fluid (igniter) or ether in the diesels to get them running. Some diesel engines had a special port or device for delivering the ether or other starting fluid to the cylinder. The usual method was to place an ether capsule into the device, then push down on the plunger. This squashed the capsule sending the ether fumes into the cylinders to enable the operator to start the engine. Once it begins firing, the high compression of the engines keeps it going on diesel fuel while it warms up.

Another event that I recall was a phony operation to lure the enemy into a trap. Most of the entire 1stMarDiv and allied units participated in this charade. I didn't even know that it had a name (Operation Mole) until two years ago when I read, "*The Coldest War*" by James Brady.

The Divisional planners were bored with the inactivity along the lines brought about by the miserable subzero winter weather. On specified days we made a great show of trucks hauling troops and equipment away from the front lines to the rear, as though the whole of X Corps was withdrawing from the MLR. We had convoys of covered trucks going out (each with a few guys sitting near the tailgate) over the south rim road in plain view of the Chinese forward observers . During the next two nights we drove the trucks back over the pass in the dark, using our blackout lights where needed, as we inched along the road trying to stay as far away from the black void at the edge. Some infantry units also hoofed it out over the pass during the day and then hiked during the night back up to the line.

As far as I could tell, nothing happened. The Chinese and North Koreans opposing us either didn't fall for it, or were just too cold to want to move out of their warm bunkers. Some of the guys in our company who worked up on the MLR with the line companies told us what was going on from time to time along the front during the winter. One cat skinner was John Chapin who told me about his work up there. He was there working on that road for days after the old catskinners blazed the trail. At night it was -42° F. and the TD-18 dozer had to be left idling all night. The ground was frozen down to a depth of eight feet. In order for him to use his dozer, the demolition men set off shape charges to loosen the ground into huge pieces of frozen soil and rock, some as big as a car. These were shoved over the side by the TD-18 until the road was completed. Jim Milliken reminds me that when the tanks first climbed up that new road, he and other engineers had to walk alongside to throw large rocks behind the tank's treads to stop it from sliding back down hill. Tanks have as much trouble on icy slopes as wheeled vehicles and infantry.

After the road up to the lines was finished, the wounded could be removed more quickly and supplies hauled up to the troops. Chapin stayed up there with his dozer to create firing pits for tanks right on the ridge line. The tank would pull in to the pit at night with the top of the turret and only the barrel of the 90mm cannon protruding. At first light, the spotters among the riflemen would show the tankers exactly where to find the embrasures of the Chinese bunkers on the next ridge and they would fire a few rounds of high explosive (HE) directly into them. The tank would then pull back, while the nearest troops hunkered down for any incoming fire from the north. The distance between the opposing front lines here was about one thousand yards—from our ridge to theirs. There were several firing pits along the line for the tank to move to each night. The Chinese could anticipate a round or two in the morning, because they could hear the tank rumbling around in the dark. Maybe this was designed to keep them awake at night. This harassing fire didn't seem to phase the enemy, since their bunkers were a part of a complex where they could retreat when things got hot.

The day that I saw the 8 inch self-propelled howitzer going north past our camp, I supposed that they were going to try to use it for direct fire from the tank pits up on the line. A direct hit with one of those shells would surely destroy a bunker. I was sure glad that big howitzer didn't set up next to us. It would have made the 105mm sound like popguns. I was also happy to know that the 155mm guns of the 11th Marines were somewhere else. Those Long Toms also made a lot of noise when they were fired. Our Army also used some 240mm howitzers. I didn't know those big mothers existed. My brother Tom watched some of these big guns in the battle for Manila. They were angled down to nearly horizontal and firing point blank at Intramuros, the Walled City. He said that the racket was deafening for bystanders, but the pounding was fatal for the Japanese holding the old fort. Unfortunately a lot of Filipino civilians also died there because the Japanese wouldn't let them out of the enclosed area.

I didn't know until a few years ago that my cousin (Cmdr. Bob Lawson) served up on the lines as a Forward Air Controller (FAC) while I was in the Punchbowl. Bob guided his fellow carrier pilots in on enemy positions. He volunteered to spend a few weeks up front with a Marine regiment. I thought that was pretty noble of him. I guess even flying a fighter bomber gets boring sometimes.

One of our engineers told me he watched one air strike by Navy and Marine carrier planes where they were dropping napalm on enemy positions. Right afterward he said, the Chinese would come out of their bunkers to make a big show of warming their hands near the oily flames. I guess they were trying to give us the impression that we couldn't kill them all.

One other work detail we were involved in when we first set up camp in the Punchbowl, was to find and destroy any possible cover that stay behinds or infiltrators could hide in and operate from. The 1stMarDiv had proclaimed an area three miles behind their lines to be free of all civilians. Any Korean civilians found there were suspected to be working for the enemy and could be knocked off on sight. However, I believe those found were held for the MPs to escort back south away from us. I transported the crews out looking for caves, bunkers, houses, or anything else we could demolish to deny cover. Most of the caves and bunkers were blown up by the demolition men. The bulldozer took care of the farm houses. Sometimes they just pushed them over and crushed them, or looped the winch cable around the whole building and pulled it down in a heap. Once the guys discovered a woman and a baby, both dead inside a house. I suppose they were the victims of the last battle that took the Punchbowl. The crew boss ordered the house burned for obvious reasons.

MINES

We did have evidence most of the time that infiltrators were at work behind the lines, although they could have been stay-behinds passed by in the push north. Dog Company (1stEngrBn) had reported that they were finding land mines, usually antitank, on the road that passed by their camp miles away to the east outside the Punchbowl. One platoon leader in another engineer letter company was severely injured when his weapons carrier hit a mine in the road. These roads had all been checked when they came into the area and all mines cleared. Months later, someone was still planting them at night even though the engineers checked the road daily for new mines. Another one of our companies had reported finding a newly laid mine right in the middle of their motor pool compound.

After those mine incidents we placed sandbags on the floor boards in all our vehicles and in the beds of the trucks used to haul troops. As far as I know, all of our casualties in Able Co. were caused by mines, booby traps or other explosives. One Marine, PFC. James Peveto, a heavy equipment trainee, was killed when he stepped on a mine 11-14-51. One of the rock bridges we built across a stream in the Punchbowl was dedicated to him with a sign on the abutment.

Another victim I remember well was a demolition man who was also quite a gymnast. Cpl. "Fitz" Fitzhugh was a handsome guy with a handlebar mustache and a great build. Whenever we were in a camp for more than a month, he set up some tall poles rigged with guy wires for his rings. He knew all of the tricks that one sees performed by professional acrobats, circus performers and the gymnasts in the Olympic games. One day he was on a mine clearing detail when a booby trapped, booby trap under a Chinese mine went off while he was disarming it. Both of his hands was blown off. He suffered facial wounds and was almost blinded. There went his career and his hobby in a flash.

One of our corpsmen was out with a mine clearing detail and as usual was standing by at a safe distance away in case he was needed. He hadn't learned the rule yet, that once you settle into a safe place, you remember the path to it and back out again. He was restless and decided to go sit somewhere else where he could watch the team at work. This time he sat down on a mine.

All mines are bad, but a bounding mine is really nasty. The bouncing Betty (BB) was designed so that once it was tripped, you could hardly get away from the shrapnel when it exploded. When activated, the main part of the BB is propelled straight up to a height of about three feet and explodes, spraying the area with shrapnel. Ordinarily when someone knows they have tripped a mine, everyone hits the deck to try to avoid being hit by the shrapnel coming sideways and up. This action does not save you from a bouncing Betty in the air. There is no escape. All you can hope for is minor wounds if you weren't too close to it.

After he tripped the BB, the corpsman probably realized that he had set off a mine and was briefly paralyzed with fear. The BB had hit him in the buns, prompting him to move, but a few seconds later it exploded on the ground spraying him with shrapnel as he stood up. It was a loss that touched everyone. When a Navy recruit decided to become a corpsman, he probably never thought he would be doing this kind of dangerous work with the USMC. Each of our corpsmen played an important role in our morale.

There may have been other casualties that I don't recall. For one thing, I was never present when someone was badly injured. It always happened on some other work detail. The victim was given first aid by the other guys, or the corpsman assigned to the detail, and then evacuated to the nearest Aid Station by vehicle—or helicopter if one was available. The victim never came back. If he survived, he went to a Navy field hospital or Army MASH unit, then off to a hospital ship, or on to a hospital in Japan and then to the USA.

Dealing with mines is a primary responsibility of a combat engineer company. When not placing mines for defense, they do the more dangerous work of removing mines. Every time our line units advanced to establish a new MLR, the troops dug in defensive positions, established fields of fire, and set out mines and trip flares. If the MLR remained static for a long period, mine fields were expanded and barbed wire stretched in front. Listening and observation posts were established well out in front, and protected with a perimeter of mines and trip flares.

Our engineers helped the line companies place mines and trip flares, stretch and secure barbed wire, and fortify bunkers. Infantry units are capable of handling the mines and barbed wire, but they appreciated the help of combat engineers to speed up the job so they could get on with patrols. Whenever a mine field was set, the man in charge drew a map of the layout showing exactly where every mine is and the type. He also indicated on the map where the safe lane was for our patrols to get safely through the mine field. Patrols tried to leave and return in the dark. Otherwise, enemy observers could watch their movement in daylight and learn where to send their patrols through our mine fields. The map played an important role in mine removal. Even with the map, it is possible that a few mines might be overlooked in the clearing process and pose a threat later.

All the talk nowadays about trying to forbid our military forces from using mines is pure nonsense. It is about time that civilians stop telling the military their business. Publicity about civilians being injured by carelessly planted mines by irresponsible people is quite touching. No one wants innocent civilians, especially children killed, and maimed by mines. However, those placing the mines are completely uncaring about those injured by their mines. The Cambodians are a case in point. All sides in the conflict between the Khmer Rouge, the Vietnamese Army and the various Cambodian governments planted mines all over the countryside. They were intended to kill soldiers, but more often than not civilians were killed or injured. According to the January 1999 issue of Parade Magazine there are over sixty million mines laying around in various countries.

For many years after the Korean War ended, farmers and other civilians were being killed and maimed by odd mines still buried all over Korea. This type of horror can best be avoided by designing new mines with a predictable time for them to render themselves inactive. At the moment, Korea is one of the few places in the world with a wide field of densely packed mines running from coast to coast along the Demilitarized Zone (DMZ).

I worked in Egypt on different assignments during the period 1978 to 1983. The last war between the Israelis and the Egyptians was in 1973. However, there were still warnings about mines along the shore running from Port Said on the Mediterranean down the Suez Canal and well past the port of Suez to distant beaches along the Red Sea. I was surprised to see evidence of mines at the beach of Ain Soukna. This was a popular beach on the Red Sea because it was closest to Cairo for tourists. The first thing we saw when we parked the car was a large area with barbed wire a foot or so high around it and rusting signs hanging from it saying, DANGER MINES. Whenever we went there we only parked where there were other cars and walked in the sand where bathers had already trod. On the beach we stayed close to where all the other people were sitting.

Every now and then while in Egypt I heard of civilians being killed or injured by mines. In some cases it was tourists walking where there were no warning signs or barbed wire. Sometimes it was an oil company exploration truck and crew that was blown up. In one case, I read of seven Egyptian laborers becoming casualties from exploding mines while clearing a beach of debris for a construction project near Port Said.

Most of my counterparts in Egypt had served many years in the Egyptian Army and had been in one of the wars with Israel. When I asked them why their Army didn't clear their own mines from the beaches and elsewhere, they had a stock answer. The Israelis left them there. I know Israelis and they would never leave anything of value or that could be carried away. If the Israelis planted mines anywhere it would have been on the Bar-Lev defensive line on the Sinai along the west bank of the Suez Canal. When the Israelis finally pulled out of the Sinai, they took everything with them except concrete walls. They stripped buildings of all wood, metal, plastic, glass, etc. and took it with them. I can't imagine them leaving even one mine.

It is more likely that after the last war with Israel was over, the Egyptian troops were eager to go home and no one thought about clearing all of the mines they had planted over the years. The soldiers with the maps of the mine fields took them home and forgot about it. In the ensuing years, no one wanted to take the responsibility of clearing the mines so they were just left there, with or without signs and barbed wire. It would have been a good training exercise for their engineers to find all those mines and disarm them.

Korean war era land mines were mainly of two types: antitank and antipersonnel. The Chinese and North Koreans employed antitank mines against us because we had tanks. The enemy used tanks very little in '51/ '52, so we rarely used antitank mines and only on roads where there might be enemy truck traffic. The enemy's antitank mines were made of wood and plastic, making it very difficult to find them with a mine detector designed to locate buried metal. Antitank mines could damage a tank, usually blowing off a tread which immobilized the tank and endangered the crew as they bailed out. Antitank mines would wreck a truck and obliterate a Jeep. The driver and passengers would either be killed or seriously wounded.

Antipersonnel mines in use at that period had two main ways of triggering them. One was by pressure, i.e. stepping on the activation mechanism, the other by trip wires. The trip wire is tied to the trigger device and the other end secured to a tree, stake or other fixed object. If the trip wire strung across path has the least bit of slack in it, it is a mine where the pin must be pulled out to set it off. Thus we knew how to deal with disarming it. However, if the wire across the trail was taut, it was most likely a device where the striker was driven home to set it off when the wire was broken or tension released.

The mine used most often was the M-3 antipersonnel mine, a rectangular block of steel, loaded with explosive. When the mine was triggered, it spread a wide swath of small pieces of hot steel, guaranteed to ruin your day. They were usually buried just under the ground surface.

Troops on patrol always carried a long thin stick held loosely in the hand with the business end close to the ground. Sometimes the point man carried the stick and examined the ground for telltale signs of a mine being buried nearby. This proved awkward for the point, because he had to concentrate his vision forward for signs of the enemy. The infantry may have solved this problem by having two men on the point, one watching ahead and the other with the stick and looking for signs of mines. If the stick suddenly jumped out of his hand, he then looked for the trip wire and traced the wire to find the mine and check it out before disarming it. If there was an engineer along, he took care of the mine so the infantry could keep moving. Most of the engineers from our platoons never went out to work without their walking sticks.

Clearing mines is always a lot trickier than laying them. When our infantry moved up in a push, engineers came into the old positions to clear the mine fields in front of the MLR and the outposts. The job was easier if we had been involved in planting the mines because we had our own map. Otherwise we were given the map the line unit made when they laid the mines. We had to be extra careful if we got involved in clearing mines that had been planted by allied forces and we trusted their maps of mine fields more if some of their personnel helped in the clearing.

Clearing mine fields that had been placed in front of and around enemy positions was the worst job of all. As our infantry took those positions, engineers went to work locating and disarming these mines, while others went forward with the line company to assist in putting out new mines and trip flares. Most engineer casualties occurred while trying to locate and disarm enemy mines. The team of engineers first fixed on the most likely places for mines in relation to each enemy bunker, foxhole, and barbed wire array, etc. They also looked carefully for trip wires and booby traps.

Because most of the Chinese mines were nonmetallic, the metal detector was useless. When Cpls. Milliken and Lopez were using a mine detector just north of the Punchbowl, the instrument was signaling constantly where no mines were found. This particular site had been fought over so much that the ground was loaded with shrapnel giving false positive readings on the detector. While they were working up on the line, Big Jim Milliken's crew ran across two enemy soldiers who surrendered to the engineer detail. In 1950 and '51, I think there were quite a few Marine engineers wounded by incoming rounds while working along the lines. I know that Big Jim was knocked unconcious and wounded in the back on a working party on the north rim of the Punchbowl.

When a suspected mine area was found, it was marked off to define its limits and the crew went to work on their hands and knees gently probing the soil carefully with a bayonet. When a probe touched something, the soil was carefully brushed aside until the top of the mine was seen. If it was one they've seen before, they knew how to render it safe. If not, they checked it out and figured out how to disarm it. The dirt was carefully removed from around the mine and under the edges at the bottom looking for a booby trap—another mine rigged to go off when the disarmed mine was lifted. Mine clearing is not for the faint hearted. It takes a great deal of patience and a steady hand to do it safely. Some guys on a mine clearing detail always carried a variety of metal pins, wires, and small nails to push into the safety pin holes on the mine's triggering device.

Another problem our troops faced with mines was trying to plant or remove them in winter when the ground was frozen solid for a foot or so. This was a problem in Europe in WWII in winter and in the coral atolls of the South Pacific where the Marines couldn't even dig foxholes into the hard coral. Under all these conditions, if they were in a hurry, the mine would be hidden behind rocks or hidden under frozen bushes

(Korea) and armed with a trip wire across a path. I've heard of mines going off on their own during extremes of temperature. The frozen soil, or the metal parts in the activator, could contract setting the mine off. On the other hand, the summers in Korea were blistering hot and some older mines would explode from the intense heat. Heavy clay soil also has a tendency to expand and heave when it is wet, which could set off a mine.

Sgt. Hepinger who lived in my tent, reminds me of one humorous incident with a mine in the Punchbowl. We had a technical sergeant who was hunting pheasants with a bird dog. While the NCO walked the dikes with his shotgun, his dog turned to cut across the paddy field and triggered a mine. The dog was blown up into the air and away from the explosion and landed unharmed, but dazed. No one was hurt by the blast, but those who saw it happen got a good laugh over the flying dog.

Our troops in WWII and in Vietnam had to cope with artillery shells that enemy soldiers rigged as mines. The son of General Chesty Puller, Lewis B. Puller, Jr. was a Platoon leader in Vietnam. He triggered a 105mm shell hidden near a trail while on patrol resulting in the loss of both his legs.

Except for the unfortunate accidents with mines and booby traps, we were generally a pretty healthy bunch. I think It had something to do with all of those shots we had to take earlier. Because of my work with equipment, my hands were always full of grease, oil and dirt. So were my clothes, which had to be washed often in gasoline, then boiled in a five gallon can of soapy water. Most of the time we were working in the field where there was no place to wash, so we just ate our meals with dirty hands. In the winter the only water around anyway was frozen. In warmer weather, if a Korean labor unit was nearby, one of the local work-ers, usually a small kid, would take our laundry down to a stream and beat the dirt out with a rock or a stick for whatever we wanted to pay them. We usually gave them some food, cigarettes, or candy bars.

During my year in Korea, I had to go back only twice to the USN Field Hospital in the rear near Battalion HQ. Once it was due to a car-buncle or some such huge boil that persisted on the back of my neck for months. At the hospital, a bunch of large tents like those seen in the MASH series on TV, a doctor looked at it and gave me some black salve, that looked like axle grease. I asked him what to do if it didn't work. He said I had to come back to see him and he would cut out the core. He showed me how it is done on an orange, "See, I just cut and X over the core with a scalpel. Then peel back these four pieces of skin, like so and then reach in and pluck out the core. That will be the end of it. Very simple." I used that salve and the thing disappeared although I firmly believe that the doctor scared it out of me with his description of how he would handle it. I didn't want anyone cutting on me.

The other time I had to go to the USN Hospital was with a severe toothache. My previous experience with Navy dentists was that they spent precious little time fooling around with fixing the teeth of Marines. It was no different here in Korea. The solution to my toothache was to pull a couple of the offending molars. but first he gave me an injection of antibiotics. Then the Novocaine, then out with the two teeth. I asked him why the antibiotics. He said that Korea was a filthy place and it was called for whenever they drew blood, broke the skin, or pulled a tooth. There were just too many pathogens in the air to take any chances.

I have a different view of Navy dentists now that I learned of one friend, who was assigned to serve as a doctor at a Marine Battalion Aid Station right next to the lines in 1953 before the war ended. There must have been a shortage of MDs at the time so they used a dentist to prepare the wounded and stabilize them for transfer back to the Navy Field Hospital. If it had been me, I would have complained that a judgement was being made that a doctor's life was more valuable than a dentist's. After all, the Battalion Aid Stations were dangerous places to work.

There was a problem with malaria in Korea and we were given chloroquine tablets to take as a suppressive. We took them regularly once a week or so with our meals. The stuff tasted absolutely awful and the only way we could get it down was to push it into a piece of food and swallow that. The corpsman stood at one end of the chow line to dole them out. The Div. HQ and the Medical Staff noted that there was a significant incidence of malaria during the summer of '51, which should not have occurred. They figured that this was due to the troops not taking their suppressives. The word came down to each company to have the Corpsman stand in the chow line and place the tablet in your mouth and watch you swallow it. I still insisted on stuffing it into a wad of bread, a slice of a canned peach, or some such. It was like having communion with the Corpsman officiating.

At that time we understood that the chloroquine suppressed the symptoms of malaria, if we caught it, so that we could carry on our work until we went home. Then if malarial symptoms appeared when we came off the drug we could be treated to get rid of the parasites..

Another way of controlling malaria was to spray areas where troops were concentrated with a fog of DDT. At the time we didn't know that DDT was dangerous to us as well as for mosquitos. The first time we were fogged, I thought we had a USMC Sikorsky helicopter coming in to crash in our compound. First we heard it approaching and then noticed that as it got closer it was spewing out white smoke from the exhausts. Then the whole camp disappeared in a white cloud of DDT and fuel smoke. The sanitary types in the helicopter were mixing DDT in some light type of oil and bleeding the mixture into the exhaust manifold of the chopper to vaporize it and create the fog. We could taste the insecticide as the fog settled into the camp to permeate every place where mosquitoes could hide. We also slept under mosquito nets at night.

THE LINE COMPANY AND THE ENGINEERS

The basic difference between an engineer company and a line company was that the infantry were in constant danger on the lines, and we, who were right behind them, were relatively safe. The infantrymen spent a lot of time out on patrols in no man's land probing the enemy defenses, trying to capture prisoners and gathering intelligence on enemy positions. We didn't have to do those things, because we were a technical support unit whose job it was to make things easier for the line companies. We did that by creating and maintaining the service roads to the front, building culverts, small bridges, airstrips, laying mine fields and stringing barbed wire in front of the MLR and the forward outposts or listening posts. We also helped the line companies in building their bunkers with timbers we brought up to them, and did anything else that we could to help them. We also had the capability to erect a steel Bailey bridge. I learned from our old salts that when our troops were evacuating the Chosin Reservoir, eight sections of a treadway bridge were dropped into the KotoRi perimeter and erected across a river by our engineers to speed up the movement of troops down to the coast. How they did it without a crane is beyond me. An old company salt named Charlie told us that he and his partner were given the job to hang around those bridges on that road until the last UN soldier and Marine were across, then dropped them with explosives so the Chinese couldn't use them. Enemy troops were already coming across one bridge when they destroyed it. Engineers units spent much of their time in building things or blowing them up.

While we were in the Punchbowl, we would sometimes see a line company passing our camp on foot in two columns with men a good distance apart. They would either be from one of our own Marine Regiments or from the Korean Marine Regiment. If heading north, they were coming out of reserve and going back on the lines to replace another unit, which would then be heading south tomorrow or the next day. If they had a rest break near our camp or near where we were working on the road, the grunts would chat with us and we'd get them water or cigarettes. We would ask them why they were walking when there were trucks available. They usually said that their Battalion or Regimental CO wanted them to get some exercise after several months sitting in their bunkers. The only chance to get exercise up there was on patrol at night, pooping and snooping in front of the MLR.

Invariably one of them would ask us exactly what we did for a living and then ask how they could get a cushy job like ours. The guys from our platoons explained about all the hand labor they did and that over half of their work involved planting or clearing mines and mine fields, as well as locating and disarming booby traps. When the infantry types heard that, they thought it wasn't so cushy after all. The grunts were often asked if they wanted to trade places with our platoon men and they declined. The mine work that they had to do when engineers were not available was bad enough. They didn't want to have that kind of work every day. Sometimes they walked by in small groups escorting captured enemy soldiers south to the POW camp.

We noticed something that has occurred to all troops in the last few wars. When they were coming out of reserve and heading back to the lines, they were more cheerful and feisty on their hike going north than going south. When I went to visit Dick Hayes when his unit in the Seventh Marines was in reserve, I asked him about that. Speaking for most grunts there, he said that there was so much chickenshit routine under the guise of training that they were always glad to be back on the line where that kind of crap was out. Their job up there was to poop and snoop and fend off enemy probes and attacks. There was no room for that other nonsense. This same attitude was mentioned by ground forces involved in WWI and WWII. So there is some madness in this method of the Division Commander to give his line troops a rest and a shower and then piss them off with the details of military drill and training so that they would take it out on the enemy when they went back up front.

On the daily work routine we were at a slight disadvantage compared to the line companies. During the long cold winter of 1951-52, the lines (both those of the UN forces and the Chinese-North Korean armies) were fairly static. It was just too cold to be moving about much and there were attempts at the same time to engage the warring parties in truce talks. For the average Marine on the line, most of the action was spent out on patrols, which were highly perilous. He usually went out on these patrols often and mostly at night, for obvious reasons. When the guys on patrol came back just before dawn, they were debriefed by the platoon leader and intelligence officer, got some chow and could sometimes sack out for a while in the bunker on the rear slope of the ridge or in one right on the ridge. Others have said that they got very little sleep most of the time.

Our situation was quite different. We appreciated the fact that we didn't have to risk our lives out on patrol. However, we did have to work all day, every day for our year in country. We worked seven days a week, sometimes 10 and 12 hour days. On top of this we had to stand watches, usually guard duty, sometimes every other day or every third day. Our company strength was about 200 men, but we were always undermanned.

So instead of having to stand guard once a week if we had a full complement of men, we had the duty much more often and then worked all day the next day.

Standing guard duty is both absolutely necessary and extremely boring, but our problem was that we still had to go out on the job and put in a full shift the next day. After a few months of this it got to be a drag, although it did make the time pass a bit faster. Also, there was very little to do around camp if you had free time except catch up on the zzzzz's. And remember there was absolutely no place to go away from camp, except to the work site.

One might ask why we had to stand so much guard duty. Our camp was isolated from all other units in a place centrally located to all of our many work sites. A free standing camp needs security covering an entire 360 degree perimeter. For one day's duty, the camp required an officer of the day (OD), sergeant of the guard, corporal of the guard, then a number of shitbirds—corporals, PFCs, and privates to man the outposts, posts within the camp and roving patrols. The outposts were usually only manned from dusk to dawn with two men to a bunker alternating the watch in two hour shifts. All of the other posts were manned on four hour shifts through the hours of darkness. Whenever we set up camp the outer perimeter was skirted with trip flares, mines and sometimes barbed wire.

Our camp was in a combat zone, because we were within the range of enemy artillery and rocket fire. Most of our rocket and artillery fire (outgoing mail) came from somewhere to our rear. It is reasonable to assume, that if we could hit them from behind our camp, they could drop stuff on our artillery and rocket outfits with counter battery fire. Short rounds from either side could land on us.

A reasonable person would assume that we don't pull a formal guard mount in a combat zone,. Guard mount is a military ritual for installing and relieving the men on a guard post with the relief shift. Normally in this case, the NCO in charge of the guard for a particular day or shift holds a formation in front of the guard house, complete with an inspection of the guard complement by the OD. The guard unit is then marched around to the various posts where a smaller ritual takes place. The relief guard marches up to the one on post and asks for any special orders for this post. The relief may be told of any incidents that have occurred there in the past four hours and is then given any special orders. The relief takes up the post and the guard coming off duty marches off with the unit on its rounds until all posts are relieved.

We had a new young 2nd lieutenant who was an Annapolis graduate, and somewhat of a prick. Some of the Naval Academy grads who became USMC lieutenants were genuine pricks. They felt that they were the best of the best, even though they didn't know shit about life in the field. We should have known he was peculiar since he was one of the few in the company still wearing leggings. He seemed to think that we were very sloppy about manning the guard detail. I found this out in a surprise visit by the prick in the middle of the night when I was corporal of the guard. It was in January 1952 when the temperature outside was hovering around -45° F. with a howling wind bringing the cold down from Siberia.

Our NCO guard detail was huddled around a small stove in the large log room we used for a galley and the mess. In pops Lt. Prick and says, "Good morning men." He has his helmet on and is not sporting the black brassard with OD in large white letters. However we all know that he is the OD. He is also wearing his duty belt with holstered .45 Colt. Someone calls out, "Attention!" That is the first and last time I heard this command while in Korea. The lieutenant was eating it up.

He sees all of us wearing duty belts (our usual cartridge belts) and proceeds to ask what we are doing in here at this hour. One guy says he is the sergeant of the guard. I tell him I'm the corporal of the guard, another guy says he's the supernumerary. The latter is the guy who fills in if a guard falls ill and also serves as a runner or gofer. The OD says, "Well, that accounts for the inside element of the guard, and what would you be doing in here?" he asks the other PFC. "I'm on post number five, sir." he says, remaining at attention. " And where is post No. Five?", the OD asks. The PFC. replies, " It's the roving patrol between posts 3 and 4, sir." "Then what are you doing in here ?" he wanted to know. "I just came in for a second sir, to get warm. My face was all frozen and the bolt on my rifle was freezing up too," he said.

Lt. Prick said that he was going to run us up. That meant the guilty PFC and myself were to be charged with dereliction of duty or some other type of military BS. We would have to report to Captain's Mast for a preliminary hearing and a sort of court process all rolled into one. He was charged with leaving his post, while on duty and I was charged with allowing him to do so.

At the Captain's Mast, each of us—the PFC, myself and Lt. Prick—told our version of events. The Skipper asked me if I actually placed this PFC on his post. I said no, that the custom since I had been in country for the last five months was for the sergeant or the corporal of the guard, or both, to take the guard duty roster around to each Marine on it and explain exactly what post he was to be on and the time he had to be there to relieve the man on duty. He was also told what time to expect his relief and who it would be. He was then asked if he had any questions about his post. Again the day of his guard duty, the sergeant of the guard would go around with the duty list once again to each man and be sure that he understood what time to be on duty and the location. The captain said he too understood that was the way we had been handling the posting of the guard. If the post watch began during the night, the corporal of the guard went to each guy to wake him up 15 minutes ahead of time and again tell him where he had to be when his watch began and exactly whom he was relieving.

Lt. Prick said that I should have taken this PFC and all the others on watch during that shift out to their post and placed them there personally. When the PFC. was asked if he knew where he was supposed to be, he answered, yes. When questioned by the Skipper, he agreed that I had explained to him twice earlier, exactly where he should be at what time and for how long. I had woken him up and he was on post promptly as ordered, and I had gone out to check on him shortly after that.

The result of this Captain's Mast, was that the PFC. was busted to private for not being on his post and I received a reprimand on page 13 of the SRB a short blurb that meant little, but branded me as a fuckup ever afterward. So you see what you get for being a nice guy? The shaft. I'm quite sure that the Skipper took Lt. Prick aside in private to explain to him that this was after all a combat zone and because we all stood so much guard duty, we knew the drill and exactly where each post was located. For us to have a formal guard mount and posting of the guard was ludicrous.

Another time after Lt. Prick had sat on a rusty corncob, he told me to accompany him around to all the posts. He was again the OD and I the corporal of the guard. It was during the midnight to 0400 watch and all was well until we reached one of the outpost bunkers. I always hung back so that if one of the guys in the bunker was clutchy, and let loose a round, I would be able to help the wounded Prick get back into Camp. After he went through the rigamarole of identifying himself, he then asked the guys in the bunker if they had seen anything unusual tonight. One of them then said, "Only you sir." The surprised Prick blurted out, "What?" The unabashed Marine inside repeated, "You're the most unusual thing we've seen all night, Sir. Nobody else ever wanders out here." All the Prick could muster was, "Very well, carry on then lads." The officers were always calling us lads and it only bothered me when the officer doing it, like this one, was the same age as myself.

It was pitch black as I followed him back to camp and I'm sure he was fuming at what was said to him. After all that was no way for a shitbird to talk to an Annapolis Grad. I was having a fit trying to stifle a huge laugh behind his frigging Academy back. When he asked me why I was mumbling, I told him it was from shivering. " I'm jjjjust cccccold, that's all. Ssssir."

The old salts in the other platoons had a way of dealing with people like Lt. Prick. As far as I know, most of the guys liked their platoon leaders because they were practical types. The incident I heard about dealt with trying to get the point across to this particular 2nd lieutenant in a way that involved no conversation. Trying to get a lieutenant to ease up by talking to him can only be done by a gunny, a master sergeant, or a gunner (warrant officer)—a Marine with years of experience and some degree of tact.

The newly arrived lieutenant had been riding his platoon for several weeks when they found the chance to make him shape up—to see the light, so to speak. They were clearing a mine field and he was right out there in the middle of it with them. While they worked from a map that they had of the mine field, he was engrossed in surveying the forward area around the front lines with his binoculars. They all stole away quietly under the excuse that it was time for noon chow. Then the squad hid behind some boulders out of sight and ate lunch. After a while they heard him calling. He had no map and was afraid to walk out of the field because they had taken the lane markers with them. They ignored him until he got the message. I guess they told him when they came back that they had forgotten he was with them. A light bulb must have gone off in his head because the incident was never mentioned again and that officer actually became a real field Marine.

FOOD AND SANITATION

I don't remember much about our meals other than C-Rations. That means the cook did a good job with all of the dehydrated and canned stuff he got from Army supply. If the food had been bad for the whole year, I would have remembered that. Little affects a guy in the military more than the food he is served. If we received any frozen food, meat for example, we must have eaten it soon after delivery because we had no freezer, although they could have used an unheated tent in winter. Our small generator operated only from dusk until taps to provide lights every night.

Our galley and mess was in a log bunker, which we used for other things, such as the guard shack. It wasn't very large, so many of us took our chow in our mess gear and ate it in our tents. The milk, potatoes, and eggs were powdered. Everything else was canned, except for dry staples such as flour, rice, oatmeal, and sugar. Once in a while we had fresh eggs for breakfast, usually fried. We devoured them even when some of them were off color, which led us to believe that they were left over from WWII. We ate a lot of pancakes at breakfast, which we referred to as collision pads. Plenty of canned maple flavored syrup helped them slide down. Another staple every service man knew as shit on a shingle (SOS) was served often at breakfast and was really quite good. It was creamed chipped beef or ground beef served on toast. Another regular was Spam, which we ate so often that the cooks had to find ways to make it look and taste like something else. I believe that the reason no one ever complained about our food was that they had seen the Korean laborers taking our garbage cans back to their tents to scrounge through them for anything edible.

A culinary tradition in the Marine Corps became a staple that I still eat whenever possible. Steak and eggs were available for breakfast on special occasions wherever I served. WWII Marine vets tell me that when they had been aboard ship for days in the Pacific, waiting to hit the beach in an attack, they knew it would be that day when steak and eggs were served at morning chow. We had this treat rarely in Korea because of the lack of fresh eggs.

There were great meals on holidays and other special occasions like the Marine Corps birthday. On Thanksgiving Day and Christmas we had a feast of roast turkey, and all the trimmings you would have had at home. I still have the Christmas dinner menu for the 1stMarDiv for 1951.

Our Skipper provided the troops with a little holiday cheer on Christmas 1951. Some enlisted men were invited in small groups into the mess for a canteen cup of eggnog. The nog was made up of powdered milk, sugar, powdered eggs, along with lots of nutmeg and vanilla flavoring all mixed together in a cylindrical 25 gallon coffee thermos container. While we stood there with canteen cup in hand, the Skipper made a short speech. Then he ceremoniously uncorked a 5th of bourbon from his very own stash (wine cellar) and poured it into the nog mixture. Our leader spiking the Wassail for the troops—it wasn't exactly like home, but it was the idea that counted.

The only damper on our holiday spirit on Christmas Day was the news about Budde. I'm glad I didn't have the Skipper's job of writing to his parents to explain how he was killed. Every time this happened to one of our own, it made the rest of us that much more cautious about where we walked, but after a few weeks some lapsed into carelessness. PFCs. Budde and Peveto were both trainees in heavy equipment and must have forgotten what they had learned at Camp Pendleton about looking for signs of mines when out walking around in suspicious territory. They should have been carrying their sticks. Christmas night was extremely quiet along the front lines. Perhaps the enemy was giving the UN troops a break. If so, we should have reciprocated in kind on Chinese New Year in February.

The company had a chuck wagon, a large trailer full of the cooking gear and much of the chow and fixings for 200 men. We moved so much, that the chuck wagon was the only way to handle the cooking and storage of food. The old salts told me that among all of the troubles they had up at the Frozen Chosin reservoir, aside from being surrounded by the Chinese and fighting in -40° F. weather, the most demoralizing incident was the capture of the Able Engineers' chuck wagon. Marauding Chinese troops ransacked the innards of it while looking for food that they recognized as edible. They said that this was worse than when the Chinese had captured the truck full of Christmas mail and opened every package looking for goodies. The Marines were really down when they found Christmas wrapping paper laying around with the names of their buddies and often their own. The wrappers and things from Mom and the family back home were blowing off to Manchuria or the Sea of Japan.

Because every Marine is trained as an infantryman, at Frozen Chosin all hands had grabbed their rifles to fight off the waves of Chinese attacking them. They were successful in fighting their way out of the encirclement but they were really pissed about the mail truck and then the loss of the chuck wagon. Luckily, there were plenty of C-rations in some of the other trucks and more were air dropped, along with ammo, as they regrouped before fighting their way down to the coast.

When we worked all the time and in cold weather, it seems that you we were always hungry. We couldn't order a pizza delivery, or run down to the base snack bar for an ice cream bar or munchies, so we had to be inventive. Here is where the 12 gauge shotgun came in. There were plenty of ring-necked pheasants in Korea. The Koreans used an ancient method of catching them in a trap. We didn't have the patience for that, so we checked out the shotgun now and then when we went to the field. Back in camp we'd scrounge some canned butter or oil from the cook and fry up some fresh pheasant. This wasn't pheasant under glass, but it sure beat C-rations. We ate "poached" pheasant often and never had to worry about the game warden, hunting license, season, or bag limit.

I was with a crew once when they spotted a pheasant quite far off in a rice paddy. We didn't have a shotgun with us so a wise ass nailed it with his M-1. The bird was sort of standing obliquely to the line of fire and when the armor piercing bullet hit it, the pheasant just disintegrated. What a waste of food. There was nothing left but feathers and feet. When we didn't have any birds and were hungry, we'd just fry up soda crackers (from the C-rations) to fill our grumbling stomachs. One of our guys who liked pheasant hunting was Billy Jo Geer. Geer was a very quiet type. When you said something to him, his usual reply was, "La Dee Da." I could tell when he had been drinking because his response vocabulary expanded to, "La Dee Fucking Da." He was indeed a man of few words.

I should not say we were short of snacks because we had plenty of pogey bait thanks to the mail and the boxes from the businessmen back home. During the winter I would often make hot chocolate by melting a Hershey bar in my canteen cup with some powdered milk and boiling water. It was a lot better than the small package of powdered hot chocolate mix that came in the C-rations, probably left over from WWII.

155

When we worked in the field or were on the move between camp sites, we always ate C-rations. A small box contained enough for one man for three meals in one day. The main course for the three meals might be a can of corned beef hash, hamburger patties, sausage patties, spaghetti, chicken and noodles, or baked beans with franks. There was always a can of fruit, such as fruit cocktail or pineapple. Small sealed packets contained either milk, tea or coffee, all powdered. There were also some crackers, or cookies, a tiny can opener, a small package of toilet paper, a packet with four cigarettes, and some matches. If you lost your can opener, someone else was sure to have one on a string. I carried mine on my dogtag chain. Otherwise cans could be opened with a bayonet or Kabar.

Some of the time we resorted to warming some canned veggies or bacon from our stash of pilfered Army rations. We cooked stuff outside in our mess gear over a fire or inside on the stove in the winter. One thing we learned fast was to open a can of C-rations before putting it on the stove. Many a new guy was surprised to find that a closed can would explode when it got too hot and he would find his beans all over the walls and ceiling of the tent. We cooked some rations unopened by putting the can in a helmet of water on the stove. This way, after we ate the contents, we had some hot water to shave or wash with.

C-rations were not much, but it was better than not eating. I didn't mind these rations, although some guys didn't care for some things like hash. There was a lot of trading going on and I always ended up with the hash, which I liked. I ate so much hash during one week, that my mouth became sore from all the grease in it. The Marines who had been through Frozen Chosin said that they found a lot of our captured C-rations opened but uneaten by Chinese soldiers. The only food of ours that they liked and could recognize as familiar, was the pineapple. Those cans were always emptied.

If people wonder why they never saw me in a photo with my helmet on, it was being used in the tent for a wash basin. I carried another in my truck when I went to work. I mentioned before that it was a long haul over the mountain to Battalion where they had a large shower tent with hot water. After a few trips back over dusty roads, it just was not worth the ride. For one thing, the driver and the ranking NCOs on the run sat in the cab, while the other dozen or so troops rode standing in the open back of the truck. There was always a layer of dust several inches thick on the road and by the time we came back from the showers, the guys in back were covered with it. So how does one take a bath without facilities while living in a tent at 40 degrees below zero?

During at TV interview Dolly Parton described the method we used, because her large family lived in a one room cabin when she was growing up. She said that in the winter a sheet formed an enclosure near the stove at bath time. She stripped from the waist up and washed from her face down as far as possible. After toweling dry and putting on a top, she stripped from the waist down to wash from her toes up as far as possible. Then she washed possible. She describes our system perfectly, except we were a tent full of guys and dispensed with the sheet enclosure. Besides we had no sheets. It became known as taking a whore's bath. I figured that in the old days, WWI and before, the troops probably learned this method from female camp followers, hence the crude name.

While reading Brady's book *The Coldest War,* I chuckled when he mentioned the downside of washing like this for weeks on end in a bunker on the lines. When he had the chance to go back to battalion, or wherever their hot showers were located he had to cope with the removal of dingleberries. I know that this will gross out some people, but dingleberries are small accumulations of fecal matter that form in small clusters on the hair around the anus. It is the result of having to live like we did. Brady said that sometimes his dingleberies were so bad, he had to cut them and the hair off with a razor blade—a very delicate operation because he couldn't really see what he was doing. This was after he had spent 45 days on the line without being able to change clothes. It must have been the same for doughboys in WWI and most of the GIs who served under similar conditions in WWII.

Speaking of camp followers, friends of mine used to ask me why I always watched MASH on TV. I told them, because that was sort of the way we lived, except there were no doctors, no officers' club, no PA system, and especially no nurses. The only similarities were the craziness of the military, we lived in tents, we were either too hot or too cold, the food was typical military, and all fabric and equipment was either olive drab or Marine green. So, my friends would ask, "What did you guys do for women for a whole year?" My answer could only be, we just toughed it out. None of us had liberty—no passes, no leave, no R & R. We were all just stuck in camp.

There were two married guys in our tent, both called up from the reserves. One was a sergeant I'll call Duke. This old-timer was so horny it was driving him nuts. A couple of times I noticed that he was gone after dark and didn't return until well after midnight. This wasn't unusual, as guys had friends in other tents where they visited and played cards. One night I woke up and found him giving himself a ProKit and washing off his genital equipment in our only washbowl, my helmet hung from the tent pole. He had his flashlight hung from the pole to see what he was doing to his own pole.

I asked Duke what the hell he was doing and he said he just got laid and he was cleaning himself. He told me to go back to sleep. I had a hard time going back to sleep wondering just where this crazy bastard had found a woman way out here in no woman's land. What about that three mile restriction we had on civilians? In the morning he took me aside and told me not to tell anyone what he had been doing. I told him that I was mad as hell that he was using our helmet for his dirty dong, when the rest of us had to wash our faces in it and use it for shaving. If he would promise to use his own helmet exclusively for his crotch douche, I would say nothing. I pointed out that the other guys would drop a grenade in his sleeping bag if they knew he was using our wash basin as a Pro Station.

I asked him just where the woman was, although I had no interest in going with him. He said she was a Korean living in a cave near her old farm and he had to walk across a mile of rice fields to get there. I asked him if he ever thought about mines. We never bothered clearing that area because no one ever went out there. Duke said he was careful by walking only on the dikes and carried the stick for trip wires. He wouldn't tell me how he found out about the woman, but I assume it was from Kim our interpreter. Or else she was a camp follower for the Korean Marines earning her stripes and campaign ribbons. I told him he was absolutely nuts and if I heard a mine go off or a burp gun firing in the dark over that way, I wasn't going out to see if he was blown away. He'd have to wait until morning for any help. I asked him if he ever thought that maybe she was in cahoots with irregular commie soldiers and one night they would slit his throat and cut off his probe and huevos. He said there was no problem and I should mind my own business.

Birty the other married guy just suffered like the rest of us only he had more wet dreams than anybody else. He was always complaining about having to wash out his starched skivvies. One time he even had one while taking a nap on Sunday when we took a break after noon chow. I guess the married guys were just a bit different from us bachelors. They were used to regular nookie back home. Birty was a nice guy, but must have been wacky the way he joined the Corps. When he went to enlist in the USMC in Pittsburgh, they wouldn't take him because he was married and had two kids. So he went to the USMC Reserve unit and joined there. Then he asked to be put on immediate active duty. So here he was with us after boot camp and Camp Pendleton.

One day while the rest of us were eating our lunch in the tent, old Birty (a truck driver) was off on a trip. The company clerk came around with a roster checking some info. He stuck his head into the tent and asked, "Is Cpl. Birty around? John O. Birty, that is." We told him no, he was gone for the day on a detail. So he asked us if anyone knew what the O. stood for as his middle name. None of us knew, but I popped up and said. "Its Orgasm. John Orgasm Birty." The clerk said, "No kidding. That's an odd name. How do you spell it?" So I spelled it with due sincerity and the dumb clerk wrote it down and left. We all had a good laugh over that and we never mentioned it to John O. I've always wondered if that stayed on his record. If so, when he was mustered out he must have been mystified to find that name on his discharge documents. Maybe it will be on his tombstone in the VA cemetery when he's gone. That name will go on forever.

In the olden days it is said that the military regularly put saltpeter in the coffee or other beverages of the troops to reduce libido to a manageable level. Some years ago when my Dad was going on 79 he was talking to my brothers, both of whom had served in WWII. He said, "Do you boys remember that stuff they used to put in our coffee?" They knew what he meant and said yes. " Well," he went on, "Its beginning to work," and then chuckled over the memory. Saltpeter is either sodium or potassium nitrate, a component of gunpowder. So it may have been used from the very beginning of warfare involving explosives. It was an easily available commodity and if the troops were convinced that it did have an effect on libido, *tant mieux,* so much the better. The old salts would call this turning real men into limberdicks.

I don't know if they really gave us that stuff or not, but I don't think is was necessary in the USMC. They had their own subtle methods for coping with raging hormones in young men. From boot camp through advanced infantry training and into Korea, we were busy every minute when we were awake and so tired we slept soundly at every opportunity. There was enough work and other physical activity to keep us all in a constant state of fatigue.

To my knowledge there was at least one attempt at devious sexual activity in another letter company. One time when I had business back at Battalion around Christmas, I ran into a guy who had been in our unit at PI and Camp Pendleton. At first I didn't recognize him because he had a taped up broken nose and two huge purple black shiners. He was sort of effeminate and I couldn't imagine him being the least bit rowdy or in a fight. Before I could ask it, he answered my question. He said, "This is what happens to you if you have a nice ass, but it's not available." I looked puzzled. He explained that there was a big gorilla in his company who had more testosterone than brains. We called a guy like that so horny that he would screw a snake if you would hold it for him.

The gorilla came up to him while he was asleep in his zipped up mummy bag and accosted him about having sex. When he refused, saying he wasn't that kind of guy, the gorilla hit him and broke his nose. I don't know if the gorilla was hauled up on charges or not, but the punchee was sent to the hospital to have his beak reset. I think that guys like the gorilla should have been issued a three day pass through the front lines and some tokens taken from Chinese prisoners to be redeemed among the communist camp followers. The special privilege tokens called fuck bars are discussed below under Lack O'Nookie.

Because we lived so close together there were no slackers when it came to personal hygiene. The guys would not put up with one person not bathing regularly no matter how cold it was outside. We shaved nearly every day. There was a rule in the 1stMarDiv to the effect that there would be no beards, although moustaches would be OK. The reasoning was that beards caused problems with treating facial wounds. It seems that infections were more likely because of a beard and the facial hair complicated the cleaning of the wound.

When I tell people that I had my hair cut only three times during my stay in Korea, they said it was not possible for an active duty Marine to pull that off. Well they just weren't familiar with living in a combat zone. For one thing, no officer or staff NCO ever came into my tent while I was inside during my whole tour of duty. The guys in my tent didn't care how long my hair was, as long as it was clean and presentable. As per regulations, I almost never went outdoors uncovered, i.e. without something on my head. In the summer it was a dungaree cap, with hair piled up under it or a helmet that would hide a mop. The rest of the year the cover was a helmet, or when it was cold, a parka hood or the Siberian pisscutter, the cap with fuzzy fore, aft and side flaps to keep your ears from freezing.

At a reunion in April 1998, Sam Camarato confirmed our long hair syndrome, but he and others in his platoon were found out in a surprise inspection by the Skipper. It was towards the end of winter when the CO had Sam's platoon fall in to a loose formation, which was very rare for us in Korea. As the captain strode to his place in front and facing the platoon, Sam, and others were wondering who this guy was. They had never seen him before, even though he had been our Skipper for the past eight months or so. No one knows where he spent his time. It was the same with officers back in the states. They only seemed to materialize at inspections, formations, parades, and of course at the head of the table on payday as the disbursing officer.

The Skipper ordered them to uncover. Sam muttered, "Madon!" He was wearing a Siberian pisscutter and when he took it off, his curly mop popped out like a giant fuzz ball. The CO had suspected as much and told them he was shocked to see this display of civilian style hair dos. He pointed to a box full of hand clippers, combs, brushes, and scissors. He told the men to pair off, pick up a set of these tools and give each other a short regulation hair cut. They turned to right there and did the job. Each barber was very careful to do as neat a job as possible while he listened to the threats of retaliation from his partner being close cropped. If anything went wrong, the first shorn would do a hack job on the second.

This had to have happened while I was there, but I never heard about it and if the whole company was involved, I must have been on a work detail. I can confirm what Sam said about the Skipper though, having seen him only twice myself in my year there. That was at the brief ceremony in the galley cum mess bunker on Christmas Day and at my Captain's Mast (trial). I told Sam about the Skipper and his powdered egg nog and Sam said he wasn't there, but heard that it was a gathering only for the drivers. Why that would be, beats me.

MAIL CALL

When servicemen go overseas, for some reason or other it takes a long time for their mail to catch up with them. It was almost six weeks before I received any letters from my family. I was really surprised, however, when I received a letter within a week of my arrival in Korea. It was a form letter from the Veterans of Foreign Wars telling me that I now qualified for membership in the VFW. I must admire them for their approach to rapid recruitment of those barely eligible. My reaction at first was one of being pissed off. If these guys can find me, just where the hell is the real mail from home?

At that time, my attitude was let's see if I survive this mess first. Then when I'm safe at home I'll think about it. How could I join this honorable organization anyway, when I had heard others calling them the Veterans of Foreign Whores. I never did join. I am not a joiner. I learned that from joining the Corps. I may change my mind, however, considering the current death rate among all veterans. It is estimated that they are dying at the rate of 1,500 per day. The obituary page of the Phoenix Republic for Sunday July 26, 1998, had 28 males listed, 17 of whom were veterans of either war. This may be statistically skewed as most of these men moved to Arizona sometime after they left the service. However, the VFW may need to look to the likes of me as a replacement draft. Otherwise their membership will dwindle away. So maybe I'd better join the VFW, soon, if they'll still have me. I should also join the Marine Corps League, the Marine Engineer Association and the American Legion for the same reason.

Packages from home also supplied us with snacks and other grub, like Ma's cookies, sausages and small cans of food. Once my sister had sent me a package with pepperoni sausage in it. It took almost ten months for the parcel to catch up with me and the sausage was still good. I would have eaten it if it was green all over.

Mail service was pretty good going in and out. It seems like it went out once a week and came in at least that often. For morale purposes, the mail is almost as important as food for troops in a war. An exception is the Dear John letter that some poor bastards received from their girlfriends and even worse from their wives. Some women just couldn't stand being separated from their men for a whole year. I wonder just how married couples coped during WWII when some guys in service didn't see their wives and kids for as long as four years—until the end of the war. For the uninitiated, a Dear John was the type of letter the poor guys received from their not-so-sweet sweethearts and wives, letting them know that they were putting and end to the relationship. In other words, the woman back home was sailing off into the sunset with some other guy. The other guy was vilified by the victim as a no good, 4F asshole, or a draft dodger who was making out with his chick while he was off serving his country and couldn't do a damn thing about it. Maybe they thought about mailing the other guy a grenade.

The mail served as a recreational outlet for some guys, especially the lover boys. If they didn't get enough mail from all the girls they knew back home they started writing to pen pal clubs. Then they would be flooded with letters from lonely girls all over the USA. When a guy bragged too much to us about his exploits, one of the men in the unit would write a letter to a magazine or the Los Angeles Times saying that he was in Korea and feeling bad because since he had gotten a Dear John letter, he never heard from any girls at all. Would someone please write to him to boost his morale? They signed the braggart's name to the letter and he would receive hundreds of letters from horny girls in every state.

The victim was amazed at the response and reveled in the attention until the Skipper called him in and said that it wasn't right for one guy to receive a whole bag of mail while only one other bag arrived for the entire company. In other words, whatever he was doing to clutter up the mail had better stop.

John Chapin may have been one of the victims of this letter writing frenzy from the states. He recently told me that someone in our tent designated him as the chairman of the Cookie Relay Team. His job was to line up Marines with the women who flooded our mail with letters. Chapin told me recently that he was shocked back then to also receive letters from Hollywood queers. That really ticked him off and he still wants to know who sent the letter to the L.A. Times and signed his name to it. I was too lazy to do something like that, so it must have been Spike. Now we know why Spike was calling Chapin "Cookie" when he saw him in the compound.

When John Chapin moved into our tent we found that he was about the straightest guy in the Corps. John was sports and health minded. He didn't drink, smoke, or swear. He must have been shocked by the rest of us, who were foul-mouthed smokers and currently restricted drinkers. It wasn't long before poor old John just gave up and slowly started to curse and smoke cigarettes and cigars. But he never cooped his beer ration for himself and continued to let the rest of us fight over it every two months. He even joined the bull sessions at night sitting on his cot puffing on a stogie while writing letters home.

There was a guy in every outfit who was afraid to let his mother know that he was in Korea, even though he wasn't in imminent danger. He insisted that Mama would worry and would never understand the situation. One guy told his Mama that he was on some Pacific island like Kwajalein Atoll. He would tell her how peaceful and serene it was and all he did was stand guard duty, swim, and lay on the beach. This guy got away with it for a while because he was a master bullshitter. At night he was always scribbling away to women he knew back home or to some he met through the mail. He often had four or five letters in process at once. One morning before we went to work he was massaging his letters, when the call went out for a mail run leaving in ten minutes.

He wanted to get a half dozen off, so he quickly addressed the envelopes, stuffed the letters inside and dropped them in the mail bag. He received rapid responses from two of his correspondents. Apparently he had put two letters in the wrong envelopes. One response was from his mother in a panic, wondering how he got to Korea and what was he doing in a Marine Recon outfit, operating behind enemy lines and in danger every day. The other letter was from a girl in another town, wondering how he got to the island in the Pacific. Was it a type of R&R he was accorded after all those harrowing experiences in combat that he described to her earlier in great detail? All the time he had been embellishing his letters to the girl with made up war stories, figuring that she would really like to make out with a hero when he came home. On the other hand, his Mom almost had a heart attack when she read about his bravery (the Walter Mitty syndrome). His return address was the FPO, San Francisco, but they had no idea exactly where he was from that, which is the way the FPO system is supposed to operate.

One benefit of being in a combat zone was that we didn't have to put stamps on our letters home—a privilege called franking. The letters had to be personal and addressed in writing with your return FPO address also written on the envelope. It is hard to believe there were a couple of guys in our company who couldn't write. They knew how to read, but for some reason never learned to write in script. They could print in block letters but they had to write both address and the return to be able to write free where the stamp went ordinarily. When they had outgoing mail, they would bring the envelope to me, or one of the other scribes, and we would write in the info on it for them and then add "free" in script up in the right hand corner.

A guy in my platoon told me that he had been talking to a couple of PFCs in our company one night and was amazed to learn that they didn't know where Korea was. They didn't even know who we were fighting or why we were there at all. I don't know who they were, but I felt sorry for them. After the war when we learned about the "turncoats", the U.S. POWs brainwashed by the Communists, it turns out that they also had a very limited education and had no idea why we were in Korea.

Although the US Military claims to have dealt with this problem of general political ignorance among enlisted ranks after the Korean War, I fail to understand what we were doing getting involved in VietNam after the French threw in the bloody towel at DienBienPhu in 1954. It was the height of conceit and arrogance to believe that we could do it better than the French. Then we proceed with a half vast war without the resolve to win it because of the heavy hand of politicians in Washington micro-managing our effort from the sea to the air, and on the ground. This time it was the military brass and civilian whiz kids like former Defense Secretary Robert MacNamara, who were politically naive in pursuing the Vietnam war with a no-win strategy. MacNamara really was a whiz at running a giant auto company in Detroit,but had no business in charge of our military in Vietnam. According to LBJ, our job was to win the hearts and minds of the Vietnamese people. At that time, one Marine general tersely told how that should be done, "Grab them by the balls. Their hearts and minds will follow." Marine leaders are not known for mincing words.

The guys in my tent must have thought that I really came from a weird family in Detroit. My family wrote often and I wrote home regularly. However, during the hockey season I would receive thick envelopes every two weeks. There was usually no letter, just a bunch of sports page clippings on the NHL scores and articles about the teams, especially my team, the Detroit Red Wings. Normally, my Mom threw in a few tea bags for me. I 'd use them, then hang them on the tent pole to dry and use them again. I knew that they were thinking of me back home, although at the time I often wondered who wrote to my Dad in WWI. He had a younger brother and I knew that Dad was a lady killer, so he must have received some mail to cheer him up. How do I know he was a lady-killer if he never mentioned them to us? We recently found some pre-1916 dance cards of his that were full of ladies names reserving a dance with him. That was the old custom at any dance. Both men and women wore these cards tied to the wrist with a piece of yarn.

COPING WITH COLD

Just how does one cope when living in tents and working outdoors in subzero weather conditions? The men who really endured under these conditions were the servicemen who were in Korea for the winter of 1950-51. There were many cases of frostbite that winter, involving toes, fingers, noses, faces and other exposed body parts. The worst that could happen with this malady was the loss of the affected part in the case of toes, feet, fingers and hands, or even death which occurred in some battles, such as at the Chosin Reservoir, where general hypothermia was a problem. The Detroit News of June 3, 1996 reports that among the 17,000 Allied troops in this 10 day battle, there were 15,000 casualties: 2500 were wounded and the rest suffered injuries from the cold. Those who had milder and treatable cases of frostbite had to endure a lifetime of pain in the affected areas. It is understood now that the frostbite afflicted are more prone to other ailments in later life than is the general population.

One photograph sums up the cold weather problem for a grunt. It was taken by David Douglas Duncan, a Life Magazine photographer who took a photo of a young Marine up at the reservoir. The lad was swathed in every bit of clothing he owned topped with his helmet and his M-1 was slung on his shoulder. In his left mitten he held a can of C-rations and in his right, a small plastic spoon. He had a puzzled look on his face as if to say, "Just how do I eat this mess? The hash is all burned (from the fire) on the outside of the can and still frozen solid in the middle."

It is rumored that a correspondent up in the Koto-Ri perimeter asked a young Marine marching out to Hungnam about his experiences up at Frozen Chosin. The reporter asked him what was his most difficult experience up at the reservoir. He asked, "Was it having to fight round the clock in severe cold weather with Chinese troops surrounding the Marines? Was it finding your buddies bleeding and dying all around you? Was it finding the truck carrying your Christmas mail and packages ransacked by the Chinese? The exhausted PFC answered firmly, "No." Finally after some thought he said softly, " My most difficult experience all the time I was up there, was in trying to get three inches of pecker through six inches of clothes to take a piss."

The new guys arriving in winter had to learn how to use a sleeping bag correctly for maximum warmth. As the weather got colder we were issued sleeping bags stuffed with chicken feathers. It came with a waterproof shell that was to be laced to the sleeping bag. I didn't bother to lace the two together the first time I slept in the bag. As a result, I was twisting around in my sleep during the night and taking the bag with me while the shell stayed in the same place. When someone woke me up the next morning I was groggy and wondered why I couldn't see anything when I opened my eyes. I was staring at the fabric of the shell's hood

Most of us figured that to be very warm at night we would sleep with a lot of clothes on, like we had been doing with only blankets. With blankets, we needed at least one under us to keep out the cold coming through the canvas cot and another on top. We soon found that we were colder sleeping in a bag with clothes on than without, but all felt that it was a bit chancy to be sleeping in our skivvies, mostly because if the shit hit the fan, we didn't want to be running outside like that at -30°F. below. For some reason or other we were a lot warmer in the bag when wearing as little as possible.

This did lead to some difficulties in relieving the bladder in the middle of the night. A piss tube was located here and there around the camp. It was a simple tube used to ship artillery shells that was dug into the ground at an angle. Some guys who slept in the buff would simply stand up in the sleeping bag and hop out to the tube to pee. However, this only took care of the No 1. It was a good thing our alcohol was limited, because it was bad enough having to go out in sub zero weather and expose your pecker to the cold wind just once in the middle of the night.

There was only one head in the camp, that I know of. It was an eight holer with a tarp roof and wooden sides. For obvious sanitary reasons it had to be located away from the tent area. The location made some guys nervous about going out there in the middle of the night. The only alternative was to go outside of the camp perimeter and take a dump in a mine field. Most of us were a little concerned about infiltrators, so we carried either a pistol or a Kabar for self defense while concentrating on the throne in the wee hours of the morning..

The nervous Nellies, however took a rather sneaky approach to protecting themselves. They would drop their spoor between the tents under the cover of darkness. Every now and then someone walking through the camp would find a pile of turds. The dirty dog who was sullying our collective nest was dubbed the Phantom Shitter. We were trying to catch the bastard for months. The bulletin board now and then had this note posted: The Phantom Shitter Struck Again Last Night. Watch Where You Step.

A redneck in the next tent had a cure for the Phantom Shitter if we caught him. He allowed that, "Back home in the hills we have a system that works well on our hound dog if he forgets and shits in the house or on the stoop." "What's that?", we asked. "Well now, it's called the corncob and turpentine treatment. You've got to catch the critter right after the event so's it'll stick in his head. Then you rough up his asshole with a dried corncob and apply a liberal dose of turpentine to the raw bunghole. If you can find him within a week after that he may not need a second treatment." What did the dog have to say about all this? " Ruff, ruff."

At one point the Phantom finally stopped. We don't know if he was shipped out, got constipated, or was caught by the gunny and given the hound dog cure. If so, he was gagged first, because no one heard an outcry from the victim. The main thing is that our health and safety was maintained in the end.

Because we had no sheets the sleeping bag had to be aired out regularly turning it inside out and spreading it on the top of the tent on a sunny day. The inside of the bag's hood got a bit grimy from the natural oil in our hair. The bar soap we used on our hair once a week should have taken all that oil out, but apparently it didn't. No one I knew then ever used shampoo. It was for women and sissies. Likewise, I never saw anyone all the time I was in the Marines wearing a bathrobe or pajamas. It just wasn't done, at least where it could be seen by the rest of us. I was married about six months after I left the Corps and my kind bride bought me a new set of PJs thinking I needed to become civilized. Its been 45 years now that we've been hitched and those same PJs are still in the drawer and have never been worn.

I've only worn PJs a couple of times in my life since Korea and they weren't mine. Once in a US Army Hospital (Thailand) and once in a US Navy Hospital (Morocco). In the former I was forced to wear GI pajamas and in the latter a SeeMore gown, even though I was a civilian both times. I guess I had to wear a GI bathrobe also when I was up and around. When the medical staff got to treating me like a shitbird, I had to remind them that I was a civilian and had to pay for my stay in their hospital.

As for getting by in the Korean winter. Sgts. Spike Bernauer and Bill Hepinger (Hep) the welders, lived in my tent so at the first blast of frozen air from Siberia, they hopped to and made us a complete fuel burning stove out of scrounged scrap from the artillery. The stove itself was made out of a large steel tube made for shipping shells. They fashioned a small door in front so we could light it. The flue was made from connected shipping containers for smaller shells and went out the top of the tent through a metal jack.

Spike and Hep also made a fuel tank for outside and copper tubing with a shut off valve bringing the diesel fuel to the burner. They also burned holes into the sides of the stove for air access. That heater kept us nice and warm all winter long. When they had scrounged enough materials, there was a stove in every tent and in the mess bunker as well. We never worried about a problem with carbon monoxide, because the tents were so drafty. The stove was a big help for heating water for shaving, washing up, washing clothes, cooking grub and for thawing out your stiff body after standing guard duty in a snow storm.

Our welders were really magicians. Sgt. Spike Bernauer had been in the Marines after WWII, but had been called up from the reserves in late 1950. He was from Amarillo, Texas where he worked with his father, mostly on oil pipelines. He and Hep kept our equipment and trucks together when things broke or came apart and had to be welded. When they weren't busy with that, they would do work for other outfits nearby. Now and then a USMC tank would rumble into our compound and Spike and Hep would fix whatever the problem was. The tankers usually wanted a piece of steel plate welded onto the escape hatch for added protection against antitank mines. Spike was a barrel chested guy who had been a guard at the brig on Terminal Island, Long Beach before he came to Korea.

Sgt. Bill Hepinger and been in the Corps since 1948, serving as machine gunner at Camp Pendleton until he arrived in Korea in the spring of 1951 while the 1stMarDiv was involved in at lot of fighting. In spite of the fact that I lived in the same tent with Hep for over 11 months, I only learned recently of some of his escapades before I arrived. Upon his arrival at Able Company, 1stEngrBn, he and his foxhole buddy from Pendleton, Dick Miller were assigned to mine clearing and booby trap details for five months with the First and Fifth Marine regiments. Hep then became a welder and Miller a truck driver. Miller ended up in Battalion G-2.

During the spring (1951) battles around the Punchbowl area, Hep was on guard duty with Cpl. Mac McClure when they caught three North Korean soldiers infiltrating their post. Hep held them at gun point while Mac went to find some help to take them away. They were not relieved of the prisoners for seven hours. In another incident, the camp fuel dump caught fire and Hepinger was trapped until Cpl. Tex McClellan cleared a path through the encircling flames with his bull dozer so Hep could walk out.

Because of his experience with machine guns, Hepinger was in charge of the two machine guns we had in camp. When we moved he set up the 50 cal. machine gun as a defense against enemy aircraft and the 30 cal. machine gun for perimeter defense. Hep was also in charge of the gun crews.

Every Marine was issued extra clothing just before it really got cold including, a tan flannel shirt, long johns, sweat shirt, wool GI sweater (mine was stolen), extra heavy duty wool socks, plus the sleeping bags. When the temperature dipped below freezing we were each issued a winter parka and waterproof shell, Siberian PissCutter, thermal boots, a pair of mittens, with a palm slot for the trigger finger, and a pair of leather gloves with removable woolen liners.

The parka was very warm. The hood front on the parka had a wide fringe of fur sewn onto a pliable wire frame so that we could shape the fur to suit the weather conditions to protect your face and eyes. The bulldozer, grader, and front loader operators were issued a light brown sheepskin rancher's coat instead of the parka. The sheepskin lined leather coat was even warmer than the parka, especially when the wide lamb's wool lined collar was turned up well over the ears. The reasoning was that while running these types of equipment, the operators often had to twist around to see where they were going while backing up. This looking over one's shoulder while moving in reverse was awkward while wearing a parka, but much easier in a sheepskin coat. When I saw these coats, I marveled that someone in the Corps had the foresight to order them for our operators. Often when I had the duty at night outside, I borrowed John Chapin's coat just for the night. The parka was better in heavy snowfall, but the sheepskin was warmer in bitter cold.

Some of our men from the south had trouble adjusting to working outdoors in the cold but I was right at home in cold weather. When I worked for the City of Detroit, we could only get out of the weather when the temperature dipped below 5°F. During ice storms, we worked day and night removing downed trees from streetcar wires, power lines, cars, and houses in weather that would shrivel one's pecker back up inside the crotch and turn the scrotum blue. We never complained because we were being paid double time. The rest of the winter we were usually in big elm trees exposed to the cold wind and snow above the housetops. In Detroit I spent my spare time ice skating or playing hockey on lakes, ponds or some neighborhood rink, or just trudging through the snow on a hike in the country.

There was little to do during off duty hours at night, especially in the winter. We were lucky in our tent because one of the guys had a Zenith TransOceanic radio. The six of us we were able to listen to broadcasts without disturbing anyone else nearby. We scrounged up six sets of earphones from the mine detectors, which were not in use at the time, and wired them to the radio's speaker. The deadlined mine detectors didn't interfere with the company's ability to clear mines, because most of the Chinese mines were made of wood and plastic and our equipment would only detect metal mines. We also found out that some of the tubes in the detectors also worked in the Zenith when a vacuum tube went out.

We listened to stateside music and the latest news while writing letters, reading or just laying in the sleeping bag after lights out. We usually picked up the Armed Forces Radio Service (AFRS) broadcasting to Korea from Japan. One program was called the Kyushu Cowboy, which played western music and another was the Honshu Hoedown mostly country and western music. It was nice to hear the patter of the DJs dedicating songs to GIs by name in Korea. Requests were called in from girl friends and relatives back home.

Some guys played cards all the time after evening chow, but thankfully not in our tent. There were always bull sessions in every tent where lots of lies were told to impress the hicks. The talk never failed to turn to women, then good home cooked food, and inevitably to what each guy was going to do when he got home. Most were going to go back to their old jobs, although the bachelors were going to marry the sweetheart who had been writing to them all this time. The married guys were going to take their wives out on the town the second night, after spending the first day and night catching up on lowering their long accumulated white count.

I had a small 45 RPM record player and had a large collection of my favorite music (classical, jazz, and country-western) were sent to me through the FPO. I kept the sound down as low as I could because I knew that no matter what I played, it would offend someone. Although I participated in the bull sessions, because I did have a gift of the Irish blarney and have never hesitated to spread some of it among the unlettered. I spent a great deal of my time reading everything I could get my hands on, with the exception of the comic books that circulated constantly. I'm not a snob about literature, but my father would not allow comic books in our house and we were forbidden to read them outside the home. My father was a self educated man and very well read, so he impressed upon me the importance of reading and education. He had explained to me that the Irish were basically a learned people and after they were forced to give up their own language by the English, they ended up many years later teaching the English how to properly use their own language.

When I was about sixteen, I had rewarded my father for his advice by quitting school in the tenth grade and going to work. He was angry about it, but I ignored him. An Arizona Game Ranger I came to know later, who was half Irish and half Navajo summed up my behavior this way, "What's the use of being Irish if you aren't ornery."

With all of the time I had to myself while in the Marines I realized I had an opportunity to pursue an education. I began this project by reading history, biographies, historical novels and a series of great books. While in Korea and later at Camp Lejeune, NC, I took correspondence courses from the Marine Corps Institute (MCI) and the U.S. Armed Forces Institute (USAFI) so I could pass the GED and be ready for college when I was discharged.

I also read a lot of the pocket books, which were circulating in Korea, because I could carry them around on the job. We had a few odd balls who did a job on some paperbacks. They could never find the place where they left off, so resorted to tearing each page out when they finished reading it. We had to reason with these guys to preserve the few reading materials we had available.

KOREAN MARINE REGIMENT

The Korean Marine Regiment (KMR), which was the fledgling unit of the Korean Marine Corps (KMC), was based somewhere near our camp, but the main part of the Regiment was on the lines on the flank of the 1stMarDiv. The only time I saw any of them was when they were marching or running by. One morning when the temperature was around 15°F., I heard some chanting on the road and went out to see who it was. I was startled to see a KMR platoon going by at double time carrying various parts of weapons on their shoulders. Some had mortar base plates, others had the tubes, the tripods, or light machine guns. They were stripped to the waist and wore only gloves and a gunny sack separating the metal parts from their skin. They were headed south and an hour later I heard them running back north chanting as they went. I was glad that I wasn't in that outfit.

We had a number of our guys working with the KMR on engineering training. I learned from them that the KMR did their boot camp and advanced infantry training right up on the lines or right behind near us where there was a level place for them to drill. Our Marines said they witnessed some pretty heavy forms of discipline. For example, if the KMR lieutenant or the DI was so inclined, he dealt out the punishment right there in ranks. The DI or officer would take off his belt or use his swagger stick and proceed to thrash the offender until he crumpled on the ground. They also used their fists or kicked the skinhead when they felt it was necessary to get him to shape up. I believe this kind of discipline was exercised by the DIs and officers in the USMC back in the old days.

One type of training conducted by our company was to show the Korean Marines how to clear and to properly lay a mine field. Among the things that they tried to teach them was to never, ever attempt to clear a mine field at night. After the first dozen or so Koreans finished the course they were sent back to their line companies to practice the fine art of handling land mines. Several weeks had passed when the KMR commander sent over a request for more of his men to be trained by Able Co. When the KMR CO was asked why he didn't use the men we had already trained, he said they were either dead or seriously wounded How come? It seems that the mine fields they wanted to clear were part of the defenses for the Chinese and North Korean lines. The KMR wanted to be able to have their patrols penetrate the mine fields to better raid the enemy for prisoners.

They couldn't very well clear a path through the Chinese mine fields in daylight, so they attempted to clear their path at night with a very high casualty rate that came not only from the mines, but from the raking fire and mortar blasts that followed the first mistake with a blown trip flare or mine. I don't know how our Skipper handled it, but he probably told the KMR that if they continued to try to clear mines at night in no man's land, then we couldn't train any more of his men.

Speaking of the night, we occasionally saw bright lights playing on the clouds in the middle of the night. We heard later that this was from a searchlight unit on our side focusing their powerful beams on the bottoms of large cloud banks. It must have been thought up by the Psychological Warfare (PsyWar) people in X Corps. The idea was to steal the night from the enemy by bouncing the beams off the clouds so that the moisture therein reflected the light onto their positions. I suppose it was assumed that the Chinese would be reluctant to mount any raids, frontal assaults or patrols when they could be plainly seen from our observers. I have no idea if this ploy worked or not. When we later moved over to the western part of the country, our military found another innovative use for a searchlight.

The Sunday before we packed up for rotation of divisions we received word from Charlie Co. to the east of us over the ridge, that they had just received a visit from a small enemy plane lobbing small bombs out the window. He was headed in our direction. There were occasional sorties like that by the North Koreans to harass us with their small Russian planes. The only damage they caused was psychological.

These planes were dubbed either Bed Check Charlie or Five O'Clock Charlie, depending on when they arrived. They were a nuisance as they flew close to the deck to avoid radar and were too slow for our jets to contend with. A Marine pilot flying a Corsair finally cleared them all from our skies.

Before leaving the Punchbowl Division HQ had decided that there were too many incidents involving the accidental discharge of firearms, usually with unauthorized sidearms. There had been several of these in our company, one in our tent. One guy fired his pistol and the bullets passed through six tents in a row, up high so no one was hit. He was a bit off his head and was sent home and given a medical discharge. Everyone had to turn in their extra sidearms to Battalion to be locked up until the owner rotated home. I traded my P-38 for a Chinese flare pistol and a French soldier's beret rather than lose it.

THE DIVISION MOVES

In March of 1952 the 1stMarDiv was ordered to pull out of the eastern mountains and make its way to a new position in the western part of Korea along both sides of a point where Panmunjom was located just north of the MLR. I guess the wheels figured we had been in one place long enough and needed a change of scenery. It took us several days to take the tents down and secure our gear aboard trucks and trailers. Extra trucks were sent up from the 7th Motor Transport Battalion so that the redeployment would be made in one move.

I heard that the 1stMarDiv's 7th Motor Transport Battalion (MTBN) was made up largely of black Marine drivers. One of our drivers said that if he called 7th MT Bn. to lay on some trucks, this is what he heard on the other end of the line, "7th Motor Transport Battalion. Dispatcher speaking. We've got two bys, four bys, six bys, semis, and them great big mothers that go shoo, shoo, shoo. What'll you have today?" The 7th MTBN carried all of the Marines from the line regiments in this big move. They also assisted in moving the artillery, tanks, amtracs, USN Mobile Field Hospitals, ammo and other supplies.

When we left the Punchbowl, I drove my Jimmy-mounted LeRoi and could stow all of my gear aboard between the cab and the compressor. The trip took a couple of days because the roads were narrow and not well maintained. Able Company was one long convoy snaking its way westward. At night we increased the interval between vehicles and camped on the side of the road. The tracked heavy equipment was hauled by battalion lowboys. The Cat grader drove right along with us. It had no cab and the driver wore goggles. The operator was covered with dust at the end of each day. That dust caused a lot of us to pick up intestinal parasites during our stay in the country. Sometimes the Korean honey buckets would leak their contents onto the roads while transporting human waste to the fields.

We got to see some Korean people for the second time since arriving in country. We passed through and near many villages enroute and the people lined the roadside to watch the show. Some old folks bowed, some younger ones even smiled. They were rewarded by our troops tossing out candy bars and cans of C-rations to the kids mainly—a typical American response to poverty and an attempt to erase the grimness of war for those who suffered the most.

Our Skipper and XO had gone ahead to scout out our new camp site. It was somewhere between the lines and Panmunjom to the North and Munsan-ni (or Mansan-ni) to the south. A nearby bridge spanned the Imjin River and provided access for our negotiators to drive to the peace talks site in Panmunjom. Munsan-ni was a railhead town and provided quarters for all of the UN and US Military negotiators, their aides, translators, interpreters, security detail, and the international press corps. Munsan-ni later became the UN Advanced HQ, through the signing of the armistice in July 1953.

In 1959, while assigned to the AID Mission at the American Embassy in Phnom Penh, Cambodia, I met Ted Liu, the Chinese Cultural Affairs Officer in the US Information Service. Ted was born in China, but grew up in the states and graduated from Colombia University. He lived at Munsan-ni when he was in the US Army where he served as an interpreter at the peace talks at Panmunjom. At one session he was surprised to see one of the interpreters on the communist side of the table, a Chinese soldier who had been in classes with him at the university. Because of the situation, they recognized, but couldn't openly acknowledge each other. They had to face each other (inscrutably) this way for months.

The terrain in western Korea was level with hills here and there, quite different from the mountainous east. We heard that because of the flatness of the topography in this area, the space separating the front lines of the Communist and UN forces was measured in miles. We didn't find out for a couple of weeks that some of us would be working just in front of our MLR with trucks and equipment.

As soon as we set up our tents and settled into the new camp, we were assigned to various projects in the area. The original steel bridge crossing the Imjin was severely damaged by sappers as the war seesawed back and forth across the area during 1950-51. The 84th Army Engineer Construction Battalion had replaced it with a low type of temporary bridge running parallel to the twisted wreckage of the old one in April 1952. The new structure was called the Freedom Gate Bridge and was guarded at both ends by ROK MPs who were backed up by a sandbagged pit containing a 30 cal. machine gun crewed by Korean Marines.

Soon after we arrived our demolition men were told to drop the one section of the railroad bridge near the south bank of the river. They did not realize that all the bridge sections were connected to each other on top of the concrete pillars in the river by steel expansion rings. When the first section was blown, one end of each of the other sections fell into the river. There would be no kudos for that job. It must have been Short Fuse Fred in charge and he just couldn't wait to blow something up.

According to Hastings in his book *The Korean War,* in April of 1951 the 29th Commonwealth Brigade, made up of British plus a Belgian unit, held off a much larger force of attacking Chinese troops on the south bank of the Imjin. The fighting raged for several days. In the battle the Brigade lost 1,000 men and the Chinese suffered 10,000 casualties while stopping the Chinese advance in its tracks.

Just in case the communist forces broke through the MLR to the north, the Fredom Gate bridge had been prewired by the Army for quick demolition to deny the commies a place to cross the Imjin. One set of wires ran to floodlights mounted under the bridge for emergency lighting for the demolition crew. Another set of wires ran to the demolition charges installed at critical points on the supporting framework. The terminus for the wiring network was at the abutment on the south end of the bridge. From time to time, a demolition crew had to make a dry run on the bridge to check the wiring and the charges.

While I was there, we made several dry runs on the bridge. These trips were never announced. One of our lieutenants would come around and tell us to saddle up for the bridge. While the demolition crew got their gear together, I hooked up the floodlight generator unit to the weapons carrier. We would roar up to the south end of the bridge, the crew jumped off and ran under the bridge carrying extra satchel charges and packs of C-3 in case it was needed. I backed the generator up to the right spot at the end of the bridge while the officer was checking the demolition circuits. Then I hooked the electrical wire leads to the running generator and threw the switches to make sure all the floodlights were working.

This always caused a big stir in the guard shack on the bridge. It seems that whenever we did this dry run, it always scared the crap out of the MPs who were not aware of what we were up to. They must have thought that we were actually going to blow the damn thing. I could see the MPs in the shack cranking away on the field phone trying to reach some Army post to find out if this was for real. The only guys there who were calm, were the Korean Marines on the machine guns. They had been in combat before and were not easily rattled.

I know that if the officer in charge was someone like Lt. "Buck" Rogers, from our third platoon, he didn't stand much on ceremony. He thought that prior notice was unnecessary if this was a practice drill. I'm sure that he did what I would have done when confronted later by the Army MPs commander. I would have said that we tried to call earlier to give you warning, but we couldn't get through on the phone. The lines were busy, or down, or no one answered at the MP end. Sorry about that!

Now that we were working around US Army units, I noticed that every piece of machinery such as tournapulls, scrapers, bulldozers, etc. had a sign painted on it in large white letters. It said," This equipment cost so many thousand dollars, TAKE CARE OF IT. Whenever we had any business at the bridge or had to cross over it, I saw a huge pile driver (tracked) sitting on a barge tied up to the north bank of the Imjin River not far from the bridge. On the back was painted," THIS ITEM COST $40,000. TAKE CARE OF IT." A few months later I noticed it was gone. It had slipped off the barge and into the river with only the top of the boom sticking out of the muddy water. So much for the admonitions. This way the GIs responsible for it couldn't see the sign. Maybe the operator had been to the waterproofing course and was checking out his handiwork. One never knows.

FUN AND RECREATION

There wasn't much for us in the way of fun and recreation. There were no other military camps and no civilian towns anywhere near us at this site. However, there were some US Army units down the road toward Munsan-ni and some of our guys with a nose for booze soon found out that one Army camp had a small EM club with beer and liquor. So they would drift down there in a Jeep in twos and threes and come back stinking drunk. This was tolerated for several weeks until the inevitable fight broke out between some doggies and the visiting thirsty Marines. So the Army CO banned any more Marines coming in for Happy Hour. I guess our Skipper either didn't hear about the ruckus or didn't care, because no one told us to desist from socializing with the soldiers at their slopchute. The Marine boozers found a way around the ban, by scrounging Army fatigues and going back to the Army EM club incognito. As far as I know there was no more trouble.

We did however, get Marines who went to the Army club to bring us back a bottle of whiskey now and then. We were not allowed to make any noise in camp after dark, and especially after taps at 10, so a few of us founded the Culvert Club under the road. The concrete culvert was about 30 feet long and big enough for us to sit up in. We would sit in there with a small candle and pass the bottle around, tell jokes and sing songs. Every now and then a military vehicle would rumble over us on the road. Those passing could hear our raucous singing and wondered where it was coming from. We could not be heard in camp and looking back, it was a pretty stupid thing for us to do. To protect ourselves from an infiltrator sneaking up and rolling a grenade inside, we took turns outside at one end of the culvert keeping an eye out for trouble. We always had a carbine or M-1 at hand. The others had to keep an eye on me though because I had a habit of wandering off when I had too much to drink. Our beer ration improved now that we were near the capital and the port of Inchon. We began to receive wooden cases of Japanese Asahi brand beer in bottles packed in straw. It was a step up from the American 3.2 canned beer.

Singing among Americans troops is usually associated with drinking. Since our access to alcohol was strictly limited, there wasn't much singing. I do remember one song we sang once in a while. It was adapted from Movin' On, an old favorite by Hank Snow. Our version of the words went something like this:

Hundred thousand Chinese comin' over the pass and the whole Eighth Army is a haulin' ass, We're moving on, We're movin' on.

There were more words but I can't recall them.

The main reason for troops to sing is to boost their morale. I still have the old feeling of pride when I hear the Marine Corps Hymn. Then

I imagine that I am back on the parade ground marching past the reviewing stand. Phillip Gibb in his book, *Now It Can Be Told*, tells of a German Commander in the 5th Bavarian Division in WWI ordering his men to sing because they looked so gloomy. This was during their march returning to the battle of the Somme, which the Germans were already losing. They were ordered to march in circles and sang only half heartedly. When they were compelled to sing *Deutschland Uber Alles,* that broke the unit down completely. The German Army near the end was completely demoralized.

We were ordered to sing only once and that was in boot camp, while we were inside the hut where we were exposed to tear gas. We went in there with our gas masks on to get used to wearing them and then were ordered to take them off to get a good dose of gas while singing the Marine Corps Hymn. After five minutes, we were allowed outside to grab some air and try to clear our vision.

While we were so close to Seoul, I thought I would go to the capital the first chance I had. When I heard that we were sending a truck into Seoul to pick up supplies, I asked my platoon leader if another guy and I could go along to see some civilization. He said it was OK as long as we came back with the truck that evening.

There was no time for us to tidy up, so we climbed onto the truck as we were— with cartridge belts, slung rifles and wearing our helmets. We never knew what we might run into on the way back in the dark. The other passenger was a buck sergeant from one of the platoons. It took us over an hour to get to the city, even though it was only about 30 miles away. The city was still full of wreckage, but was slowly being rebuilt. We pulled into a large military parking lot where the truck would be until it went to the warehouse for loading. We were to meet the driver back there in the afternoon.

The sergeant and I wandered around for a few blocks gawking at the debris and the buildings. We hadn't been away from the truck for ten minutes when a shiny Jeep pulled up with AIR POLICE markings. Inside were two spiffy looking young airdales (airmen) about 20 years old. They wore starched fatigues with AP brassards, white duty belts, white holsters with 45 cal. Colts and white leggings over shiny black boots. To top it off they both sported white scarves in their open neck shirts. They were a sight to behold and I guess they thought the same of us two raggedy-assed Marines. It must have been something like a couple of fancy boys running into Willy and Joe in France in WWII.

Compared to these two neatniks, we must have really looked bad. We weren't exactly clean. Our dungarees had seen better days and we were covered with dust. On top of that we both needed a shave and a haircut. All they asked us was what outfit we were with and where we were headed. We told them Able Engineers and that we had our CO's permission to come to town just to look around for the day. When they found out we didn't have a pass, they escorted us back to the truck and told us to stay with it until it left town. We were highly pissed at being stopped from our visit to the capital, but even angrier at being rousted by a couple of spotless airdales wearing white frigging ascots. So went a short bit of liberty in Seoul that would have pissed off Cinderella. If you want to know why we knew nothing much about the very country we were sent over to save, there it is.

When the word got around the 1stMarDiv that the Army and the Air Force troops were given a five day Rest and Recreation (R&R) leave to Japan, many Marines were really steamed. This was becoming a morale problem because we read the Stars and Stripes and saw the articles about doggies and airdales from Korea enjoying themselves in Japan. So what did the USMC HQ in Korea do? They ordered every Marine Battalion to have each company select two guys to go on R&R to Japan for five days. When the lucky few made the trip, the USMC/PR (Pubic Relations) machinery went with them to report the big deal in the next issue of Stars and Stripes. From then on, no more Marines were allowed to go on R&R. As far as HQ was concerned, the problem had been taken care of, so shut up already. I didn't know of one Marine who went on R&R while I was there.

WORKING ON THE FRONT

When opposing forces settle into static defenses, they both seek the ideal terrain for defense, but at they also require high points for observation of the enemy's movements. Our (UN) air forces were essentially unopposed by the communists, so we could use our aircraft for observation of their activities at least during the daylight hours. This lack of control of the air on the Chinese-North Korean side forced them to seek the highest ground for their MLR in the western sector of Korea.

Because I was a peon, I have no idea why our MLR was situated out in the flatlands. This choice probably had something to do with where the Army forces found themselves after their last push north. The fact that truce talks were in progress at Panmunjom also entered into it, because it was just inside North Korea but across the UN MLR. A perimeter a mile or so across was established around the town of Panmunjom as a neutral area because of the truce talks. No aircraft were allowed to fly over that area, and there was to be no aggressive military activity within the perimeter. That meant no patrols and no firing of weapons of any kind. Any violation of these conditions by either side would threaten to halt the truce talks.

In order to mark the Panmunjom location for opposing forces, there was an aerostat of the old barrage balloon type tethered at the site of the truce talks. It floated a couple of hundred feet above the ground during the day. It could be seen for miles. At night a powerful searchlight plied its beam straight up into the sky and could be seen from a greater distance.

While the truce talks were going on, the fighting continued on both sides of the Panmunjom site. The infantry patrols on both sides must have appreciated the presence of the beacon at night to help them find their way to their objectives and back to their bunkers before dawn. It gave them a fixed point in the air for orientation.

The wide space between our MLR and that of the Chinese had been traditionally used for rice fields. The lay of the land threatened to allow runoff from the coming summer rains to flood Marine bunkers and trenches. Division HQ had our engineers study the possibility of using earth moving equipment to haul dirt just in front of the MLR to build up a 12 foot high berm for hundreds of yards in front of their trench to protect our infantry. Engineer officers said that it could be done, but only if we used our trucks and dozers from the crack of dawn until mid morning and only if the dump trucks were driven slowly so that no trails of dust would attract the attention of the Chinese artillery forward observers. I was not assigned to this project, probably because there was no drilling and blasting to be done. The dozer operators and truck drivers who worked out there for several weeks, kept us posted.

By this time spring of 1952 we were receiving our first draftees, FNGs. The USMC was not getting enough volunteers in 1951 and they were taking men who were drafted. I don't know if they had a choice of the Marines or Army or they were ordered to the Marines, but it was not a happy occasion for those men. The USMC also came to regret this decision. It is one thing to put a draftee into an outfit that is full of them such as the Army, and quite another to push them in with an all volunteer outfit. Because the Marines and the Army Airborne were originally all volunteer units, the training command could do just about anything to them in the way of discipline. They couldn't however, abuse draftees in the name of training and discipline. After all they didn't choose to be in the military at all, whereas we volunteers did so opt and were bound to put up with whatever was dished out to us.

Some draftees were OK, others simply didn't measure up. We began to refer to them as sloppy selection, because of the letters SS (Selective Service) in front of their serial numbers. We had one draftee FNG driver, just in from the states who brought us unwanted attention. He thought he was hearing things when his new duties were described to him, The gunny explained that he was to drive his truck out to the project site in front of the lines. The trucks would be loaded with fill and they would then all drive very slowly, so as not to raise any dust, to the berm and spread the dirt on top. He was also told to drive with the windshield secured down on the hood. When the FNG asked why drive slowly with the windshield down, the gunny gave him the business. He told the him that if you drive fast enough to raise the dust, or if you drive with the windshield up so the sun is reflected from it, the Chinese FOs will start lobbing shells at us.

The FNG was no fool. When he got out there he made a few trips back and forth hauling dirt and drove slowly with the windshield down. As the morning light grew brighter and he thought about it, he figured that the Chinese aren't blind. If they can see the glint from a glass, and can see our dust, then they can sure as hell see us right now. So he began to speed up to get the work over with. The other drivers tried to wave him down to tell him to slow down he was making too much dust. Finally the Chinese, who knew what we were doing anyway, thought we were poking them in the eye. They lobbed a few shells in on the berm. No one was hurt but the work had to be secured for the day. The guy in charge sent all the trucks back and told the senior driver to tell the gunny what happened. He wanted that FNG run up on charges of disobeying orders and endangering everyone on the job.

Nothing ever came of it because of the FNG sloppy selection status. He was simply given other assignments to the rear. The heavy equipment section was headed by Staff Sgt. Pappy Admunsen, a portly fellow with a cherubic face and handlebar moustache. He asked for volunteers to take a dozer out on this job. The dozer was parked behind a small hill out of the sight of the enemy most of the day, but worked on the berm in the early dawn under the fog and haze. The operators Irwin Grossman, John Chapin and two others, took turns operating the TD-18 until the work was spotted by the Chinese FOs. The Chinese decided to lob a few shells into the work area while the dozer was leveling and compacting the dirt on the berm. The first round whistled over, probably as a warning. Then another came in to bracket the dozer. Before the third one was on its way, Pappy had Chapin's attention and he was able to leap off the dozer. They took cover in the trench but the TD-18 was damaged by an airburst. The shrapnel cut the hydraulic hoses and damaged some other soft parts like the radiator. When the harassing fire stopped, they turned off the engine. The disabled dozer was taken out after dark by a tank retriever and dropped off in our company compound. I don't know why they didn't use a tank dozer from the Tank Battalion for this job in the first place, but I'm told by a friend, Walter Rockwood, a former captain in Army armored, that they are too slow and of limited capacity in moving dirt.

I recently learned that Sgt. John Chapin was awarded a Bronze Star at Camp Geiger in 1953 for his work under fire in front of the lines. John was surprised to find himself the center of attention at a ceremony complete with the band playing. Chapin believes that three others in Able Company were later given the Bronze Star for the same project in Korea. If I knew who they were I would honor them here as I do former Sgt. John T. Chapin for having guts. One of them may have been Sgt. Irwin Grossman from North Dakota. John says that at the time, he didn't think much of it while waiting in the front line trench for the enemy to stop firing. He felt that he was only doing his job.

LACK O'NOOKIE

Because we were now in an agricultural area and not too far from what was left of Seoul, we were more apt to run into civilians even though the USMC tried to keep us away from them to keep down any untoward incidents. It also helped to keep the VD rate low among Marines in Korea at that time. I recall being on one work detail where we came across a family trying to farm a plot. There was a small hut here and a large field of corn. There were four of us walking through the property looking for an old gravel pit we had been told about.

As we spotted the hut and approached it out of curiosity, we saw an older couple and a young woman. We were all gawking at the young Korean and I noticed the sergeant who was with us showing a little too much interest in her . He was already drooling. I sensed from his attitude that this is the first woman he had been close to for maybe ten months and he was going to screw her whether she agreed or not. When he let us know what he had in mind, we began to argue with him. We went back and forth. He told us he was going to fuck her right there and we told him that he would have to do it over one of our dead bodies. While the four of us stood there waving our rifles around, the three Koreans stole off into the high corn. When the sergeant noticed they were gone, he was angry and pointed his carbine toward the cornfield yelling for them to come back or he would blast them. The three of us were finally able to calm him down and we told him if he gave it up, we would not mention it to anyone back at camp. I'm sure this type of incident has gone on in every war, but with sadder consequences.

A GI who claimed to have access to info derived from interrogating Chinese prisoners, told me the Chinese Army didn't have a problem with horny troops trying to screw any civilian woman they came across. For good behavior, hard work and acts of valor, the Chinese soldier was given a fuck bar, that when redeemed at the local camp followers' tent, entitled him to so many lays. It was a small cast metal token they could carry with them and was inscribed with whatever the soldier was due.

They called it the key to the Jade Gate. I have no way to confirm this story. How wonderful for them. And all we got were Hershey bars—but with nuts for acts of valor.

Now if you don't believe the Chinese fuck bars, I can document the existence of a girly unit in the French Army fighting the Vietminh in Indochina. I quote no other than Bernard Fall, PhD, a military historian and an expert on the politico-military situation in Indochina. He devotes chapter 6 of his book, *Street Without Joy,* to The Women. It is written from his diary and he refers to the traditional, although unofficial, outfit of French Colonial Forces called the BMC, the *Bordel Mobile de Campagne* (Mobile Field Brothel). BMC used to stand for *Battalion Medicale de Campagne* until it was coopted by the duty broads. The women in this unit not only offered their charms to the troops, but also fought their way out of ambushes with their French escort unit, served as auxiliary nurses at the battle of Dien Bien Phu, and worked as intelligence operatives for the French Army. The native women came primarily from a tribe in North Africa. I met Dr. Fall who had an apartment in our compound in Phnom Penh, Cambodia in 1960-61. He was killed by a mine while on patrol with a US Marine unit in Vietnam in 1967. It was unfortunate, because he was a Professor at Howard University in Washington, D.C. and as such, one of the few Frenchmen that the politicos in that city would listen to about our half-assed involvement in Vietnam.

Further evidence of actual field brothels during WWII was recently brought to light when a number of Korean women conscripts, shanghaied by the Japanese, brought a lawsuit against the Japanese government for damages. They were kept by the Japanese troops overseas as sex slaves and were called comfort girls. In their testimony they added that they were also physically abused in many ways. Japan had completely dominated Korea at the time WWII broke out. For details read, "*The Battle for Manila,*" by Richard Connaughton, et. al.

Although my father never talked about the subject, I understand from all the accounts I have read of WWI, that women were available to troops. Normally this would occur when they were in a rest area, in immediate reserve just behind their battalion on the lines, or in some movement to new positions. There were cafes, called *estaminets* located in some towns, even in buildings that were half destroyed. Since Dad could speak French, I imagine he tried to make out with the local women, just like the rest of the guys. When facing death constantly, you think that every piece of tail might be your last, so there is a certain abandonment of moral strictures previously adhered to by most. French men apparently didn't complain, since they understood that their women were a bit hard up after hundreds of thousands of French soldiers had been killed between 1914 and the time the Americans arrived in three years later.

According to Fussell, in *The Great War and Modern Memory*, the British Expeditionary Forces (BEF) in France and Belgium during WWI adhered to the British caste system. Tarts were readily available in the towns near their billets with the blue light for officers and the red light for other ranks.

Other things I heard about the Chinese and North Koreans from guys in line outfits was that as POWs under our control, the Chinese and North Koreans lived well after they were captured compared with our guys on the lines. The POWs lived in a secured compound surrounded by guards and barbed wire, but they had three hot meals per day, slept on cots and had electric lights in their tents. We suspected that our POWs, however, were treated very badly . The facts came out at the end of the war, when we learned from the few ragged survivors about the torture and abuse of American and UN troops at the hands of the enemy. Many of our men died simply because their wounds and ailments were left untreated or they were forced to wallow in their own filth for months and years.

The summer months of 1952 were much the same as in 1951, lots of rain, mud, mosquitos, sweltering heat and boredom when I was not sleeping or working. When there was a dry spell we ate dust every day. I was told to report to a special training session for drivers, which was to last a week. It was held near the Imjin River under the leadership of a lieutenant from the 7th MT Battalion. Some engineer had figured out a way to waterproof vehicles, which was an important development for an amphibious force.

We attended lectures on the waterproofing system and spent several days working on adapting various types of vehicles so they could be driven in very deep water. There wasn't much application for this idea in Korea, unless we were going to make another landing as the 1stMarDiv had done early on at Inchon and at Wonsan.

The system involved the sealing of any part of the engine that needed to be kept dry to function while running. A properly waterproofed vehicle could be driven off an LST or other landing craft through water that would cover the engine compartment. Extension tubing was attached to the carburetor air intake and the exhaust pipe and then fixed to the sides of the windshield and extended a couple of inches above it. The distributor, coil, plug wires, and other electrical components were sealed with a type of plasticine that stuck to the surrounding metal and plastic parts. The plasticine was also attached firmly over the air breather valves on the transmission and on each of the differentials on the axles.

We took turns testing the vehicles in some of the shallow waters along the edge of the river bank where there was a gentle slope. On the first day when a big Jimmy 6X6 had been completely waterproofed, the instructor had the driver inch his truck up to the river's edge. No one was sure of the water depth away from the bank at that time and the officer was uncertain about having the driver go too far. A Korean was paddling around in the water about 15 feet from the shore in front of us. The lieutenant called out asking him how deep it was by motioning with his hand up at his neck. I doubt that the Korean understood English and as he dog paddled, he started nodding and motioning with his hand up at his neck as he saw the officer doing. He accepted that as the water level and assumed the guy was walking around on the bottom, so he told the driver to drive slowly into the water.

The driver put the truck in gear and went slowly into the river until the point where he was pretty wet, but kept going. Then the truck disappeared entirely while the driver floated away and swam back to the shore. The water was a lot deeper than that Korean stood tall. Water had flooded both the carburetor and the exhaust system when those tubes went under the surface and that killed the engine. By the time we pulled the driver in, the Korean swimmer was gone. He may have been from the North Korean Dept. of MisInformation. Some of our swimmers hooked a chain to the rear end of the drowned Jimmy and we pulled it out with the winch—an engine rebuilding job for the mechanics back at Battalion.

All of our trucks and dozers were equipped with power take off (PTO) winches. They were in front between the bumper and the grillwork on the vehicles and on the rear behind the driver's seat on the dozers. Because our winches saved us from a lot of hand labor moving heavy objects around, we had to gave them special attention in preventive maintenance. When in use, we had to be sure that the cable didn't kink anywhere as this would ruin the cable. When we finished using the winch, we carefully wound the cable back onto the drum so that it wasn't binding in a small loop somewhere. Then the wound cable was covered with a light coat of motor oil or grease and covered with a piece of burlap which was secured with wires. This kept the cable from rusting and the cover kept the road dust out.

ROTATING OUT

I was not due to leave Korea until just after the first of August 1952. But in the middle of July, the gunny (Tech. Sgt. Peacock) told me and a few other guys who came over in my draft to stand by to be rotated out in a few days as soon as the paperwork came down from Battalion. I didn't ask any questions and went around saying goodbye to buddies here and there. By this time I didn't have much personal gear to organize and my clothes were pretty well worn out. I stowed a few things in my pack and turned in my rifle, ammo, 782 gear and whatever else the government owned and sat on my cot waiting for transport.

A truck pulled into the compound with some guys going home from other companies. I shook the hands of a few Able engineers who came out to see us off then climbed aboard for the first leg of the trip home. We stopped at some other camps enroute to Munsan-ni or some other railhead. We boarded a train that was similar to one described by my father for moving US troops around France. In France the box cars were known as 40 or 8's, *(quarante ou huit)*. They had a capacity of 40 men or eight horses. The doughboys and tommies referred to them as "carrots or wheat," a corruption of the French pronunciation.

Our train had cattle cars that still had straw all over the decks. There were two choices, either sit on the straw or stand all the way to the port. Most of us stood because we were restless and the view of the countryside was better. Some, like myself were wondering if there was some mistake in the orders and when we got to Inchon, we would be shipped back to our outfits.

We arrived at a siding on the outskirts of Inchon and were taken by trucks to a huge replacement depot, comprised of course, entirely of tents. Here we would go through the motions of decontamination and processing before boarding the troop ship. We formed in long lines and as we came to one point, we were told to undo belts, open your pants, and uncover (remove your cap to you civilians). Try doing all that at once. There was a Marine standing there with a Flit gun filled with a white powder, probably DDT. He shot one burst into my hair, which was so long it took several. Then a burst into the cap in my hand. When my pants were open he shot a dose of powder into my crotch. I knew that they had a terrible problem with cooties in the trenches in WWI, but I wasn't sure about Korea. I guess the USMC was not taking any chances.

At one point we were also dewormed. The medical people assumed that since the roads were so dusty, we were all bound to have worms. Everyone in Korea was breathing the dust so we were given some medicine to act as a vermicide. If you want to know what good that does, it kills *verms* . That's German for worms.

Next we went to chow. Then off to the showers with hot water to start the process of removing the crud from our skins. Before we went into the showers we stripped bare and threw our clothes into a huge pile. We were told that they would be burned, which is what they did with the clothing of captured enemy troops. We were told not to linger too long in the showers. We could come back anytime to soak in the hot water. As we left the shower tent, we were issued new USMC dungarees to wear on the trip home.

We were at the RepoDepo for about five days of processing. At one point an officer asked me how I felt about going home? I said that I was overjoyed. He then told me that I wouldn't be allowed to board the ship until I got my hair cut. I went straight to the camp barber and was properly sheared down to the scalp.

One of the RepoDepo regulations explained to us the day we arrived, was that we were not permitted outside of the fence to fool around with civilians. The CO said that the consequences to offenders would be dire. The really horny guys there could smell women in the nearby shanty towns and took the risk. Those who were caught going under or over the fence were in fact severely punished. They were sent back to line outfits for another two months. If a guy hadn't been in a line outfit before, he served his extra two months in one.

The sad thing is that the shit hit the fan in August and September and the two opposing armies went at each other with a vengeance. I wonder if any of those fence climbers became casualties just for a piece of nookie. Try explaining that back home when some friend asked how a guy got his Purple Heart. He would have to say, " Well, I was OK until I went under the fence from the RepoDepo to have my white count lowered. The next day I was in a fire fight and got hit. I was patched up, sent back to the lines and a month later was hit by mortar fragments. All because of the lure of a woman."

Most of the guys on the way out were reunited with their seabags. For some reason, my own had disappeared. I was issued a new set of nearly everything in the way of clothing, except winter woolen greens. I needed some khakis in case we pulled liberty in a Japanese port.

The day we left the RepoDepo it was raining. We were trucked down to the port, where we stood around on the top of the sea wall for hours. There were few ships about and no wonder, because the tide in the Inchon area could vary 36 feet from low to high. Most of the cargo coming into port is brought in by lighters and unloaded by hand. We found that we would be going out the same way, but in landing craft. Our transport was anchored out in the mist somewhere in deeper water.

It continued to rain as we climbed down the sea wall and clambered aboard the LCTs (Landing Craft Tank). The seabags had been sent to the ship so there was more room to cram us into the landing craft. It was after dark as we circled around the harbor for a couple of hours waiting our turn to approach the ship. Those of us lucky enough to hold on to our ponchos stayed dry from the knees up but the others were drenched. When we got to the ship, we scrambled onto a flat barge tied up alongside and then filed through a side hatch into the ship's bowels.

This troop ship, the USS General Black or some such name, was twice the size of an APA. It was belonged to the Military Sea Transportation Service (MSTS). The troop complement was about 50:50 Army soldiers to Marines. The lucky Army troops had been hastily sanitized at some base in Inchon and would be going to Sasebo, Japan for a week stay at their own Repo Depo. The lucky Marines were destined to be going straight home, even though we had convinced ourselves that we would be going on a three-day liberty spree in Japan.

I now realize why I was allowed to rotate out of Korea two weeks early. Instead of going home on a little APA, the MSTS sent this huge ship, which had to be filled up for the trip back. So the call went out from X Corps and 1stMarDiv HQ to round up the 11th draft men and send them home early. This ship had just delivered thousands of replacements to the RepoDepo in Japan from the west coast and then brought a lot of processed FNGs from Japan to Inchon.

The trip from Inchon to Sasebo only took a day and there was little friction between the Marines and the Army. When we pulled into port and began to unload the soldiers there, we got the word that the ship would only be there long enough for the soldiers to get off. We then took on another bunch of soldiers that had been left there a week earlier. So there would be no liberty for any Marines. There was a lot of grumbling but no sparks as we gazed out at the city and thought about what might have been a great liberty. I suspect that the USMC brass wanted to spare the nice people of Sasebo a frontal assault of several thousand horny young men. It would be more diplomatic to have them blow off steam back in the states where they would be absorbed into the vastness of an understanding home population. To appease us somewhat, we Marines could draw some of our pay even though there was little to buy at ship's store, except cigarettes at eight cents per pack.

Although the US Navy in fact ran the ship, a large part of the crew were contract employees of the U.S. Merchant Marine. This meant that we would not be on a lot of shit details such as chipping paint. Because most of the Marines and soldiers on board were returning from combat, we were all left pretty much alone.

Most of our time was spent resting, reading and watching the nightly movie on deck. The below decks accommodations were just as packed as they were in coming over, but the ship was much larger than an APA so it tossed and pitched less. The meals were good compared to the field chow in Korea, even though we were back on the two large meals per day because of the large number of troops aboard.

There were a few jobs announced for those who wanted them. I chose to work in the carpenter's shop as a gofer. My most memorable day on that detail found me delivering a large sheet of plywood from the shop amidships to a compartment forward in the fo'csle. I have long arms and can easily handle a four- by-eight-foot sheet of plywood. My problem was that I only weighed 145 pounds and I was on the wrong side of the sheet as I went forward. I was outboard and carrying the plywood to the inboard side. Everything was fine until I passed the end of the superstructure on the port side and was exposed to the wind ripping across the deck from starboard. The plywood nailed me to the railing and I was stuck there for about five minutes. I was hollering for help, but the sound was carried off with the wind. A sailor on watch on an upper deck saw my predicament and sent a couple of guys to pull it off me. That scared the crap out of me and I still wonder if this landlubber wasn't set up by the carpenters just to blow me away. If that railing had been a simple cable as on some ships, I would have sailed off into the Pacific with only the plywood for a raft.

There were so many Marine veterans of the line companies on the ship that I decided to let the snorers make as much noise as they could at night. Many of these men were combat weary and a bit punchy. If a rear echelon type like me started shaking them in the middle of the night to stop their snoring, I just might get a Kabar stuck in my throat and if I survived, there wasn't thing one I could do about it.

A lot of guys drew some pay and spent the whole trip gambling. I don't understand how it can be against regulations to gamble with money on government ships and installations and still have the winners go up to some ship's officer and ask to put a couple of thousand dollars in the safe until they got home. We were allowed to put certain other items into a common secured locker for safekeeping. We were not allowed to bring home any captured weapons as souvenirs. The guys who had personal sidearms in Korea had to bring them aboard unloaded and store them in the safe room. I had traded my Walther for a captured Chinese flare pistol. I didn't want to have it confiscated so stashed it in the empty battery compartment of a guy's Zenith radio. Once aboard he placed it in the secure personal property compartment. When we got off the ship, I found that someone had stolen my only war souvenir. The Chinese used flares along with bugles to signal their troops when to begin an attack.

The crossing toward home was much faster than going over. We made it back in nineteen days from Japan to California. The rumors were flying about where and when we would land. At first we heard that we would all get off in San Diego. Then we heard that we were headed for San Francisco to let the Army off and we would then go to San Diego. That caused a stir among the Marines, especially the few married guys A few days out from port we learned that it would be San Diego and we were elated. There was a mimeographed sheet issued every other day with world news and military items of interest to crew and passengers. I recall that when we were a day out of San Diego, we noted a crisis in the Mojave Desert in California. There had been an earthquake that morning at Tehachapi. It was so destructive that part of the wall at the state womens' prison fell down. Many prisoners made off into the desert and the surrounding mountains.

Most of the Marines aboard forgot about the big deal of landing on US soil, all they were talking about was volunteering to go to Tehachapi straight away and help round up the female poojies. These horny men who had not seen a woman for a year wanted to spend some quality time in the chaparral with women who had not been near a man for several years. What a laugh that gave us, but some turkeys were dead serious about rescuing those women.

STATESIDE

The port of San Diego looked a lot better to us this time than when we left just over a year before. There were some small Navy vessels sent out to greet our ship and we lined the railing taking it all in. It was sunny and warm at midday and we really felt good about coming home. Just looking at this wonderful city from the middle of the harbor made everyone forget about chasing female prisoners at Tehachapi.

While the ship was being secured quay side, we went below to gather up personal effects. Our seabags would be off loaded and delivered to our quarters in San Diego. As we filed through the hatch and onto the pier I noticed a scattering of civilians, mostly wives and parents waiting to greet their loved ones. One of my buddies nudged me and pointed to a very pregnant young woman. He said, "If her husband is getting off with us and has been gone a year, she has some explaining to do." I told him that I would not want to see his expression when he sees her.

I went over to a small stand offering refreshments and was handed a cup of java and a fresh donut by a middle age woman. She said it was with the compliments of the Gray Ladies. For me it was a grand welcome home. Like the returning Vietnam veterans, there would be no band, no parades, no banners, no hoopla like that given the WWI and WWII vets. The woman's simple gesture of hot coffee and a dunker was good enough for me.

No more riding in cattle cars and in the backs of trucks. USMC buses took us through San Diego straight to the USMC Recruit Depot (USMCRD). We pulled up to an area of Quonset huts where we would stay until we were processed out of here within a week. While we waited for our seabags to arrive we went to the mess hall for lunch and spent the afternoon standing around in front of the huts watching the new boots go through their troop and stomp routine.

For us salty vets who had gone through Parris Island (PI), the MCRD at San Diego was known as the place that turned out Hollywood Marines. Due to its prominent location, very close to civilization, this boot camp had a reputation for being less harsh than PI. If a DI really harassed a skinhead here, it would be in full view of civilians in and around the base. At PI, a DI could do just about anything to a boot out in the open air and no one would hear or see it except other Marines, sea gulls, and of course the sand fleas. Near our huts we discovered a set of 72 perfectly aligned foot prints painted on the tarmac in the position of attention. Our first thought was that these west coast boots must really be dumb to have that done for them.

Every one of us off the ship was chomping at the bit to be off on liberty in San Diego. However, there were a number of things that were involved in the processing so we couldn't go ashore until the next day. We had no money and had to wait for pay call. We had to take a brief physical to make sure we didn't have any oriental diseases to spread around the US. The medics were still looking for *verms.* Those who lost their ID cards had to be issued new ones and we needed liberty cards to get off the base. I must admit that the base admin types went all out to get us on our way home.

Our seabags were delivered that afternoon. My khakis were all brand new and had been rolled up in the bottom of my seabag. Another guy dug out his old khakis and put them on as I did with mine. We laughed at the sight of these rumpled uniforms and decided that we would never be allowed off the base by the MPs at the gate. We still looked like Willy and Joe, even though we were clean shaven and our hair was close cropped. The only part of our uniforms that would stand inspection were our shoes, which we had two weeks to spit shine, and regulation socks. We couldn't find an iron to press our clothes anywhere in the area.

We didn't want to be sitting around the huts on our first night back in the states, so we decided to go to the movies on the base. There shouldn't be any problem with that. We pulled into the lobby of the base theater about 15 minutes before show time. There were a lot of brown-bagger Marines and dependents waiting for the doors to open. We felt their eyes running over us slobs and we ignored them. A few minutes later a staff NCO came over and said that he was from Special Services. His khaki uniform was crisply starched and very squared away. He sported only a Good Conduct Ribbon and a Sharp Shooter badge on his shirt.

He said he managed the theater and told us that we couldn't be admitted inside because our uniforms were a mess. I explained our situation to him with some chagrin. What a welcome home this was. We can't go to town. We can't go to the slop chute, because we have no money and we would be highly pissed if we couldn't even go to the free movie. He told us to calm down, then said that he would let us in only after everyone else was seated and the lights were out. In the meantime he told us to go around the corner outside the building and wait there were no one could see us. I thought I heard him muttering about Willy and Joe as he left. Welcome home Korean Vets! We're so very proud of you that you have to hide outside then sneak into the movie on the sly so no respectable people can see your wrinkled uniforms. Damn the brown-baggers! It was still good to be home.

The next day we were paid, issued new ID and liberty cards,and given a chance to iron our khakis. Those who had been promoted in the past year, including me, were given new stripes, which had to be sewed on. We were also given something else we didn't have before we left, campaign ribbons. One was the Korean Service Medal, with three battle stars. Another was the United Nations service ribbon. I've just found out that we were supposed to be issued the National Defense Service Medal or ribbon, but I've never seen either one.

All the time we were in Korea and all the way back on the ship there was a lot of talk about what everyone would do as soon as they were let loose in the USA. Some would head for the bars and get sloshed. Others wanted only to go to a fine restaurant and order a thick steak with a baked potato and fresh vegetables. The cockhounds would try to charm some wanton woman into bed. The first day I was ashore in San Diego, I just walked all over the city looking at everything. For some reason all I wanted to do was drink fresh milk and then pig out in a good restaurant.

While we were aboard ship we were given a form to fill out about our next assignment. The gist of it was that we were to list our first three choices of duty stations after our tour of duty on Korea. Like a fool, I thought they (Personnel at USMCHQ) were serious, but they had already made decisions for us before they saw our completed forms. On my form I had listed Terminal Island, Treasure Island, and Barstow Supply Depot. These were all Marine posts, the first two on the California coast and Barstow out in the Mojave desert close to Tehachapi (pure coincidence). I'm sure that USMC gave a lot of thought to my selections. When I received my orders they read, "Thirty Days leave, then report to the 2nd Engineer Battalion, 2nd MarDiv, FMF, Camp Lejeune, NC."

I should have known that the choice of duty form was probably only meant for officers and staff NCOs but only a sop for us EMs. The new posting was at the convenience of the government. I found later that one was assigned to eastern posts if your home was east of the Mississippi. Everyone from west of the mighty river went to western posts more or less. Also, I had an MOS that was needed by the engineers and I was a natural for Camp Lejeune.

Cpl. Dick Hayes at tent camp. Battalion in reserve from the 7th Marines on the lines. Winter 1951/1952 near the Punchbowl.

"Bones" Ginnelly with ringneck pheasant to share with tent mates for a change of rations. Western Korea, May 1953.

Sgts. Spike Bernauer and Bill Hepinger, Able Engrs. welders. Punchbowl Jan. 1952.

Cpls. John Birty, Bob Callahan, Monty Cessna, John Chapin standing. Punchbowl, North Korea, Mar. 1952.

Cpls. Milliken and Lopez on mine clearing detail frustrated by shrapnel giving false readings on mine detector. North Rim of Punchbowl, Oct. 1951. Photo: Jim Milliken

Marine Corsair after a controlled crash landing on new emergency strip built by Able Engrs. Punchbowl, North Korea Feb. 1952.

Cpl. Jim Milliken's mine clearing detail captures two North Korean soldiers on the North Rim of Punchbowl. Oct. 1951. Photo: Jim Milliken

Taking a bath, washing up as far as possible. Life in the Punchbowl, Oct. 1951. Not much privacy!

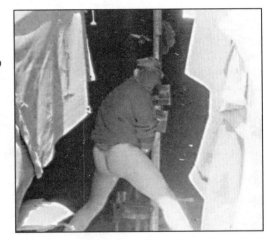

Able Engineers' camp West Korea. Cpls. John Chapin and "Bones" Ginnelly. Ssgt. Pappy Admundsen standing near Chapin's dozer damaged by enemy artillery airburst. April 1952

Cpl. Sam Camarato (Ration Raider) and platoon mascot. Able Engineers camp in the Punchbowl, March 1951.

Jim Kramer, Engineer in 11th Marine's firing pit next to Able Engineers' camp in Punchbowl, Dec. 1951. The 105mm fired over our tents at night. Photo: Jim Milliken.

The Able Engineer's drill team: "Bones" Ginnelly, Jimmy and LeRoi ready for the day's drilling and blasting. Punchbowl, N. Korea, 1951

Korean Marine Regiment machine gun crew guarding the southern end of the railroad bridge across the Imjin River. The Freedom Gate bridge is seen below. May 1951.

Railroad bridge with spans in Imjin River. Adjacent Freedom Gate Bridge built by 84th ECB 8th Army, 10 Mar 52. Photo: US Army (via NARA, Washington, D.C.)

"Bones loading his truck with the Allis Chalmers front loader. Korea, June 1952.

Able Co. Engineers escorting Marine tank up to the lines on the north rim of the Punchbowl, North Korea, winter 1951-1952. Photo: J.M. Milliken

PART THREE
SECOND MARINE DIVISION
FMF

PART THREE: SECOND MARINE DIVISION, FMF

 ## HOME LEAVE

MY ACCUMULATED PAY OVER THE PAST YEAR amounted to more than $1000, so I spent the whole month's leave in Detroit having a good time. Some of my acquaintances around the old neighborhood really pissed me off when they greeted me. They would say," Hi! Where ya been these past few months?" I just fumed and didn't try to explain that I had not been in Detroit for 16 months and hadn't seen any of them for at least 18 months. That didn't tick me off half as much as some friends asking me if I wanted to go camping while I was home. I had to explain to them that I had been living in tents since early Feb. 1951, eating canned and powdered food and going camping was not my idea of a good time. I had another 17 months to go in the Corps and that would likely include plenty of camping opportunities.

I grew up in a neighborhood full of Finns and had become accustomed to regularly taking a sauna bath. After a year of bathing in a helmet and with very few hot showers, I figured I was a candidate for a good old Finnish bath. The drill is that you sit on the bench at whatever level was comfortable and pour cold water onto the hot stones on the stove. The steam is not visible but you can feel it. It is not uncommon for the temperature at the top seat to reach 200° F. Often it got so hot the air was scalding my lungs, so I learned like the young Finns to cover my mouth and nose with a damp washcloth and breathe through that. Otherwise you had to move down to the next bench or the lowest one.

I went to the sauna with some Finlander friends. Taking a sauna is a social affair for them. After ten minutes I was amazed to see the brown crud coming out of my pores all over. That was Korean dust and dirt being forced out and sterilized in a Finnish steam room. A few more minutes of steam and I began flogging myself with a small pine bough to improve the circulation under the skin. The pine boughs are for us kids. The old Finns still use a birch switch on their tough hides. In other places like the Upper Peninsula of Michigan, when the Finns are through in the sauna they go out and roll bare-assed in the snow. In the summer they just jump into a cold lake or a horse trough. That would separate the faint hearted from the real Finns. I had to settle for a cold shower. Afterwards I felt like a million dollars and had probably washed away a pound of Korean dirt.

I did go out to swill a few beers with Ted Kilberg, the guy I had enlisted and gone through boot camp with. When I went off to Korea with the rest of the guys in training at Camp Pendleton, I lost track of Ted. During his session there, the Training Command found out that Ted had played hockey in and around Detroit and Windsor, Ontario. So they put him on the base hockey team. He played there for quite a while until one night he was run over on Hwy.101. Ted said he was celebrating and perhaps reliving a hockey game. He was hit by a car while trying to get the puck out of the middle of the road. Perhaps he mistook the yellow line for the blue line. His leg bones were badly fractured and the doctors had to put them back together with pins and steel rods, etc. Here he was back home with a medical disability discharge and going to the VA hospital for rehab treatment.

He had to wear a large brace on that leg from hip to foot and was hobbling around the old hangouts when I got there. By the end of the first evening, I was slightly ticked because Ted was making out with women falling all over the injured Marine. I guess that they just assumed that he had been wounded in Korea so he needed some TLC. I was concerned that he would never play hockey again and he lived for that game. Ted recently told me that he was able to coach hockey teams around the Detroit area for many years and five of his players ended up in the NHL.

Most of our old friends were now off in Korea or somewhere else in the military, so I decided to spend more time with my family before heading off to my new post.

CAMP LEJEUNE

I arrived at Camp Lejeune, NC in September and reported to the central office with my travel orders. I was taken by Jeep to the HQ area of the 2nd Engr. Bn. A personnel type in HQ Co. talked to me about the outfit while we waited for a Jeep to take me to Charlie Co. The Jeep driver was W.T. Martin, a good natured bear of a man who told me that he was from Fancy Gap, Virginia and he welcomed me to Charlie Co. W.T. took me into the company office where the company clerk took my orders and introduced me to Master Sgt. Rozier who asked me a lot of questions and gave me a rundown on the company. He informed me that as in Korea, I would be in HQ platoon as a truck driver—and given any other duties that they could think of as needed.

The HQ platoon Sgt. showed up and escorted me across the street to the barracks and told me to choose any empty locker and rack nearby. I then went off to supply for a set of sheets and blankets. When I got back, the squad bay was filling up with guys coming in from work at the end of the day. I introduced myself to those near my new rack and began to stow my gear. Next day I felt a little better when I found two guys in Charlie Co. who had been in other platoons back in Able Co. and had rotated home a month or two before I did. They were Sam Camarato from Cleveland, Ohio, and Jim Milliken from Enola, Pennsylvania. This gave me someone to relate to, with regard to the experience in Korea.

I was surprised to find that my original seabag showed up from the great storage limbo across the Pacific. The supply man, SSgt. Harry Reed asked me how I got along without it for the past three months and I explained the second issue of clothing at the RepoDepo at Inchon. I asked him if there was a problem about having two nearly complete issues of uniforms. He thought that I had been around long enough not to ask any questions like that. If the great supply honcho at USMC HQ wanted some of it back, they would let me know.

I fell into the work routine, which at the time seemed to center around making our trucks look pretty. We had a platoon leader who insisted that we coat all of our trucks with a light film of diesel fuel when we were preparing for an inspection. It reminded me of an old salt's saw, "Fall in with dress blues and tennis shoes, clean tie ties, and a light coat of oil"—a spoof on idiotic commands. The coat of oil had to be applied to the deadlined trucks, even though they were not running. During my first few months at Camp Lejeune, I had some difficulty adjusting to the routine of living in a barracks and all of the other crap like parades and inspections.

I didn't know how to cope with this stateside nonsense, and I thought that maybe Korea wasn't so bad after all. So I asked to see the top and told him I wanted to go back to Korea as soon as possible. He looked at me as though I was off my rocker and said that I should know that there is a line ahead of me. He said that as soon as every Marine stateside who had not already been there was sent to Korea for a tour, then I could go back. About a month later the top asked me if I still wanted to return to Korea. I said that I did. He asked the clerk for my SRB and when he got it, he looked for something and told me to stand by. He said that he'd found a way for me to do it.

It seems that a flyer had just come in from the Office of the Commandant HQ, Washington, D.C. circulated to all posts. The message was that there was a shortage of platoon leaders in the Corps, especially in Korea and to solve this problem the personnel staff at USMCHQ had decided to lower the GCT score from 120 points to 115 to qualify an EM for OCS at Quantico, VA. Officers Candidate School there turned out new second lieutenants to serve as platoon leaders throughout the Corps. The top looked up my GCT score and noted that it was 119. Where this would not do when I was in boot camp, all of a sudden it was my entry to OCS and a return trip to Korea. I asked the top if I could think about it first and he said there was no hurry.

I went back to the barracks and thought it over for one whole hour. It should not have taken that long to figure out that this shortage of platoon leaders in Korea was due to the high casualty rate among them. I also had to wonder why I would want to try to become a 2nd lieutenant when I did not like some of the ones I came across. Then I pondered the fact that an officer is commissioned for life and serves at the pleasure of the President. In other words, after one's initial active duty hitch as an officer, one is in the reserves until he retires or resigns his commission. Whereas when my three year hitch was up, I was to be honorably discharged and my obligation to the military was over. I would be out in 15 months and off to college and a career as a civilian, so I said screw all this stuff. I went back and explained my decision to the top and then fell into the stateside routine with some satisfaction. I was going to be a 20 year man all right: three in and 17 out.

Someone high up at USMC HQ had the great idea that Marines must learn how to make amphibious landings in all kinds of weather and unusual conditions. To this end they began a series of annual visits to Goose Bay Labrador, courtesy of the US Navy amphibious fleet, and with the permission of the Canadian Government. These landings were held during the very coldest months for maximum training effect.

When I got wind of these maneuvers, and that I was a candidate to go along in one of the soon to be ice encrusted LSTs in December 1952 and January of 1953, I began scheming to get out of it. My platoon sergeant sent me to see the top. When I explained that I had spent the winter of 1951-52 living more or less outside in one of the coldest places on earth, I had become very allergic to the cold and thought that I have already qualified for cold weather training in the rough. I didn't go into the medical condition caused by the Korean cold, as my scrotum was still somewhat blue and wrinkled.

I added that many of the guys in Charlie Co. who had not been to Korea would benefit from the pleasure cruise to Goose Bay. They put their heads together and decided I was right. The next day my name was removed from the Goose Bay roster and placed at the top of the volunteers for the amphibious landings on Vieques Island, Puerto Rico. I was elated. Out of the deep freeze and into the sunny tropics. It pays to complain in a diplomatic manner.

In retrospect I was also lucky enough to escape being sent on another "volunteer" assignment, which has eventually resulted in the slow death of some of the participants. I refer to the atomic bomb tests at the Nevada test site, and some of the atolls in the Pacific Ocean. Several times while I was at Camp Lejeune the call went out for volunteers to travel to these sites and stand around in trenches, albeit at a "safe" distance from ground zero to measure the effects of the bomb's radiation on troops.

For a number of years now, there has been overwhelming evidence that the radiation from these detonations has seriously affected the health of not only the GIs who were exposed to them, but to civilians who lived downwind in Nevada, Utah and Northern Arizona. I would never have volunteered for this duty and I thank God that I was not ordered to go, because I would have gone.

AMPHIBIOUS OPERATIONS

Sometime in January 1953 we got the word to prepare to ship out the following week. We needed at least a couple of clean sets of khakis for whatever liberty we would be allowed down there. We would be living back in tents again in Vieques, which called for dungarees all the time. In any case we took our field packs and dress shoes along. I had to prep the truck I would be driving for the landing and load my gear into it along with my rifle and field gear.

The trip to the port at Morehead City didn't take long, even though our convoy drove slowly with a good distance between vehicles to allow the civilian traffic to pass. We sat around for seven hours waiting for our LST to arrive from Little Creek, Virginia up near Norfolk. When it did pull in a Navy lieutenant came ashore to jaw with our Skipper. He was the Load Master for this trip and would direct the vehicles and equipment to designated spots on both the upper and the lower decks.

While we were loading I wandered among the vehicles checking things. Almost every truck was pulling a trailer of some sort—water tank trailers, generators, communications gear, and cargo trailers of various sizes. Even the Jeeps and weapons carriers were towing something. Some trailers had tarps drawn tight to keep out the rain and dust. I wanted to see what was in one of them and untied the lashings. When I peeled back the canvas, I was shocked to see cases of antifreeze. Now I know why we had no antifreeze in Korea for the first half of the past winter. Some rear echelon supply poge at USMC HQ on the Potomac had looked at a map in the summer of 1951 and scratched the extra antifreeze requisition from 1stMarDiv HQ, Korea. Why? Because he saw that Korea was on the same latitude as Washington, D.C., so the winters couldn't be all that bad there..

So they had been sending the extra allotment of antifreeze to the Caribbean where a dip of the temperature below 65° F. constitutes a cold wave. Now I was glad I wasn't going north to Goose Bay, Labrador for that landing. They'll be wondering where their antifreeze is. Maybe this was to stop the enlisted Marines in Korea from drinking it for want of a proper grog ration.

Everything going aboard the LST had to be backed in very carefully. Sgt. Paul Goehle supervised the loading of the bulldozers. As each vehicle or machine was jockeyed into position, it was lashed down with chains to slots in the deck by the duty deck force of the LST with the Chief Bosun Mate supervising. They left enough space between vehicles for a man to walk through on watch. The lower tank deck was filled first with most of the heavy stuff. When my turn came, I backed my truck up the ramp to the upper deck and watched as it was secured down with chains.

I was officially aboard so went looking for the gunny for my bunk assignment. The crews' and Marines' quarters were strung along the space between the hull and the lower deck's bulkhead. At least it was better than our quarters on a troopship. The compartments were small, but roomy and the bunks were only four high. Loading went on until well after dark. Right after chow, the Gunny called us together to read the duty roster for the trip. We were to stand two hour fire watches day and night for the duration of the cruise.

As I've said before, there is good duty and there is bad duty. Standing fire watch on the upper tank deck was the good, but was normally done by sailors. Doing the same stint on the lower tank deck was the pits because of sea sickness. On a huge ship like a battlewagon, cruiser, or carrier it is fairly easy going for most. The smaller the ship, the more likely it will pitch and sway and bob and weave. The worst ship to be on, when there are anything but calm seas, is a flat bottom tub like the LST.

I have made some lengthy sea voyages and was never really seasick, even on the LSTs. One thing I learned from the old Navy salts is that if I started feeling queasy when below decks in heavy seas, then head for topside in the open air. It worked every time for me. If I couldn't get topside, then I headed for the galley and asked the cook for some soda crackers. Those work most of the time, I guess by absorbing the liquids sloshing around in the stomach. The only thing that made me slightly queasy was having to smell the diesel exhaust fumes while standing in the chow line on deck. I've hated the smell of diesel fumes ever since.

The chow line formed up out on the deck and wound through a passageway in the superstructure. When the sea was up and we were about to enter the hatch into the mess area, we could see all the way through the ship from one side to the other. For a few moments all I could see through the opposite hatch was sky, then as the ship rolled, the horizon would appear. Then all I could see for the next few moments was the ocean until the cycle started again. Those with weak stomachs were advised to direct their gaze somewhere else or risk losing their meal after they ate.

The thing that I disliked most about cruising on a loaded LST was having to stand fire watch in the lower tank deck. It was like being in a huge closed metal warehouse that was pitching and yawing while I hung onto the railing at the top of the ladder. That was the best place to keep an eye on everything because I was slightly above the tops of all the cargo and could easily spot trouble. It was also the safest place to be in case a bulldozer, tank or truck broke loose from its chains. There was a ventilator bringing fresh air in from one of those funnels on the upper deck, but it didn't do much good.

Every vehicle and large machine carried either gasoline or diesel fuel in its tanks. The movement of the ship kept all that fuel sloshing around allowing the vapors to escape from the tank's vents. The whole of the lower deck was rank with these noxious fumes. A guy could get a bit queasy down here from all these fumes, so the watches were kept short. I never went into the lower deck unless I was forced to do so and I never saw any sailors down there, except for the deck crew assigned to the chaining down of cargo at loading time. They must have figured that it was our equipment, so we could watch over it.

During the night we were inched off the beach by powerful winch pulling the LST back out to its anchor. When we woke up the next morning we were well away at sea and in the company of seven other ships in convoy—mostly APAs, AKAs, and LSTs. The weather was windy and chilly, but the seas were not too rough. It was a good thing we brought our field jackets.

Four days after leaving port we headed due south between the Virgin Islands and the main island of Puerto Rico. More ships had joined us during the voyage and there were now dozens of vessels in the invasion fleet. We passed close to a small island called Culebra (Snake), where the 2ndMarDiv, used to hold its landing exercises. An old friend of mine, Jack Burch, told me of his unit in the 8th Marines making these landings in 1949.

The next day we stood well off the target island of Vieques. We watched AKAs and APAs off loading their landing craft as dawn broke. Then the infantry scrambled down the cargo nets into the Mike boats and LCVPs. Amtracs, also known as alligators, were driven fully loaded with infantry off the ramps of some LSTs into the water and made the first wave of assaulting craft up and onto the beach. When the beachhead was secured, two LSTs plowed into the beach and artillery batteries and tanks were offloaded and directed to their positions.

Our LST was equipped with two huge steel causeways, one strapped to each side of the ship. These steel rafts were almost as long as the ship itself. One edge of each causeway rested on a heavy steel flange just above the LST's water line. Each causeway was winched up so that it was even with the ship's railing on the top deck. Each was held in place by a series of one-inch cables running from the flange around the bottom of the causeway, over the railing, across large blocks of wood and secured to the deck with a turnbuckle.

The LSTs equipped with these causeways carried a small contingent of SeaBees who had installed them. As our ship neared the beach, one Seabee stood at each of the eight blocks of wood that had the taut cable running across it. Every SeaBee held a heavy axe at the ready. When they received the signal from the bridge, each swung his axe blade down on the cable severing it. The causeways, made of tons of steel, threw up a huge splash as they fell away on each side of the ship, but the launch was so well timed that the LST rocked very little.

The causeways were quickly tethered to the ship and a huge diesel powered outboard engine was attached to the aft end of each to maneuver it into position on the beach. Instead, however, one causeway was moved around the LST and attached to the other. Then they were lashed to the side of the ship, which moved them forward then cut them loose to coast onto the beach by their own momentum. After the Seabees secured the united causeways to the shore, the LST nudged up to them with doors open and main ramp partly lowered. With a signal from the Seabees, the ramp was lowered to rest on the end of the causeway.

Thus we were able to take every bit of equipment and vehicles ashore without getting tires or tracks wet. The only trick was turning our vehicles to go from one causeway onto the other where they were tied

LST unloading on beach Vieques Island, Puerto Rico. 2nd Shore Party Bn. equipment in foreground. Feb. 1953.

together. So much for my schooling in Korea on waterproofing vehicles for landings. The Beach Master's guides from the Shore Party Bn. showed us which tracks to take to our camp area.

While waiting on the beach I watched a couple of amphibious trucks (Ducks) of the Shore Party come ashore to lay wire matting on the beach. Each Duck carried a load of the matting connected in segments. There was a rack of steel angle iron built over the Duck. The matting came up from the Duck's cargo truck onto the framework. At the water's edge the first segment was laid down and as the Duck drove onto the matting, the tires and front end of the vehicle pulled the rest of the matting down across the beach. The other wheeled vehicles then cross the sand from landing craft without getting bogged down.

Charlie Company took over several rows of pyramidal tents that had been set up set up for the whole landing force and we settled in. The next day, I was told to report to the company office tent. The gunny and top asked me about what I had done in Korea. I told them I drove trucks

"Bones" Ginnelly, acting electrician standing by at Charlie Co. Cat. generator on Vieques Island, Puerto Rico. Feb. 1953.

but spent half of my time on the compressor, the generator, and flood-light unit. The latter three were lumped under stationary equipment, which gave me a secondary MOS as an operator of same.

The top said, "See, I told you we'd find one." I asked them, " One what?" The gunny said," You're now electrician." All I could think of was, "I didn't know that." The top said, "If you ran the generator and floodlight unit in Korea, then you must be an electrician." I allowed that this was a stretch, but the words were theirs, not mine. They explained that the chief electrician, a staff sergeant was ill and had to be evacuated. I was to report to a Cpl. Don Hensick who was the evacuee's assistant and would show me what to do. This was my assignment until we left the island, because the chief electrician wasn't coming back.

Hensick gave me the skinny on his former boss. The guy was a lush and had smuggled several fifths of booze onto our LST in his seabag. This was a violation of the regs, but so was drinking the stuff enroute. Maybe he was getting rid of the evidence. The day we came ashore the NCO was falling apart with the DTs. Our Corpsman turned him over to the doctors at the hospital unit and they had him flown out.

Hensick was a laid back guy from the Polish enclave of West Allis, Wisconsin. I dazzled him with some Polish words and phrases I had picked up from people I knew in Hamtramck in Detroit. He knew his stuff about electricity and told me that the work was easy. All we had to do was to wire up every tent in the entire tent city and put a socket and a bulb in and that was it. We had to help tend the generator also, but that seemed to run along pretty well under the care of Max (Pappy) Fullen from Tennessee. He was the Stationary Equipment Operator and we filled in when he was off duty.

At the reunion of C Co in April, 1998, Pappy reminded me of an incident that occurred on Vieques. The officers had tents on a small hill where they had a reefer for their beer. They needed power and ordered a line from the generator up to the reefer, which ran on 220V. This was done and the duty electrician then plugged the wires into the 440 volt outlet on the panel at the dynamo side of the generator. Pappy didn't know this and when he let out the clutch to engage the generator, the 440 volts surged through the wires, causing a big ball of blue flame that traveled all the way up the line to the reefer. There it turned orange as it burned out the reefer's electrical stuff in a puff of smoke. I guess the officers had to drink their beer warm like the rest of us. I expect that anyone near the generator would have headed for the beach or Isabella Segunda.

Hensick handed me the electrician's tools and showed me what to do. They included: a steel gizmo with handles that clamped the wires firmly together so they could be spliced, a Navy issue electrician's knife with two blades, one of which had a screwdriver at the end, a hefty pair of electricians pliers, called side cutters, and a large roll of black tape. This kind of work was right up my alley. The main tent camp was huge and I had to report only to Hensick. We worked as a team most of the time and no one ever knew where we were. When we weren't out on a wiring job, one of us was usually near the generator to check it out. If anyone wanted to find us, they could follow the wires. Otherwise they could locate the generator from the racket it made or the diesel fumes it gave off.

This cruise on Vieques was better than being back in Korea. It was warm and sunny every single day we were there and as it began to warm up in the afternoon it would rain and cool things off. There were few formations and I don't recall any inspections—not even a roll call. There was no place to go on a small island.

Hensick and I went from tent to tent stringing wires and splicing pigtail sockets onto a drop cord. It took a couple of weeks to get them all done. After that it was a routine job to check for short circuits, re-place bulbs and help Pappy. I recall only one job that was out of the ordinary.

We were called to the quarters of a brigadier general to wire his tent and another he used for his office. He was out somewhere doing what-ever generals do on maneuvers so we started at 1030 hours and finished just about noon. We were packing our gear to head back to the Charlie Co. mess for lunch, when a sergeant in an apron and a white cook's cap appeared. He had just talked to the general's aide de camp (ADC) on the phone and he and his staff would not be back for lunch. The ADC had invited us to have the lunch he cooked for them.

So we entered the general's tent after washing our grubby hands, and sat at his field table with the cook and his helper. The lunch was really great and we asked the cook if the general always ate like this. He said, "The general eats the same food that you guys get at your mess tent. However, I prepare his meals in smaller quantities, which allows me to add more flavor to the basic GI grub by mixing in special ingredi-ents. For example, I added grated cheddar cheese to the powdered po-tatoes to make them more palatable. I notice that you have each already had three helpings of the spuds." We both nodded in agreement be-cause our mouths were full.

I wondered if the general's aide didn't arrange our meal so we would get the message that the general's food was made from the same fixings that were available to us grunts. In simpler terms, he ate the same food as the troops. I'm sure that is what he wanted us to tell all the other peons. The only difference was that he had an alchemist cook to turn the basic canned and powdered stuff into palatable food. Because we didn't want anyone else after our jobs, we never told a soul about the gluttony that we were partakers of. A guy has to protect his flanks and his rear, and his food. Was our food in the mess really that bad that this is the only meal I can remember eating during two months on the island? Go figure!

While I was acting as an electrician, the rest of the division was making a couple of more practice landings—storming the beach. Once in a while I bummed a ride out to one of the ships to fish off the fantail and watch the landings. If any one asked me what I was doing I'd say, "I'm on standby for the chief electrician." I never did catch a whole fish from the ship. Just as I was reeling in my catch a barracuda would zip in and whack off as much as he could swallow. Seeing all these barracudas made me a bit uneasy about swimming from the beach.

One of the ships in our landing fleet was a fat wallowing tub known as a Landing Ship Dock (LSD)—a floating dry dock. The center of the ship could be flooded to bring in certain types of landing craft, park them in cradles and pump the water out so they could work on the hulls or transport them some distance. On a weekend the crew would flood the center space and allow us to swim in their pool. We didn't have to worry about barracudas or sharks.

The history of Vieques is interesting. The USMC and the US Navy decided back in 1950 that they needed a place to practice landings with naval and air support. The requirement was a sizeable island without any civilian population who could be injured, maimed, or even molested by off duty Marines and sailors. Vieques fit the bill except for the civilians living there. They had to be moved. The USMC and the US Navy convinced almost all of the locals that having ten thousand horny Marines anywhere within sniffing distance of their women would not be a good thing. I have read about this perceived injustice and a group of clergymen in the US has been working to rectify the situation so the folks who were pushed out could have their island back.

In any case, troops on Vieques had minimal liberty available in a town across the island called Puerto Isabella Segunda. I didn't go there, nor did I bother to go on liberty on the main island of Puerto Rico where most of the liberty hounds went. I just hung around Vieques and went to the beach on my days off. I was saving myself for whatever exotic port we would visit on our way home. There was a wild rumor that our ship would visit a port in Central and maybe even South America. Dream on young Marine! You know that the recruiter spoke with forked tongue about seeing the world.

We had several Puerto Ricans in our outfit who were in seventh heaven being near home. Every weekend they were off to see families on the main island. The only one of these Puerto Rican Marines that I remember was pug ugly. We'll call him Pancho, because it is the closest thing to punchy that I can think of. At one time he must have been pretty handsome, but he was a boxer and had served many years as a sparring partner for Kid Gavilan, the Cuban light middle weight champ. He had two huge cauliflower ears and a Roman nose that was roamin' all over his face.

Unfortunately for him and for anyone standing in front of him, as in the chow line for example, he was very goosey. There is goosey and then there is very goosey. A very goosey person reacts rather violently and may sock the person immediately in front of him. The effect is amplified if the gooser shouts something at the same time he applies the goose. When this happened to Pancho, he would leap forward swinging with both fists at anything or anyone there. It was so bad that when he got behind me in the chow line, I would bug out and go back about ten places to be out of range. This kind of horseplay may seem silly to civilians, but was part of the routine in any camp and was good for morale. Maybe not for the goosey one, but for the rest of the outfit.

I learned early on that when I had to wake up Pancho in the middle of the night for his stint on guard duty, he might just leap out of his sack and start choking me. He was fast and strong so I didn't want to screw with him up close. I found that out one night when I was the corporal of the guard and had to wake him up the first time for the midnight to 0400 watch. I shook him and he leaped out of his sack with a baseball bat. When my flashlight beam lit up that piece of wood, I was out of there and back at the guard tent in a flash to get some help. When I told the sergeant of the guard, he said, "Why do you think I sent you? He almost got me the last time." So we went back together and were able to get him out to his post at right shoulder bat.

I figured out a way to wake Pancho up the next night without endangering any of us. Because he was really rocky, no one else would sleep in his tent, not even another Puerto Rican. The tents on either side of his were also empty because of the racket he made when we woke him up.

I found a long piece of rope and when Pancho wasn't around, I tied one end to the upper part of one leg of his cot. I ran the other end under the sidewall of the tent. When it was time to wake him up, either I or the sergeant of the guard would quietly close and secure the tent flap and then pull on the rope to shake his cot. He would leap up in the dark swinging his bat around and bashing the tent pole until he woke up and started to cuss. Then we could talk to him calmly from outside and get him out onto his post. I sure would like to be around if some 2nd lieutenant sneaked up on him in the dark doing his OD duties. He'd wake up in sick bay with a cracked cranium.

Like most of the other Puerto Ricans in our outfit, Pancho spoke English like I spoke Spanish, half assed. Someone in the chow line was telling him how ugly he was because of his ears, nose and facial scars. He was obviously mad and wanted to tell this gringo off once and for all.

He clenched his fists and gritted his teeth while he mulled over the English in his head. Then he blurted out, "If jou don like mya face, then fuck it." Everyone was in stitches, but Pancho was very pleased with what he had said and gave us a big smile. No one teased him after that and he was now one of us.

I found out months later that while I was on Vieques my brother's ship was somewhere in the vicinity. He was aboard the USS Hoist, a rescue and salvage vessel (ARS). They were trying new methods to raise a sunken vessel by experimenting on a German U-Boat resting on the sea bottom. John was a Quarter Master First Class (QM1) with ten years in the Navy. The Hoist carried a number of master divers and also a decompression chamber for saving divers and rescued submariners from the bends, the dreaded nitrogen gas bubble affliction.

MARACAIBO, VENEZUELA

We were ordered back on the ships the first week of March for the cruise home. It took all day to load our LST with tanks, other vehicles and our heavy equipment. Our LST (509) and one other weighed anchor and steamed off to the south as darkness fell. We had no idea where we were going until the next day when the Skipper announced that we were headed for Venezuela.

Caracas is an hour over the mountains from the nearest port of La Guaira and the Venezuelan Government must have decided that we should make Maracaibo our port of call. It was more used to dealing with foreigners than Caracas. This was to be a goodwill visit. Can you imagine sending FMF Marines on a goodwill visit? One day out from port we gathered to hear the word. This would be only the second time that a US Naval vessel was allowed to call at Maracaibo. It would be the first time ever that U.S. Marines were allowed ashore. That is with the exception of the Marine Guard detail at the American Embassy in Caracas.

Our platoon leader explained the situation ashore. Venezuela was an oil producing country and its economy was in a highly inflated state at the time. Everything was imported from the states and the prices of those goods were three and four times the sale price in the USA. We were advised to avoid all discussions about this issue and the low prices of goods in the USA when talking to the locals.

Naturally we were told to try to avoid becoming involved in discussions about politics. Venezuela was run at that time by the last of a long line of dictators, an Army general. We also got the standard lecture on our behavior while ashore.

We were not to be staggering around bothering the locals, harassing their women and fighting with the men. There were bound to be some problems with communication. The language was Spanish and the only men aboard who could speak it were the Puerto Ricans. There was a money changer on the pier, where we could change our US dollars for Venezuelan Bolivars. Their currency was named after their most famous hero, Simon Bolivar, the man who liberated Venezuela and Colombia from Spain.

Everyone was on deck as we neared the coast of Venezuela. We came from the north passing by the coast of Colombia which was very green compared to the island of Vieques we left behind. The sun was close to setting as we steamed between the Peninsulas of Guajira in Colombia to starboard and Paraguana in Venezuela to port. This was the Gulf of Venezuela where we slowed to pick up a pilot.

It was dark as we neared Maracaibo. The city was well lit up and the first neon signs we saw were advertizing cerveza. At least we were assured that there was lots of beer in town. That night and the next morning were spent pressing our khakis and shining shoes for a much-anticipated liberty.

The ship's company had to have port and starboard liberty, while the Marines only had to leave a few men aboard for fire watch in the tank deck. This kind of liberty was very rare, i.e. a few hundred GIs ashore in a city of 350,000 people.

The next morning we had our uniforms on early to be the first ones off the ship. A few of us were standing around on the upper deck when we were called over by the ship's executive officer (XO). He told us that there were two reporters and a photographer aboard from the local newspaper who wanted photos of us with the Skipper and XO who were talking to the press. The article was in the paper the next day, El Diario de Occidente, dated March 11, 1953.

We were told that there were many people in the city who would like to entertain us for the weekend. If we were interested, we should line up in front of the American Consul General's building and someone would pick us up. Another newspaper article had asked the general public to welcome the American servicemen by coming to the Consulate from 0900 to noon to pick them up and take them home, out on the town, or whatever.

I went ashore with the wily, wiry electrician, Don Hensick. We first changed our money, then passed through the Venezuelan Navy's gates into town. We were surprised to be saluted by the guards at the gate and we returned the compliment smartly. As we walked around the port area we were saluted by all manner of uniformed men and we responded in kind. This was the first time anyone had ever saluted either of us first. These people didn't understand our rank insignia, nor we theirs. I gather that their CO told them to salute any *NorteAmericanos* they encountered in uniform.

After I thought about it, I realized that any dictatorship has a large military force, thus, all these guys in uniform. In Venezuela, aside from the Army, Air Force, Marines, Coast Guard, and Police, there was a large contingent of a Spanish type unit, La Guardia Nacional. It is a special type of quasimilitary national police force.

At 1030 hours Hensick and I joined the line of Marines and sailors on the sidewalk in front of the Consulate. It was easily found because it had a large American flag flying from the pole in the front yard. As others in front of us were picked up by *Maracainos*, we moved to the head of the line. A new four-door DeSoto pulled up driven by a Polish fellow named Jerzy with his wife Nicole who was from France. Hensick and I got in the back.

They took us out to lunch at a grand club of one of the oil companies, I think it was Shell. Jerzy found us a table and we were joined by some other *petroleros* (oil people) . The men worked for various oil companies and were themselves from the USA, Holland, and Belgium. The Dutchman told us that the Americans were perhaps the cleverest of all of the oil men. We asked why that was and he explained, "You have probably noticed all of the oil wells surrounding this huge lake. They belong to the European companies, primarily Royal Dutch Shell Oil, who first made the strikes in these rich fields. Years later the Americans began to show up and found no available land free for further drilling."

"The Americans saw this vast lake in the middle of all these European wells, and surmised that this was the best place to drill. The concession authorities gave them lease contracts on the whole lake, even though everyone knew that there couldn't be one drop of oil under it. Who ever heard of drilling through water for oil? So once they started drilling in this shallow lake, they began to hit oil all over the place."

To the American oil men-geologists, it stood to reason that if the depression that allowed Lake Maracaibo to form went well below the subsurface, then they couldn't miss the oil if it was in its own lake way down there underground. It wasn't long before the Americans were admitted to the local brotherhood of *petroleros* and were lauded for their cleverness and persistence. The American oil companies were expropriated in the 1960s by the government along with all other foreign owned oil firms.

After lunch, we went to Jerzy's apartment to pick up their dog, a Pastor (German Shepherd). They then took us on a tour of the City on the Lake. I was amazed at the design of the houses. They were ultra modern and painted in bright colors that one would find only in the tropics. Most of them were covered with red or terracotta tiles. The streets were very wide, which was a good thing, because most of the drivers were pretty wild. We had been in the city now for a whole day and I noticed that we had not heard one car horn. I couldn't believe this was possible in a city this big with so many crazy drivers.

I asked Jerzy about the quiet and why we didn't hear any car horns. He said, "Aha, you have no doubt heard of our general, el Caudillo? Our supreme leader in all things. He lives in Caracas, but some time ago when he came to Maracaibo for a visit, he was highly irritated by all the horns blowing all day long. So he issued an edict that no one may blow their car horn in the city for any reason. Now if anyone blows his horn, he will be pounced on by the police. The driver is taken away to jail for four or five days and his car is left on the street. It only took a few arrests to get everyone else in line. If your car was gone when you got out, too bad."

On our tour we stopped by a playground where Venezuelan kids were playing basketball and other games. We got out to walk around the perimeter and Jerzy's dog was going crazy tugging at his leash and barking like mad. I asked Jerzey why he was doing that. He told me that his dog didn't like Venezuelans. I couldn't figure that out. Here is a foreigner living here where he probably bought the dog and the dog hates the locals. Maybe it had to do with him training his dog that way because his wife was home alone for ten days at a stretch, while he was out looking for oil.

Jerzy and Nicole took us home for dinner, which surprised us when they didn't serve it until 2000 hours. Between 1800 and 1900 hours they served us drinks with cheese and French bread. The first time I had to use their head, I came back and asked Hensick if he noticed anything odd in there. We wondered why they had a toilet opposite another toilet. Maybe they sit there one on each throne and play chess. We didn't want to bring it up in front of the lady, so we asked Jerzy while she was in the kitchen cooking. We didn't know it at the time but we had just seen our first bidet. Jerzy explained its function.

When Nicole served dinner, she brought Hensick and I each a steak with French fried potatoes and steamed veggies. Both of them had some beef about as rare as it comes. They each had a huge serving of steak tatare, which neither of us gringos had ever heard of before. It was a mound of about a half pound of raw ground steak, with a hole scooped in the top and a raw egg sitting there staring at us like a big yellow eye. The base of this mountain of meat was surrounded with chopped raw onions.

They apologized for serving us a different dish, but they had learned from other Americans in town that we wouldn't eat steak tatare. I explained that a hungry Marine would eat anything as long as it didn't move, but thank you we were pleased with the steak she so thoughtfully cooked for us. They served wine and French bread with the meal and we had some coconut confection for desert followed by rich coffee grown in Venezuela. Later, I thought to myself that they needed all that raw meat because they probably went at each other like wildcats when he came in from his ten day stint crawling around in the jungle with his divining rod. Dowsing for oil deposits that is.

After dinner, they served a digestif. I chose Sambuoco and Hensick a brandy. I've had Sambuoco before with Italians in Detroit, but they usually served it with coffee. Here mine was served in a small glass with four coffee beans floating on the surface. The beans are roasted when a flame is applied to the liquor. Munching on the beans when the glass had cooled was a delightful way to mix the flavor of coffee and anise.

That night our hosts took us back to the ship just before midnight. This was getting to be the most interesting liberty I had been on yet. The next morning we hung around the ship in the morning working over our uniforms for the day. It was about 0900 hours and there was a good-will tour coming aboard made up of civilians from town. Venezuelan military dignitaries had been aboard the day before at the invitation of the Skipper. While I was shining my shoes, I noticed a small crowd of sailors and Marines gathering under a large air grate in the overhead. Those lechers had heard that the civilian visitors was made up mostly of young women wearing dresses. As I came closer to the group staring up, one motioned to me with his finger to his lips. Silence. I nodded. This was going to be an old fashioned Navy shipboard beaver shoot. As they trooped along directly over us following the ensign on tour, we sure got to see some nice legs. One sailor whispered, "Nice gams." Another added," The trouble is that those legs run right on up to where they make an ass of themselves." I know it sounds very sophomorish, but that is the way you get from living with a bunch of guys on a ship.

Speaking of women in Venezuela, one didn't see them very much on the street. A few of us went for a walk in town and ended up having coffee in the restaurant of the Hotel Detroit. I asked for a coffee on the house because I was from Detroit. The waitress laughed and gave me a bill anyway. The only women in the place were the waitresses and the cashier. Some Venezuelan men came over to talk with us and were very nice. They took our checks and paid our bill. They saw us making eyes at these good looking girls and asked us what we thought of them.

When we told them of course we would like to go out with them, one man said that if we were lucky enough to have this arranged, we would be surprised to learn how these things are handled in a Latin country. We would only be able to walk from the house to the Plaza Bolivar with the girls and then a promenade around the statue of the Liberator. Of course we would be accompanied by three or four members of her family—most likely by a grandmother and a couple of aunts.

217

A young man couldn't be alone with a young woman until they were engaged to be married. All we could say was," Things sure are different down here."

Jerzy later took us to the beach on Lake Maracaibo. The beach was lined with rows of tall coconut palms. For lunch Jerzy took us to a thatched hut that specialized in a delicious local dish of fish cooked in coconut milk. It is still served in small restaurants all around Maracaibo.

The day before our departure Jerzy escorted us to the center of evening social activity for some *Maracainos*. The grounds were typical of a tropical garden with the sweet scent of jasmine wafting through the palms. The compound had a country club atmosphere, which is what it was during the day. The main building contained a night club, which served fancy meals, a dance floor and a large bar. Coming in through the covered porch, we were struck by large oil paintings on the walls. There were more of these elegant art works hanging in the main room. I noticed that the paintings were all of women—some clothed, some in the buff, and some in various stages between.

We sat down to dinner with Jerzy and some other *petroleros*. During dinner I looked around the room and saw that there were no women anywhere. Men at the tables and the bar and women on the walls. As we finished a great meal, a feast for us Marines, there was some applause as a band began to play a vaguely familiar air with a Latin beat. With that, a single file of well dressed women filed onto the dance floor and each took a bow. I was expecting a night club act, but they dispersed into the room to talk to the diners.

I asked Jerzy what was going on here. Was this a floor show? A French petrolero at our table spoke up saying, *"Mon ami,* you see the tall Madame talking to the band leader, the one with the coif of gray hair. She is what we call *La Mere des Tortues,* the mother of the little turtles." Jerzy explained that she was indeed the madam of the place. He told us that this was a high class bordello to which ordinary military enlisted men were not admitted. Only officers and gentlemen were allowed in as patrons. But of course we were welcome because of our status as honored visitors. The men at our table nodded in agreement and told us that our meal and drinks were already paid for by the *petroleros.* We stood up as they offered us a toast to the friendship *(l'Amistad)* between Venezuela and the USA. Some Venezuelan military officers at the next table joined in and raised their glasses towards us with *"Salud."* Not knowing what that meant or what else to do, I acknowledged the toast by raising my glass to them and bowing slightly.

The name of the tune the band was playing earlier suddenly came to me. It was their rendition of, "When the tarts come marching in." Hensick wondered at the variety of women in the room and we were told that they came here from all corners of the world. We were also warned not to be carried away by their beauty, since they were too expensive for any peons to spend any time with. Oh well, we had to remember that we were here on a goodwill visit and under the restrictions of Cinderella liberty. It was back to the ship by midnight or it would turn into a huge gray pumpkin. We never mentioned the evening to anyone else on the ship, because they had been in the waterfront dives and would not have believed us.

When we left Maracaibo the next morning, there were a lot of people to watch the ship depart. I assume that many of them were the folks who had taken us in as guests and treated us as friends. I was so charmed by this visit, that I swore to myself I would someday return to this country to live. I took me 33 years, but I made it back to live in Caracas one year and in the llanos of the interior for another. In my work I had to make several trips to Maracaibo. The city has now swollen to over a million in population.

During the night we joined the other vessels from the amphibious fleet. When we passed between Puerto Rico and the Dominican Republic we were joined by still more ships departing from Vieques for the return voyage to North Carolina or Little Creek Virginia.

I can only recall two events on our LST during the trip back to the states. One dealt with one of the Navy's exercises coming apart. A fleet tanker was going to those ships that required additional fuel and lubricating oil to make it back to home port. Refueling moving ships is a complicated affair, and requires the utmost in team work and cooperation between the officers and crews of both ships involved, especially if there are rough seas.

We watched as the tanker closed on us on a parallel course and slowed somewhat to match our speed. The duty deck force on the LST crowded around the point where the fuel lines from the tanker would come aboard and be connected to the fill valve to our tanks. The tanker was putting out the booms carrying the hoses out to our ship. The seas were not smooth, but rather normal for refueling. For some reason, the deck crew on our LST fumbled three attempts to make the connection of our hoses to those from the tanker.

We could see that the Skipper on the tanker's bridge was livid with the screwing up of a routine refueling drill. He ordered his ship to secure the fuel booms and lines and they were pulled in. By now, he was probably telling the Skipper of our LST on the radio to get his act together and when his deck force was properly trained in refueling he could order more fuel and oil through channels. With that, the tanker pulled rapidly away to starboard and went off to refuel another ship. I gather that the Skipper of the tanker outranked ours.

Two days later I learned from our officers that they had been approached by the ship's engineering officer and the Skipper on the subject of obtaining some oil from the Marines. Apparently the ship had enough diesel fuel to reach home port, but they were running low on badly needed lubricating oil for the engines and whatever other machinery used it. So we set to draining oil from various engines that would not be running until we were back in camp. We also found some cases of oil we had in reserve for oil changes on trucks, tanks, bulldozers and other equipment. It was enough to get us back to port. Otherwise the Skipper of our LST might be in serious trouble if there had been a problem with the engines due to lack of lube oil.

The ship's crew showed their appreciation for our help by donating their entire stock of ice cream to all the Marines aboard as mere passengers. This was done one day out of port and the gesture was accepted with the usual grace attributed to Marines traveling on Navy ships. We would have preferred beer or whiskey, but gobbled up the ice cream with relish.

We steamed north in fairly heavy seas after the session with the tanker and ran into a storm which really set the LSTs to rolling and wallowing. The worst vessel to be aboard in a storm at sea is the LST. It was designed with a flat bottom so it can slide into shallow waters and offload its cargo at the beach. Because of that design it bobs around like a cork in heavy seas, making life aboard quite miserable.

A tank broke loose from its chains on the lower tank deck. The Marine on fire watch sounded the alarm as the heavy tank skidded sideways into a deuce-and-a- half Jimmy to one side of it and then into an IH dump truck on the other side. As the ship rolled it would smash into the side of one of our trucks then go crashing into the other one on the return trip. The Seabees aboard managed to round up some timbers that were thrown in next to each truck to close the gap and steal some momentum from the loose tank. Between the duty deck force under the Chief Bosuns Mate in charge of damage control, Marine engineers and the Seabee contingent, the tank was subdued and secured to the cleat holes in the deck. When we unloaded later, one of the trucks had to be taken off with a wrecker. The tank was only scratched and left under its own power.

I liked to go out on the upper tank deck on warm clear nights while we were underway, climb onto my truck and sit on the steel headache over the cab. It was great to sit or lay there with the movement of the ship reminding me that I was going home. One night while I was watching the stars and checking the position of the other ships in the convoy, I heard a swishing sound of wings as a huge bird flew over me a few times. Another driver crapped out on the next truck over yelled, "Hey Bones! What the hell was that?" I told him I didn't know, but it was too big for a bat. Then while the bird was coming over us again really low, the driver lashed out with a length of rope and brought the bird down with a crash on the hood of my truck.

The mess area on most Navy ships is used for after hours recreation every evening after the last mess call. This night it was full of Marines and sailors playing games. The other driver and myself had tied the legs of the huge bird together and we had his wings pinned as we brought our trophy into the mess to show everyone what we had caught. As soon as the crowd had seen our prize and realized what it was, the sailors all split the scene, except for a Chief Bosun Mate who started ripping in to us about some taboo or other that affects sailors. He told us to get that damned bird out on deck and let it go or there would be a jinx on the ship. I couldn't believe that, but we did as we were told and released it from the fantail. He had followed us to make sure the bird was gone. He then told us that it is an old superstition among seafarers from the days of the sailing vessels that it was bad luck for the ship and the crew to mess with an albatross when at sea or any other time. I don't know how he expected Marines to know all that Naval lore. Now that I think about it, this happened before the aborted refueling operation with the tanker and also the episode with the wild tank on the lower deck. One never knows.

The only other incident aboard the LST that sticks in my mind, was a lesson in unit politics and social decorum in the Marine Corps work place. After the evening meal I wandered into the mess area to see if anyone wanted to play cribbage. Instead, I was asked to make a fourth in a pinochle game at one table and I agreed since I knew two of the players. I didn't know the old fellow who sat across from me, but he was about as sour a person as I had ever come across. To be an old guy in the Marines at that time, meant that the guy had to be a master sergeant or a gunner (CWO) or some such senior rank. He was such a pain during the game, that I decided I'd had enough of his complaining and was waiting for a chance to shut him up somehow. A wild thought for a mere corporal. I didn't know his rank because we were all in skivvy shirts due to the heat, so he couldn't have been a CWO.

We were playing for some small stakes and the game was cutthroat pinochle, with every man for himself. If some one was set—didn't make his bid, for example—he had to pay to the pot. As the game went on, the old guy dealt and I ended up with a double pinochle and some power. Since I sat next to him and the other guys passed, I decided to pass too, dumping the game on the dealer. Well, he had no meld and no power and so he went set. When he saw my cards as I played them, all that meld plus the power to gobble up tricks, he blew his stack.

He was so mad he started turning red. He pulled out some bills and threw them at me, then stomped out of the mess area cursing me and shouted that I had not heard the last of this. The other guys who knew him had already left as soon as he jumped up yelling. I had crossed the line. Not only was this guy the first sergeant of a company in another Battalion, but I was told he was an absolute nut case. He was in Korea with the 1stMarDiv for the entire war, having shipped over and stayed for three tours of duty. Now that is certifiably crazy. But not half as crazy as the lowly noncom who stuck it to him. Actually, I thought it was hilarious at the time. On the other hand, maybe he had heard what I said about him when I first saw this poor excuse for a Marine NCO, "That a good piece of ass and a bicycle ride would finish him off." He might have been a fine Marine at one time, but he should have retired when he started to go downhill. Maybe it was the three tours in Korea that did a job on his personality. I could sympathize with him on one point—I had wanted to return to Korea myself. In him, I could see myself in 20 years if I stayed in the service.

I heard no more about it and never thought about the game again. That is until we arrived back at our quarters at Camp Lejeune. The following week I was told by our top that as much as he regretted having to do it, I was to serve the next 30 days on mess duty. After all, the tops had to stick together when one of their rank is taken on by a mere corporal. The order came directly from battalion. When I showed up the next day at 0400 hours to report for duty, the head cook (a master sergeant) took me aside and wanted to know what I did to warrant this lousy duty. "Come on, " he said, "You know as well as I do that corporals don't stand mess duty unless they really offended someone of rank. Come on now, you can tell me. If it was someone who has rankled me, it may even make it easier on you for the next 30 days." So I told him. He knew the turkey and was pleased to see him lose his cool. So it was that I drew some relatively easy duty in the mess hall for the next month.

Like every other detail in the service, there are varying degrees of liking the work one is assigned. The chief cook told me to report to the cook in charge of the spuds and salads and that sort of thing. I thought, oh no, not peeling potatoes like Sad Sack on KP. It really wasn't bad because we had a machine to do the job. All we had to do was to feed the beast. It was built somewhat like a centrifuge, but much slower moving and held about 50 pounds of spuds at a time. At the bottom of the thing was a very uneven disc with an abrasive surface that rotated providing the motion to move the spuds across its surface, thereby rubbing the skins off. The spuds were all in motion, moving through the pile so that sooner or later all were peeled. A lever opened the door near the bottom and the peeled spuds fell into a container. They were then de-eyed and went off to the cook to work his magic. My only observation was that plenty of useful bits of potato were ground off with the skins and went down the sewer. But I was not paid to think at this job.

Coming from an Irish family, I was raised on meat and potatoes. I had no experience in making salads, so I had to follow the instructions of the cook. In order to make a salad for 1,000 troops at lunch and dinner, we had to have huge bowls, and plenty of fixings. The most popular salad was mixed lettuce and tomatoes. Next was a large wedge of iceberg lettuce with french dressing, followed by ground up carrots with raisins and mayo. For the wedges, I must have whacked up 250 heads of lettuce. The carrot dish used up at least a 100 pounds of carrots. The stainless steel bowls we mixed the stuff in were about four feet across and two feet deep. The first lettuce and tomato salad I made filled the bowl and I had to use my arms up to my elbows to mix it up. I followed the vague recipe by adding a few tablespoons of vinegar, which I had no taste for then. When the cook came by to check me out he tasted the salad and said, "Not enough vinegar." He grabbed the quart bottle and poured the whole thing into the salad. I mixed it up and he tasted it again and said, "Its OK now."

The bad side of being on mess duty was that I had to get up at 0330 hours to get cleaned up to show up for work at 0400, but that didn't bother me, because I was an early riser. If I got my galley area cleaned up by 0900 after breakfast I could go back to the barracks and crap out for an hour or so before reporting back to start fixing the spuds and salad for lunch. Same deal after lunch. A couple of hours of down time, then back to work at 1530 hours preparing food for dinner. The other down side was that I was too tired for liberty at the end of the day. All I wanted to do was sleep.

Sam Camarato tells me that I was wrong about being too tired for liberty. At Camp Lejeune, the liberty just wasn't worth the effort. Sam was on mess duty at Camp Pendleton before he went to Korea and loved it because he could go on liberty every night to San Diego and all the other good spots around Pendleton.

The best thing about being on mess duty was that I got plenty to eat. I was skinny, but ate like a horse. Another benefit was my name would not appear on any roster for guard duty. If I didn't offend any of the cooks, I had it made and they tried to make it easier for me. However, if anyone tended toward the goof off side, they had special jobs waiting for them. One of the tough jobs was riding the range. There was no horse involved. We're talking commercial type cooking ranges, which measured about three feet wide and seven feet long. When they got through frying 1500 hamburgers or several hundred pounds of bacon, ham, or fish, the surface had to be cleaned for the next meal. This could only be done with a scouring type of steel wool pad and it took a lot of elbow grease. There were six of those ranges.

Pot walloping was another type of lousy duty. If you didn't like helping your mom scrub a few pots and pans at home, then you definitely don't want to have to scrub those great big mothers used in a mess hall galley. The cooks could dirty those things faster than you could clean them up again.

The worst type of job for a guy on mess duty was having to clean out the grease trap. When the ranges were in use, the frying grease ran off the surface into the concrete grease trap outside of the mess hall. When the stuff had turned into a solid greasy mass, it had to be scooped out into barrels for disposal. It was a smelly and messy job and usually was given to the guy on mess duty who showed up late or sneaked off early before his work was done for the day.

Once we settled into life at Camp Lejeune after the cruise back from Vieques, we had a chance to compare liberty ports. While some of us were lucky enough to be on the LSTs for the historic visit to Maracaibo, Venezuela, the rest of the landing force steamed into the port of Colon in Panama. We had a great time in Maracaibo, because that city could easily absorb our liberty hounds. However, in Panama there were so many Marines and sailors going ashore at one time from the troop transports and other ships from the Amphibious Fleet, that they were stumbling over each other in Colon. On top of that, there were a large number of American soldiers living in the Canal Zone. This overcrowding always leads to some friction, especially when loose women and demon rum is added to the mix of sailors, soldiers, Marines, and indigenous personnel.

Sam Camarato told me about one incident involving Jim Milliken, Jim Grafton, Sam and some friends. They were in a bar drinking when a ruckus started up in the back where some Marines and soldiers were swinging at each other. Jim G., Sam, and Jim M. decided to go to the front door to make room for the Shore Patrol, which would surely show up. While they were minding their own business just outside the door, a soldier ran up from the bar and sucker punched Big Jim in the jaw. Big Jim didn't see the guy coming and his head snapped back, hitting the brick wall. Then he slid to the ground and was out cold. The local cops showed up and hauled them all down to the calabozo and locked them all up. That, by the way, is where our word calaboose comes from. When the cobwebs cleared from Jim's head, he was gabbing away with a soldier next to him on the bench in the holding cell. Sam asked him, "Jim, what are you being so friendly with this doggie for? He's the one who coldcocked you." They were fined several hundred dollars each and released. Since no one had that kind of money there must have been some arrangement with the US Military or Consulate to pay the fines and the men would be docked the amount from their pay for several months.

CADMID EXERCISE

A couple of months after I came off mess duty, we got the word to saddle up for a short seagoing trip from Morehead City up to Little Creek, Virginia. The operation was an annual event called the CadMid exercise. We were to put on a demonstration of a typical amphibious landing for the senior class of midshipmen from Annapolis and the cadets from West Point. During the operation, the cadets and middies would be on bleachers facing the beach so they could watch the whole show unfold. The next day, they would don their field garb and accompany the Marines out to the ships. This was their chance to participate in a landing, storming ashore with the bleachers occupied only by the press and the brass. The landings were made on a beach near the border of North Carolina and Virginia.

The infantry and other troops went ashore in the Landing Craft, Vehicle and Personnel (LCVP), the smallest of the amphibious vessels and in Amtracs. The LCVP could carry one or two jeeps or a small weapons carrier or 30 men. In order to condition the troops to handle emergencies in a landing, now and then the Navy coxswain driving the LCVP would stop it just short of the beach and shout, "Ramp failure!" He would not drop the ramp so we could jump off on the beach, so we had to climb up over the gunwale and fall into the water on the side. This was a pain when we were loaded down with a weapon, a heavy pack, ammo and all that stuff. All we could hope for was that the LCVP was in shallow enough water so we could touch bottom and wade ashore

We thought the coxwains were getting carried away with this drill and just doing it to gig the Marines, but they had orders to pull the ramp-failure drill every so many trips for proper training. Quite a few of us got dunked the first day and more on the second.

We had one Marine 2nd lieutenant who was a recent graduate of the Naval Academy. He was so gung ho, he couldn't sit or stand still aboard ship. He was going to show those cadets and middies how it was done. Out on the APA we were groaning from his enthusiasm. He was rallying the troops around him long before it was our turn to go down the nets into the bobbing LCVPs.

When we did hit the beach on the first day, this lieutenant really was the first one into the water. The coxwain didn't call for ramp failure, but he lowered the ramp for a better view of the beach line when he wasn't in near enough for us to unload. The shavetail was so eager that he rushed off the ramp, yelling, "Follow me men." He disappeared over his head—he wasn't very tall anyway. When his helmet didn't show right away, someone jumped in after him and helped the soggy figure onto the beach. He sure made an impression on the bleachers. The viewers learned one thing anyway. Don't leap off the ramp until the coxswain says its OK or you feel the craft touching the bottom near the beach.

After a couple of days of demonstration landings we boarded the ships and headed for Little Creek, Virginia, the U.S. Naval Amphibious base for the East Coast fleet. Ships normally tie up parallel to the piers, but at Little Creek a dozen LSTs were tied side by side and with bow up to the pier. In this way, the bow doors could be opened and the ramps dropped for loading and unloading supplies and airing the lower tank deck. The ships were only about a foot or two apart.

Most of the LSTs lined up next to ours carried the steel causeways secured to the sides. If we wanted to visit another ship we could, if nimble enough, just jump from one to another instead of going out through the front ramp and around. One day some of our ship's company told us about an ensign they had as a division chief who was a pain as far as they were concerned. It seems that he was going to visit an LST several ships down but, when he went to step over onto the next causeway, he misjudged and fell into the water between the ships. He made a lot of noise hollering for help, but no one seemed to hear him. In fact, they were ignoring him as long as they could to teach him a lesson.

A CPO heard him shouting and ordered the sailors on deck to find out who was in the water and get him out. The white hats wanted this ensign to get a good soaking so took their sweet time getting a line thrown to him. They finally got him hoisted out and hopefully he got the message and behaved as a young Navy officer should toward his men after that. The sailors knew that he wouldn't be crushed between the ships, as they moved from side to side, because the causeways would touch first and were above the water line. But he could have drowned if he panicked and thrashed around, maybe whacking his noggin against the hull. They watched him traipse across the deck leaving a trail of water as he headed for officers' country. He was embarrassed, but perhaps a better man for the experience.

We stayed ashore in some Quonset huts while in Little Creek and were allowed liberal liberty. My brother John's ship, the USS Hoist was based in Norfolk as its home port. I met John in Norfolk and he showed me around the city for a couple of days. It seems that every ship of the fleet with had its home port in Norfolk had a special bar where the crew hung out. He took me to the Hoist's bar and I met some of the crew. I was wearing my khakis and he was in his whites. There could have been a problem with a lone Marine going into the sailor hangouts, but being with my brother, who was really a salt, made it easier.

After we had made the rounds of quite a few bars and then two restaurants for lunch and dinner, John took me to his ship to look it over. With so few officers assigned to the small ship, the CPOs and first class POs (like John) stood the OD watches in port. After I entered the quarterdeck and saluted the OD and the ensign aft, I noticed a bronze plaque on the bulkhead. It read,

No Muff to Tough
We Dive for Five
On the Bottom with Bad Air

I asked John what that was all about and he said that was the ship's motto. I came to find out it was really the crew's motto. The chief master diver standing OD duty said, " We get five bucks an hour extra duty pay for every hour we're diving. Hazardous duty pay you might call it. The rest you can figure out your own self."

We went to the bridge, which is where John stood most of his watches as QM. We stopped where he bunked and John whistled up a bottle of whisky from some hidden spot. So we had a few more drinks and went to look at the business end of the ship, which is rescue and salvage. The deck from the superstructure to the fantail was where the divers and their assistants work. They showed me the typical diver's suit, helmet and supporting gear, the type used for deep sea or hard hat diving as opposed to SCUBA diving.

In order to go to greater depths than normal, a special helmet is used which allows the diver to breathe a mixture of helium and air. This atmosphere does something to the sound of the divers voice which sounds very squeaky when he talks by telephone to the support team on deck. John tried to get me inside the decompression chamber so they could seal me in and show me what it felt like to be down to over 200 feet. I begged off claiming to have a real bad case of claustrophobia which is heightened whenever my brother is tipsy and wanting to experiment with my life.

The next day we were wandering around Norfolk when a voice called out from a passing car, "Hey Geek." I just thought it was a sailor trying to start something because he saw a sailor and a Marine steaming along together—a rare sight. The car did a U-turn and came back to park where we were standing. It was Lt. Weller the XO and deck watch officer when John served aboard his previous ship, a fleet oiler. Things were informal enough aboard a smaller vessel for the second in command to be calling the QM1C by his nickname (Geek).

He said, "Pile in and I'll show your brother around Norfolk. It was his hometown and he knew it well. No wonder he was career Navy. He drove us around for a while and then took us to his mother's house where we headed straight to the kitchen to have something to eat, drink a few beers and tell sea stories. Compared to these two old salts, with twenty Navy years between them and some of that in WWII, I couldn't compete in the BS category. But I held my own.

Another day while John was busy on his ship, I went on liberty with Jim. We were in a bar or restaurant talking to a couple of young women who worked there. One was a blond with Lydia tattooed on her fore-arm. That wasn't her name, but it reminded me of the Burl Ives song about Lydia,The Tattooed Lady. We asked her why she had a tattoo and she said that it was done when she got drunk once. The other woman was a slight, dark haired Italian. We asked them why they spoke without a southern accent and they told us they were from Newark, New Joisey.

We found out they got off work at ten PM. So we said we'd be back then. When we showed up they took us to the public beach in their car. They had gone home to put their bathing suits on under their clothes so they went swimming while we sat on the beach and watched. The beach was fairly well lit and when the blond, who looked like a singer from a Wagnerian opera, took off her skirt and blouse, I almost fell over. All she needed now was a spear. She had large tattoos all over her thighs from suit line to knee. I was flabbergasted. There were crossed American flags, a Marine Corps emblem, and I don't know what all. For all we knew there were some campaign ribbons with battle stars tattooed on her cheeks.

I looked at Jim and said, "She got drunk once and got tattooed, Eh?. Must have been drunk a lot to have all that done." I asked him what he thought of Brunhilda and he said, "I bet she can trip you and beat you to the deck." He asked me what I was thinking and I told him I thought they belonged to a motorcycle gang and we'd better scram before the bikers show up. He agreed. We told them we had to be back at the base at midnight as we were shipping out tomorrow and we shoved off.

The next day was Sunday and everyone was sleeping in. The Quonset hut was very quiet until about 10AM when a woman's shrill voice out-side started calling, "Giannelli. Hey, Giannelli. Come on out here, you guinee bastard." She kept this up for about ten minutes while I pulled the pillow and covers over my head. The guys who were still sleeping started to yell at me too, "Bones, go out there and tell her to shut up." Then she shouted,"Giannelli, I'm pregnant. If you don't come out, then I'm coming in there." That was the last straw. I got up and got dressed while a few boondockers were thrown at me by those whose sleep was being disturbed.

I went out to find Brunhilda and her spear carrier standing near their car. I went over to talk to them and they wanted to know why we bugged out last night from the beach. I told them a story and said that we were told to standby to ship out today. They finally left and I went back inside and was given a lot of flack from the Marines who were woken up. I couldn't understand how they found us or how they got onto the base. I had told the Italian only my name. They knew we were on an LST, so they came to Little Creek and tracked us to the hut. So much for base security.

There was only one casualty that I know of on the Little Creek cruise. It was one of our platoon sergeants, only he didn't know it until he got back aboard ship. It seems that he found a young woman in Virginia Beach who was ready, willing, and able to spend a late evening on the beach with him. They had a good time, with some serious rolling in the grass up a little draw near the beach. Now its one thing to have sand in your way while you're engaged in such activity, but the ultimate insult is to become infested with chiggers in sensitive places. He told me about it when we got back to Camp Lejeune. His case was so bad that the Docs at sick bay had to have him come in every day for a week to excise the little buggers out of the skin on his pecker and his huevos. To add to his misery he got some nasty letters from the girl who was not immune to the chiggers in her private parts. He probably had to steer clear of Virginia Beach for a long time—after they both stopped scratching.

CAMP ROUTINE

Camp Lejeune was an extremely boring place for a single Marine in his off duty hours. There was a slopchute located near our barracks where we went for a beer and sandwiches in the evening. There were some pool tables and a primitive bowling alley where we took turns setting pins while someone else bowled. The setter stepped on a pedal which forced a small rod up through a hole in the deck. The setter had to place each pin on the rod in its proper place, then release the pedal and hope the pins didn't fall over, which they often did. Those alleys must have dated from WWI or earlier.

The local folks in the area surrounding both Camp Lejeune and Fort Bragg sixty miles to the west had that typical attitude towards servicemen. We like you to spend your money in town but stay the hell away from our women. There were probably thirty thousand Marines at Camp Lejeune and a like number of paratroopers at Fort Bragg. That many young men could have a decimating effect on their women folk, so we were warned to keep our distance from them. The following ditty from mountain music explains the situation well. It is a farmer addressing a Marine on base and the latter's response to his plea.

Father: Are you the one that did the pushin'
 Left the bloodstains on the cushin'
 The footprints on the dashboard upside down
 Since you've screwed my daughter Nelly

She's had trouble with her belly,
So I think you ought to come around and settle down.

Marine: Yessir
 I'm the one that did the pushin',
Left the bloodstains on the cushin',
The footprints on the dashboard upside down,
But, since I've screwed your daughter Venus,
I've had trouble with my penis,
So I think we're fifty:fifty all the way around.

— *Anonymous*

There was one truck driver, Jack W., who invited me out to his place for the weekend once in awhile. He was a brownbagger who lived in a trailer park off the base. Married Marines were called brownbaggers because they brought their lunch to work in a paper sack. He had a wife and a little kid and was just scraping by on his pay and allowances. It was nice for me to get off the base now and then and see how the other half lived. They would feed me a meal or two and I bought the beer.

They received some special kind of allotment to help them support a family and some other deal called commuted rations or ComRats. When they were on the base they had to pay for their meals if they chose to eat in the mess hall. If they went aboard ship or we were out in the boondocks on maneuvers, they could eat the USMC chow without paying.

The only time I didn't appreciate staying with Jack was when I was sound asleep at one end of their trailer and the thing started moving in the middle of the night. I'm a very light sleeper and the first time this rocking motion started, I thought it was an earthquake tremor. Then I thought maybe they were behind in their payments and a tow truck was repossessing the trailer. Jack weighed over 200 pounds and I guess they were in their bedroom at the other end, going for two falls out of three. This kind of marital grabass can be a bad thing to be doing in the presence, albeit invisible of a single, healthy, and horny Marine. It just brought home another reason we bachelors didn't like brown baggers. They had a nice warm, soft woman waiting at home every night and we single guys had to go hunting far and wide just to find a woman to talk to or look at.

I stopped going out to his place for a long time. When he asked me when I was going to spend the weekend again, I told him it depended on the day. I said I would only come out on tag team night. He scratched his head and asked what I meant by that. Because I didn't want to broach such a delicate subject directly with him, I just said that I only wanted to come out when tag team wrestling was on TV. "Oh," he said, "Is that it. OK, I'll let you know."

Liberty in the nearest town of Jacksonville left much to be desired. There were not more than two restaurants and a bar or two. I went to town often just to get off the base. I usually went in with buddies like Sam Camarato, Jim Milliken, and Frank Cannon. We drank beer and ate pizza most of the time. I recall having guys in the barracks ask me to bring them back a pizza for a midnight snack, but they never asked me to do it again.

If I could remember to order their pizza, I was already three sheets to the wind. I liked lots of crushed Italian hot red pepper on my own pizza and thought everyone should enjoy this treat. When the pizza was ready I sprinkled it with red pepper and took it back with me to the barracks. I always returned well after 2200 hours when there were no lights in the squad bay and the victim couldn't see what he was eating. I would shake him to wake him, tell him it was the pizza delivery guy, set the pizza on his bunk and then hit the sack. The smell of fresh baked pizza was overwhelming and the victim would wolf down the first slice and then start gasping to catch his breath. Then he'd start cursing me while running to the scuttlebutt to quench the fires. When confronted by the burning mouth, I'd just say, "It must have been the cook who did it. I know nothing about it." Invariably they gave me the rest of the pizza telling me to just try it myself and see how I like that hot stuff. I'd stow it in my locker for a snack the next day. Needless to say that I always made them pay for the pizza beforehand.

Liberty around the camp was so bad that many of us went farther afield on the weekends. The main options for us Yankees was to head for home or Washington, D.C. In Washington, Marines could sleep at the Marine Barracks at the Naval Gun Factory nearby. The capital was closer than going back to Detroit and it was reported that the single women there outnumbered the men. I only made the trip to D.C. once and quickly learned that there were indeed plenty of women there. The problem was that nearly all of the single women there worked for the government, were twice our age, and most still lived at home with mother.

I preferred to go back to Detroit on weekends. I rarely took the bus, sometimes hitchhiked, and usually rode with a Marine from Michigan who owned a car. Sgt. John J. Mazany came from Saginaw and always had a carful of Marines who shared the cost of gasoline for the trip. Hitchhiking was not bad as long as the weather was good. I've stood out in the rain and snow for hours waiting for a ride.

We never knew what kind of a ride we were in for until we were in someone's car. I've been picked up by all sorts of drivers, queers, religious zealots, drunks, but most of the folks were quite decent. If I sensed trouble, I'd get out of the car at the first opportunity. On the other hand,

I had one family drive off the main road and I was concerned until they told me to relax. They were taking me to their nearby farm for dinner. Then they took me to the next city where I caught a bus.

On a weekend pass, we would leave the base at 1700 hours on Friday and had to be back by 0700 on Monday morning. It was a 15 to 18 hour drive one way from Camp Lejeune to Detroit to cover about 900 miles. I would spend most of Saturday and Sunday at home before heading back. We all took turns driving so others could sleep. Most of the driving was on two lane roads, and much of that in the mountains, with the exception of a couple of hundred miles on the Pennsylvania turnpike. One time on our way back from Detroit we were in the middle of the highest tunnel on the turnpike when we ran out of gas late at night. We were able to coast over 25 miles to the next gas station.

There were a lot Marines involved in serious auto accidents during these weekend rushes to get home and back on time. The Provost Marshal decided to remind us to drive safely by placing a Marine's wrecked car on a platform on the median just outside the main gate. It was the last thing we saw on leaving the base and the first thing on returning. The demolished car carcass was replaced with a new one each month and dubbed the "Wreck of the Month." We were so pressed for time trying to get home and make use of every moment there and trying to get back to the base before morning roll call, that we paid little attention to the wrecks on display.

I shudder when I look back on the way we drove coming back to camp from a weekend pass. We drove as fast as we could on ice, snow, in driving rain, through fog and the black of night. I recall driving through Pennsylvania, West Virginia, Virginia, and North Carolina in dense fog at 70 MPH. Sometimes we were guided only by the reflection of our lights on the power lines strung along the road. If another car was driving at a good clip ahead of us we just followed his taillights. Chances are it was another Marine on his way to camp. If at any time those power lines or the car in front of us veered away from the road we would have crashed in a heap. Another candidate for the Wreck of the Month club. This behavior was quite idiotic, but that was the way we lived at the time.

In those days there were many opportunities to use a drive away for transportation from Detroit toward Camp Lejeune. People from other states bought new cars in Detroit and had a firm there contract with travelers to drive them to the owner's city. The drive away firm paid me for the travel expenses. Once I drove a 1950 Studebaker from Detroit to Norfolk. The car had been repossessed by the bank. It was then a short hop by bus from Norfolk to Camp Lejeune.

When the Corps decided we should spend time in team sports, we called it organized grabass. Everyone had to participate. On weekends we often had small groups of guys playing tag football or baseball outside the barracks. This was unorganized grabass and I liked to play football along with the usual suspects from Charlie Co.—Al Gonder, Ed Urban, Don Schott, Don Riegel, et al. Once I cracked a couple of ribs and had to go to the emergency room (ER) to have my chest taped.

A couple of weeks later I went in to have the corpsman remove the tape. He grabbed one end of it while I stood there and he spun me around like a top, ripping off the tape and taking some small pieces of my skin with it. I asked him if that was normal procedure. He said, "No, the corpsman who put on the tape had forgotten to spread some special salve on the skin to prevent the tape from sticking so tight." I looked at it as another form of Navy discrimination against Marines. I figured they only used that antistick salve when taping up sailors. The Marines could just tough it out.

The only other time I had to go to the ER or sick bay was when I had my nose broken playing football. The Doc placed tubes up my nostrils, pushed the cartilage back in line and fixed it with a tape. He said the swelling would go down in a few days and the black eyes in a week or so.

During the late summer of 1953, Charlie Company moved into the field on the base to build a pontoon bridge across the New River. Once we got the rubber pontoons inflated and anchored to the shore—and some to the river bed—we laid the treadway road surface across them in sections and bolted it together. Sgt. John Chapin was there from Camp Geiger operating a crane to lift the treadway sections into place. We had just completed the bridge and were finishing work on the abutments when we got the word from Battalion HQ to bug out. It was a hurricane advisory and the storm was due to come in the next day. We didn't have time to disassemble the bridge so the Skipper, Lt. Driscoll, ordered us to let the air out of the pontoons and allow the weight of the treadway to press them to the river bottom. The anchor ropes to the trees on each bank were slackened slightly to let the bridge down.

We then turned to our tents, which we collapsed and placed our foot lockers on top of the canvas to keep it from blowing away. We then headed for mainside where we holed up in a Butler building to ride out the storm. We brought our cots with us so had a place to sack out. Ordinarily no one minded the sound of rain on the tin roof and sides of a warehouse, but being inside a Butler building during a hurricane was something else. The noise was continuous, with the wind and rain pounding on the metal. Now and then a piece of debris or a tree limb would slam into the wall. It was a sleepless night for most of us.

The storm moved away from the base the next day and we moved out onto the base proper to clean up the debris. When we had the roads cleared of tree limbs and trunks, we went into Jacksonville to help the city workers do the same. It was about a week before we could return to the work site out in the boondocks to reinflate the pontoons, raise the bridge and complete other engineering projects. The first thing we had to do was put our tents back up and dry out the canvas. Not much water got into our footlockers but my dress shoes, which were left out in the open in the rush to get back to mainside, were green with mold inside and out. Now they would match my woolen winter uniform.

In spite of my dread of the routine of living in a barracks stateside, I recall relatively few inspections and that sort of thing which I deemed unnecessary nonsense. There were a few rifle inspections, usually when one was on guard duty. Since we were a specialized technical unit, most of our inspections were of our gear and equipment. Sometimes there were inspections which went on behind our backs so to speak.

There was one 2nd lieutenant in our company who had a penchant for inspecting our rifles while they rested in the rifle racks in the squad bay. If he found a rifle that was dirty or had rust on it anywhere, he would gig the Marine by restricting liberty on the weekends. The most frequent victim of these sneak inspections was Max (Pappy) Fullen who came from the border area of Virginia and Tennessee. The problem was that the officer would find a bit of rust on the butt plate of his M-1 often enough to cause Pappy to be restricted to the base on many a weekend when he could have been enjoying himself ashore.

Anticipating the end of his contract with the USMC, Pappy told me what he would do when he was discharged. When he got home he would find an M-1 butt plate somewhere and fix it to a rock in his back yard. Every morning he was going to go out there and piss on it just to watch it rust.

I don't remember if it was the same lieutenant, but one at least showed up for a surprise inspection in the barracks while we were still in the squad bays. One might say that I was a bipolar Marine. I stuck to the regulation way of doing things in order to avoid any trouble. On the other hand, I tried to get away with as much as possible without bringing anyone of rank down on my case. The idea of going without haircuts in Korea was taking it to the extreme. Thus I was as neat as was required, but in my heart, I was a slob, and a closet slob at that. So it was that I had two wall lockers when we were each entitled to only one in the barracks.

The one that had Cpl. Ginnelly's name on it was neat and always ready for inspection. The other was a mess with everything just thrown in there in a pile. I kept a bottle of whiskey in a boot on the bottom, which was against regulations, having the whiskey that is, not keeping it in a boot. The tag on the door only read Cpl. Bones. Both lockers were always locked. The day the lieutenant (probably the one known as Jungle Jim) came through the squad bay, he wanted only to inspect wall lockers. After he checked out and passed my official locker, he came to the next and said, "Where is this Marine so we can have him open the lock?" I volunteered, "It belongs to Cpl. Bonez and he is on leave at home in Puerto Rico, Sir." He nodded, tapping the Bones name tag with his swagger stick and just said, "Very well lads, carry on then." As he went on to look in other lockers, the guys around my area were having trouble controlling their collective urge to laugh out loud. I knew what they were thinking; that Ginnelly would go to any length to protect his alter ego.

In August 1953, the company clerk, Sgt. David Gangeri asked me if I wanted to come to work in the office with him. I told him I'd think about it and a couple of days later the top called me in to ask me the same thing. Master Sgt. Rozier was a real gentleman, which some tops were not. I knew that it was not a good idea to refuse assignments when one is asked by the ranking NCO in the company, so I said I would do it and reported for duty the next day.

I have no way of knowing why they asked me to work in the office, since I had no experience in this line of work. Almost all of my work life had been spent in some outdoor activity and I didn't think much of office work, which kept me indoors. I started out working on the morning or daily report, which every unit in the US Military has to complete. This was a big challenge for me because I couldn't type one word.

As soon as the morning formation was dismissed, we had to know the status of every person on the company rolls. The gunny collected all this information during roll call and turned it over to the CO, or the XO, who turned it over to the top, who gave it to us to type. The morning report dealt entirely with personnel. The name, rank and serial number of each person not in the morning formation had to be entered on a line with a comment on where he was—in sick bay, on leave, AWOL, on TDY or special assignment elsewhere, in the brig, on mess duty, guard duty, etc.

This report had to be typed up in ten copies, using carbons and it had to be completed by 1000 hours with no errors so that it could be taken to Battalion HQ and sent on to Division HQ. Initially, I was somewhat intimidated by the manual typewriter and the first few days, I must have spoiled a couple of dozen sets of the forms because of typos. So for about a week, our report was always late, until I got the hang of it and made fewer errors. In those days we didn't have correcting fluid or any other type of aid for covering over typos. Corrections had to be done laboriously on each of the colored copies and the original with an eraser.

Usually, most Marines sort of look down on company clerks and refer to them as office pinkies. This is probably due to the fact that most Marines live outdoors and have ruddy complexions, whereas the clerks are always indoors with pasty faces or pink skin from lack of exposure to sun. I didn't get any flack from my buddies for going to work in the office, but I sure got a lot of it many years later when I told other former Marines that I did a six-month stint as a company clerk.

The other guys in my outfit knew that there were a lot of perks for a clerk. They knew who made out the guard, mess and other duty rosters. Although the top or the gunny or both, were supposed to make these lists, it was normally left to the clerks who gave it to the senior NCOs for approval when finished. The clerks were able to get out of a lot of other things such as, field problems, field days (cleaning up the barracks and policing the grounds), guard and mess duty, routine inspections, and parades. I finally got the better of the brown baggers on that score. That is, I was able to get out of work details that they could not.

One benefit for me was that I got to know our CO First Lt. Bernard Driscoll was a really great Skipper and had an unusual ability to lead men. In the course of my clerk duties I frequently had to go into the service record books (SRBs) of most of the EMs in the company. The Skipper, platoon leaders, top, and gunny were always asking for someone's SRB or for us to look up some info in them. In the process, I noted that many of the EMs in the company had not been to Korea and had not even been in the Corps as long as I had, yet they had been promoted to sergeant. I wondered why I had been passed over the last few times and figured it was because of that blip on page 13—the reprimand from Lt. Prick in Korea for letting a PFC. on post come into the guard shack to get warm at subzero temps.

I figured that when my SRB was passed around to the officers on the promotion panel, each one just flipped through it and if they noticed any writing at all on the disciplinary page, they didn't even bother to read it. They just assumed that for anything to be written on that page, then that Marine must have been a fuck-up and he was to be passed over.

The government and military has a system of dealing with things that affect the flunkies. It is called going through channels. I couldn't take this matter up with the CO, without first going through the levels of command. So I talked it over with Sgt. Gangeri, then discussed it with Gunny Bowman who told me to go to the top. I showed the blurb on the page in the SRB to Top Rozier and explained what had happened in Korea. He agreed with my conclusion as to why I had not been promoted earlier in 1953. The top took my SRB and went in to talk to the Skipper about it. He also thought it was a lot of nonsense, and I was soon promoted to buck sergeant.

I tell you, a guy has to look out for himself. Naturally my buddies hooted and started calling me a rate grabber for abusing my office as temporary company clerk to get another stripe. Yes, there were definitely advantages to working in the office. Of all the officers I had served under, or who were in the same company during my three years in the Corps, I remember only Lt. Driscoll. Why? Because he is the only one I can recall who did something for me, rather than to me. I met him at our reunion in May 1998 at Camp Lejeune and learned that he had stayed in the Corps and had advanced to Lt. Col. serving as a C.O. of the 2nd Engr. Bn, 2nd MarDiv. He died of cancer in October, 1998. He was a great Marine

Now that I think about it, my old man was a rate grabber back in WWI, which made me look like an amateur. Dad enlisted in May, 1917 and reported for basic training at a camp in Texas. In ten weeks he was a corporal. After all the basic and advanced infantry training, he shipped over to France in June 1918. His unit, the 37th Buckeye Div. went into on the job training supporting the French Army behind their section of the lines. He was promoted several times enroute, and it didn't hurt that he had learned French and German in high school and college. By the time his Regiment (145th) went into the trenches in

1918 he was a top sergeant for Mike Co., 4th Battalion. By his 22nd birthday in Oct. 1918, he had been in several major battles and was now the Battalion sergeant major. I asked my Dad how living on a farm enabled him to handle his men as a sergeant. He said that he gained the experience from rousting horses, mules, and cows from an early age.

If one wonders about such rapid promotion, it was probably due to the fact that when the U S entered that war, thousands of men either enlisted or were drafted and there were not enough NCOs to handle them all. I think that another reason was that Dad had finished two years at Cornell University and was better educated than many who went into the Army at the same time he did. Moreover, in those days a top sergeant and a Battalion sergeant major had a lot more authority over the troops than they have had in recent times. In one ferocious battle in the Meuse Argonne sector, every officer in Dad's company was killed or seriously wounded. He assumed command as the ranking NCO and led the troops through the rest of the fight, which lasted for several days, until some replacement officer relieved him. For this he was awarded the French Croix de Guerre with bronze star. This is the second highest military honor in France.

I have often wondered what is the matter with our military establishment when it allows a foreign government, (in this case France) to decorate American soldiers for bravery while serving in their country, while our own military gives them no equivalent or comparable honor. There were no American officers around at the time to make the necessary recommendations for my Dad and he would never press such an issue himself. As far as he was concerned, he was just doing what was expected of him and what he was trained for. The French officers in the units nearby must have recommended him for the medal.

The Marine Corps birthday celebration of November 10, 1953 is a vivid memory. It was the one meal and ceremony that demanded a Marine's presence unless he was on guard duty or in the hospital. I had to attend in spite of the fact that I had a hell of a hangover. I entered the mess hall with some trepidation and unsteady gait. The tables were decorated and covered with extra goodies. It was going to be a sumptuous banquet, perhaps to get me to ship over. But it was a waste of time in my condition. The officers were wearing their dress blues, while the rest of us were in winter woolens. The guy sitting across from me said my face was as green as my uniform.

The ceremony began with the band playing the National Anthem, followed by the Marine Corps hymn. The Battalion CO made a speech, the chaplain said grace and we sat down to eat. It was the usual fare for festive days, with baked ham, roast turkey and all the trimmings followed by choice desserts. However, I couldn't eat a thing. I just sat there and drank tomato juice. When everyone was finished with the main part of the meal, the colonel stood up to cut the decorated cake with his sword. He made a brief speech and called on the oldest Marine present to come forward to get the first slice. Then he called for the youngest Marine present to come forward for the second. Then the rest of us came up to be served by the CO. This ritual takes place every year on Nov. 10, at every Marine post around the world, including those American Embassies with Marine Guard detachments. I participated in quite a few of these later while serving abroad as a civilian.

At each place there was a special menu card proclaiming the event. There was a package of cigarettes on the napkin. I felt so lousy looking at all that food I couldn't eat, that I felt I had to do something meaningful today. I gave my pack of cigarettes away and quit smoking forever. Actually I really did quit cigarettes, but the next day I felt a bit better and so I started smoking cigars instead. So when anyone asks me when I quit smoking cigarettes, I can still tell them the place, the day and the exact time.

In December of 1953 I went home for my last leave and bought a 1940 Mercury convertible. I was on the way back to Camp when I stopped to see PFC. Lee Tomasek in Lorain, Ohio. Lee was in Charlie Co. also but had requested a transfer to Korea and was on leave before shipping out. In the evening we went to the Italian Club and had one beer. We left there to drive around town and I pulled past a stop sign and we were T-boned by another car. Lee was thrown from the impact and landed in the yard of a house. I was thrown clear and landed on my feet. Both cars were demolished. Lee was taken to the hospital and I left there to talk to the chief of Police. When he found out I had no place to stay, he said you can sleep in the lockup tonight if you want. I spent my first and last night in jail with a cell full of Puerto Ricans who had been arrested for murder. I slept in my uniform and went to see the JP in the morning. I paid my fine by selling a Winchester carbine to the Police chief. I had just purchased the rifle from Big Jim the week before. The next morning a local representative of the Marine Corps Reserve saw to it I was on my way back to Camp after I went to the hospital to see Lee. His arm was severely injured and he was soon transferred to a Navy Hospital.

When I got back to camp, First Sgt. Rozier gave me holy hell for getting Tomasek in an accident. The top had gone to a lot of trouble to have Lee transferred to Korea and now I'd messed up the kid. That accident and the injury to Lee has bothered me ever since.

DISCHARGE

In 1953 the Marine Corps made a concerted effort to get individuals to reenlist when their enlistment was up. My due date for discharge was February 5, 1954, so the process began by having a senior NCO or officer interview me about every six weeks beginning in August 1953. The first time I met with my platoon sergeant to discuss it. The next time it was with the gunny. Later with the top and then one time it was with my platoon leader. The final attempt to get me to reup was with the Skipper.

I told them all the same thing. I saw no future for me in the Corps. I already knew how to walk for long distances before I enlisted. All I have done of any interest since I came in was get on and off landing craft and LSTs. When not doing that, I spent a lot of time on the beach waiting to embark, or waiting after having just disembarked.

I also felt that I was still being treated like a shitbird and I wanted to get a good education. At the time there seemed to be little possibility for me to do this in the Marine Corps. In 1966, while serving in the American Embassy in Rabat, I went to the U.S. Naval Hospital at Kenitra to have a hernia repaired and spent five days there in a room with a gray haired Navy lieutenant who had the same operation. Every day, the lieutenant was visited by an older Marine major. When the major found out I had been in the Marines earlier, he started chiding me for not staying in to become a lifer. After he heard all of my many reasons for getting out, he finally said the both he and the Navy lieutenant had been enlisted men who were LDOs. They had become officers under a program called Limited Duty Officer, where qualified enlisted men could rise to the rank of major or lieutenant commander in the Navy. I told him that no one ever told me about it and in any case, I wanted to go to the university without any military obligation, once I was out. I must say that all of us enlisted men had the greatest respect for those officers known as mustangs who had come up through the ranks. They had known the rigors of the ranks and so they made better leaders and role models for the rest of us.

Another beef that I had was that I had every other tooth missing in front on top. Some of them were extracted at the convenience of the Navy dentist. Both the Marine Corps and the Navy refused see to it that my teeth were fixed, saying they were bad when I came in and they couldn't be bothered upgrading them. So the Corps expected me to be well fed and nourished so that I could hump over the hills when necessary. I asked them, "How can I do that, when half the time I cannot chew the tough meat you serve in the mess hall?" So, they thought I was fit enough for cannon fodder when I enlisted in 1951 when they needed warm bodies, but since I survived and the war was over, they felt no need to bother with fixing my teeth. In other words, they had no further need for my warm body, so why should I even consider staying in the Corps. It was cheaper for them to find a new recruit with good teeth, perhaps a young lad more malleable than myself.

You could tell when a guy was being called in for the "shipping over" interview because he would be discussing his options with his buddies. Another sign was if he started humming the tune to Four Leaf Clover. If we actually heard him singing the gyrene's words to that tune, we knew he was a goner. The first lines went like this:

I've thought it over and I'm shipping over 'cause I really love the Corps.

I don't remember the rest, but even the guys who wanted out, sang it anyway because it was a catchy tune.

So what did the Marine Corps get out of me? They had my warm body at their disposal for three years out of my young life. I was fortunate not to have served in a line company in Korea, although I would have done so if ordered. So I didn't become a casualty. I learned something about military engineering and was again fortunate not to get blown up, step on or drive onto a mine, or get frostbite, malaria, dengue fever, Hanta virus, hemorrhagic fever, or the dreaded Hong Kong dong.

The most important things I learned in the service had to do with 1) appreciating my own capabilities and limitations and 2) learning about a diverse group of individuals, primarily in how to get along with them and 3) how to get others involved in a team approach to problem solving.

One of the best things that three years in the Corps did for me was to give me time to figure out what to do with the rest of my life. I knew by now that the service wasn't for me. I was too much of an independent person and not well suited for a life of regimentation. One has a great deal of time on one's hands in the service, just waiting for something to happen. I made the best use of this time by reading everything

I could get my hands on and taking Marine Corps Institute (MCI) and US Armed Forces Institute (USAFI) courses. Just before I was discharged I took the week-long test for the General Equivalency Diploma (GED) and was graded in the top percentile, ranked with high school seniors all across the USA.

This made me laugh because Central High School in Detroit had to give me a diploma six years after expelling me in 1947. My mother went down to the school to pick it up and if I know her, she stuck her tongue out at him, after the principal handed her the errant son's diploma. But she probably said, "Thanks, turkey. See, he didn't even need to attend your damn school to graduate from it." He's lucky she didn't deck him.

When I compare my service to that of my brothers and my Dad, I came off pretty well. My Dad was in some pretty heavy fighting and had to put up with cold wet weather in soggy trenches, with cooties crawling all over him. Constant immersion of their feet in water led to trench foot which was debilitating. On top of dodging bullets and shells, he was gassed by the Germans along with many in his unit and suffered from lung problems all his life. So I was glad to have come through unscathed.

POST USMC ADJUSTMENT

On February 5, 1954 as promised, the USMC handed me my honorable discharge from the Corps and I went out the main gate exulting in my new found freedom. As I passed the guard shack, I turned and saluted the Wreck of the Month. I first went to Philadelphia to visit Lee Tomasek in the Naval Hospital there in pretty bad shape. He never regained the use of one arm. Going to see him was the least I could do. Then I went back to Detroit and moved in with my older sister. My folks were pretty smart. If you weren't out of the house by a certain age, they threw you out. There were six of us kids and every time one left home, the folks moved to a smaller place. When I came home, they were living in a two bedroom apartment with my 13 year old kid sister. My brother John, just out of the Navy, lived nearby in an apartment.

I had problems readjusting to civilian life. The main thing was that I sort of had a chip on my shoulder from being sat on for the past three years. I promised myself that I wasn't taking orders from anyone ever again, no matter what. I returned to my old job with the City of Detroit with an attitude. The Forestry admin types made the mistake of sending me out on a crew whose foreman was a complete jerk and hard on his men. Whenever he started leaning on me I just gave him a ration of crap, which later reflected on my efficiency report. Shortly after that one of the City Foresters drove out to the job and said he wanted to talk to me about that report. He said that he knew me well before I went in the service and I always had very good reports. "What has happened to you?", he wanted to know. I told him that I react to miserable, inept supervisors and that this one was a proper bastard. I told the bigwig that my proficiency reports always reflected the character of the supervisor who rated me. If he was a jackass, I reacted to that and gave him a bad time at every opportunity. If he was a good leader who treated his men right, then we got along just fine and I worked harder than ever for him. As a result I was transferred to a small (two-man crew) where we were left alone to roam the city working on special forestry projects. I considered it to be a promotion and was happy there until I got married and left for Hollywood, California where my bride lived.

Some veterans of the Corps probably saved a lot of mementos from the days of their service. I am not one of them. Because I have moved 37 times since leaving the Corps, I lost my discharge and the DD 214 originals among other reminders.

The main thing for me is that I came out of the experience with my body and soul intact. All of my keepsakes can be put into the French soldier's beret I brought home. Included are: my mess kit spoon, a name stamp, a few emblems, a few campaign ribbons, my dog tags, and a C-ration can opener, which I have carried all over the world. I do cherish quite a few photographs that I took with an old Argus C-3 camera, some of which are in the book. Among the items that have disappeared along the way and which I would have liked to keep are my Kabar and the Chinese flare pistol. I didn't become too attached to anything in the service, especially that way of life.

Like other veterans, there were a few changes I wanted to make in my life when I was set free. First of all I had a list of things I didn't want to eat for some time, such as pancakes, hot dogs, spam, cold cuts, and chipped beef or creamed hamburger on toast (SOS). However, I did continue to eat steak and eggs several time a week. There were a few other pet peeves that my new wife found difficult to understand. I absolutely refused to stand in any line for any reason. For many years she was frustrated because I wouldn't stand in line at a good restaurant or even for a good movie.

When I returned to Detroit right after my discharge, I went down to the Veterans Administration to convert my life insurance (NSLI). When I saw the long line of veterans and dependents waiting to be taken care of, I shuddered and left. I'd rather give up my insurance than stand in line. After the six months had passed for me to convert, I was married and living in Hollywood, California and I thought perhaps I should have that insurance since I now had a dependent. I went to a small office in Hollywood where American Legion volunteers helped with VA problems. An old veteran looked into it for me and said that even though the deadline had passed he was able to keep my insurance in force. He found that I had accumulated enough dividends over nearly four years to pay for my premiums all this time. All that without standing in line.

One of the questions some people have about basic training in the American military has to do with discipline. In other words is all that strict and rigorous discipline as I have described it, really necessary. My answer would be yes and no. It all depends on the situation and the terrain. Actually it all depends on the types of people one is dealing with and the ultimate goal of the training and the mission of the branch of service. I am a strong advocate of discipline in our fighting forces. I also believe in universal military training (UMT) for all US citizens when they turn eighteen years of age.

From the time I was discharged until Feb. of 1959, I was in school. I went to night school in Detroit to round out the GED diploma. In Los Angeles I went to LA City College for one year while working full time. In Sept. of 1995 I entered the University of Michigan at Ann Arbor and graduated with a BSc in Fisheries Biology. During registration for my first semester at Michigan, I ran into one of our former platoon leaders from Camp Lejeune. I went up to him and said, "Hi lieutenant, remember me? I'm Sgt. Ginnelly from Charlie Company." He had a surprised look on his face and shook my hand with some reservation. He politely asked me what I was doing here and I told him. He was registering in the graduate school in electrical engineering. He wasted no time in making tracks and I can't blame him. Out of 200 men in our company, he could not remember me and perhaps I was a Marine he had to deal with in a court martial and I might be out for revenge. Our CO, Lt. Driscoll told me last year he used to call this lieutenant Jungle Jim. Lt. Driscoll said that Jungle Jim was a brilliant electrical engineer and one summer at Vieques he straightened out all their electrical problems in the camp. I wonder if it had anything to do with the officers' beer reefer and the flaming ball on the wires.

My Marine Corps service stimulated my interest in other countries so I joined the Foreign Service and was assigned to the American Embassy in Phnom Penh, Cambodia in the fall of 1959. The State Department had wanted to assign me to Korea, but I convinced them that I wasn't ready for that just yet. I served in Cambodia until the spring of 1964. I also served three years in Morocco with AID and on long term contracts with AID in Egypt and Thailand and other private contracts in New Zealand and Venezuela. However, now that I'm ready to return for a look at Korea, I'm getting too old to have any interest in travel. It is time to call it quits unless the Koreans decide to have a 50th year reunion for those of us who went over there to help them. Then I'll reconsider my travel plans. Meantime I still adhere to the motto: SEMPER FI to all Marines, former Marines and ex-Marines.

EPILOGUE

Recently I dreamt that I was attending the next reunion of Charlie Co. at Parris Island, SC in the spring of the year 2,000. As we were walking around the MCRD my former nemesis and senior DI SSgt. Sicklick suddenly appeared as a phantom to threaten us with his ever present prop. Only this time, it wasn't a swagger stick, nightstick, or broomstick, but a cane. Think he's gone old and feeble, eh? He comes at me to strike with the cane, only this time I try to defend myself by grabbing the end tightly. I pull on the cane, unwittingly releasing the sword hidden inside. SSgt. Sicklick flicks the sword around yelling. "*En garde* skinhead. He lunges forward with the bared sword while I tried to fend him off with the sheath. He may be old and gray, but he's still in control with a sword cane. Then I woke up sweating. Maybe the whole three years was a dream. That's why I couldn't remember anything for four decades. Maybe I'll cancel out at the last minute on the next reunion. That is unless the MCRD at PI can assure me that SSgt. Sicklick will not be visiting there at the same time.

REFERENCES

Averill,Gerald P. Mustang. *A Combat Marine.* Simon & Schuster 1987

Blair, Clay. *The Forgotten War.* Random House, Inc. 1987

Brady, James. *The Coldest War.* Orion Books, NY 1990

Chung, Donald K. *The Three Day Promise.* Father & Son Publ. Talla-
hassee 1989

Dyer, Gwynne. *War.* Crown Publishers, Inc. 1985

Fall, Bernard. *The Street Without Joy.* Stackpole Books, Harrisburg, PA
1961

Fehrenbach, T.R. *This Kind of War.* Macmillan Co. 1963

Fussell, Paul. *The Great War and Modern Memory.* Oxford University
Press 1975

Hastings, Max. *The Korean War.* Simon and Schuster 1987

Hoyt, Edwin P. *The Bloody Road to Panmunjom.* Stein & Day 1985

Manchester, Wm. *Goodbye Darkness.* Little Brown & Co. 1979.

Russ, Martin. *The Last Parallel.* Rhinehart & Co. 1957

Thornton, John W. *Believed to be Alive.* Paul Eriksson Publ.
Middlebury VT 1981

Toland, John. *In Mortal Combat: Korea 1950-53.* Wm. Morrow NY
1991

ORDER FORM

For your copy of A Cruise in the Corps; the View from the Ranks, by Gerald D. Ginnelly, send your check or money order for $14.95 plus $2.00 Standard rate or $3.20 priority mail to:

DANO & DAD
P.O. Box 2052
Prescott, AZ 86302

Your book will be shipped promptly on receipt of your order and payment.

Name _____

Address _____

City _____ State _____ ZipCode _____

Please indicate desired shipping:

☐ Standard rate: Add $2.00 (4-6 weeks)

☐ Priority mail: Add $3.20 (2 days)

For international mail, please check with Postal Service and add appropriate amount.

Sales Tax: Please add 7.5% sales tax for books shipped to Arizona addresses.

No. Copies	Unit Price	Total
	$14.95	
Sales tax (AZ res., 7.5%)		
Shipping		
	Total	

ORDER FORM

For your copy of A Cruise in the Corps; the View from the Ranks, by Gerald D. Ginnelly, send your check or money order for $14.95 plus $2.00 Standard rate or $3.20 priority mail to:

DANO & DAD
P.O. Box 2052
Prescott, AZ 86302

Your book will be shipped promptly on receipt of your order and payment.

Name _____

Address _____

City _____ State _____ ZipCode _____

Please indicate desired shipping:

☐ Standard rate: Add $2.00 (4-6 weeks)

☐ Priority mail: Add $3.20 (2 days)

For international mail, please check with Postal Service and add appropriate amount.

Sales Tax: Please add 7.5% sales tax for books shipped to Arizona addresses.

No. Copies	Unit Price	Total
	$14.95	
Sales tax (AZ res., 7.5%)		
Shipping		
	Total